THE BAGPIPES

RICHARD McLAUCHLAN

The Bagpipes

A Cultural History

HURST & COMPANY, LONDON

First published in the United Kingdom in 2025 by
C. Hurst & Co. (Publishers) Ltd.,
New Wing, Somerset House, Strand, London, WC2R 1LA
© Richard McLauchlan, 2025
All rights reserved.

Distributed in the United States, Canada and Latin America by
Oxford University Press, 198 Madison Avenue, New York, NY 10016,
United States of America.

The right of Richard McLauchlan to be identified as the author
of this publication is asserted by him in accordance with the
Copyright, Designs and Patents Act, 1988.

A Cataloguing-in-Publication data record for this book
is available from the British Library.

This book is printed using paper from registered sustainable
and managed sources.

ISBN: 9781805262848

www.hurstpublishers.com

Printed and bound in Great Britain by Bell & Bain Ltd, Glasgow

To Donald Mackintosh,
a scholar and a gentleman,
but more importantly,
a piper and a friend.

CONTENTS

List of Illustrations   ix
Acknowledgements   xiii

Introduction: More than an Instrument   1

1. Origins: From the Profane to the Sacred and Back
   Again   7

2. Getting to Scotland: Resisting National Boundaries   17

3. You'll Take the High Road and I'll Take the Low
   Road: A Diverse and Fluctuating Culture, 1500–1700   31

4. Piping in Jacobite Times: The Sound of Divided
   Loyalties, 1700–46   45

5. Pipes, Power and Patronage: The Enlightened
   Reimagining of the Highlands, 1746–1830s   57

6. A Time for Giants: Developing a Tradition of
   Innovation (and Madness), 1830s–1900s   75

7. Everything Changes: The Great War, Women and the
   Standardisation of Tradition, 1903–39   99

8. Piping Characters of the Old World on the Cusp of the
   New: Rousing the Romance from Within, 1939–1970s   115

9. Breaking Free from the Shackles of Convention: The
   Bagpipes Redefined, 1970s–1994   139

10. Yesterday, Today and Forever: The Health, or Otherwise,
    of Scotland's Contemporary Piping Culture, 1994
    Onwards   161

Conclusion: A Global Instrument Worthy of Mystery   183

Notes   195

Bibliography   239

Index   253

LIST OF ILLUSTRATIONS

1. Bust of Roman Emperor Nero, Capitoline Museum, Rome, restored in the seventeenth century. CC by 3.0, https://creativecommons.org/licenses/by-sa/3.0/.

2. Pig bagpipe, adjacent to Percy tomb, Beverley Minster, c. 1340. Photograph by Ian Pittaway, earlymusicmuse.com.

3. *Belles Heures of Jean de France, duc de Berry*, Limbourg Brothers, early fifteenth century. Public domain via Open Access, The Metropolitan Museum of Art.

4. Marginal doodle, *De Caelo, De anima*, 1487. Public domain via picryl.

5. 'The Bagpiper', Albrecht Dürer, 1514. Public domain via Open Access, The Metropolitan Museum of Art.

6. 'The Fool', *The Dance of Death*, Hans Holbein the Younger, 1523–5. Public domain via The Project Gutenberg eBook of The Dance of Death.

7. 'The Peasant Dance', Pieter Bruegel the Elder, 1567. Public domain via Wikimedia commons.

8. Haddington town piper, mid-eighteenth century. Courtesy of East Lothian Council Archives Service.

9. 'Piper to the Laird of Grant', Richard Waitt, 1714. National Museums of Scotland, Image © National Museums Scotland

10. Frontispiece, John Geoghegan's *The Compleat Tutor for the Pastoral or New Bagpipe*, 1743. National Museums of Scotland, Image © National Museums Scotland.

11. Iain MacGillivray piping on Culloden Moor during the filming of *Outlander*, undated. Credit: Iain MacGillivray

12. Malcolm MacPherson, 1880s.

13. Piper George Findlater, The Gordon Highlanders, winning the Victoria Cross at Dargai, 1897', Edward Matthew Hale, 1898. National Army Museum, Out of Copyright.

14. Shyopat Julia, Jaipur Literature Festival, 2023. Photograph by Abhimanyu Rathore.

15. Belarusian bagpiper, undated. Public domain via Wikimedia commons.

16. Elizabeth 'Bessie' Watson, Women's Suffrage March, 1911. The Women's Library at LSE, image reference 7JCC/O/02/022.

17. St Laurence O'Toole Pipe Band, 1912.

18. Piper Daniel Laidlaw, The Illustrated London News, 1915. Public domain via Wikimedia commons.

19. Dagenham Girl Pipers pipe band, 1933. Valence House Museum, image reference BD7/10.

20. Bill Millin, 1944. Public domain via Wikimedia commons.

21. Seumas MacNeill and Catriona Campbell (now Garbutt), early 1950s. Credit: National Piping Centre.

22. Alex Currie, undated. Credit: The Learned Kindred of Currie.

23. Josef Režný, 2007. CC by 4.0, https://creativecommons.org/licenses/by-sa/3.0/

24. Galician bagpipe and drum group, undated.

25. 78th Fraser Highlanders' celebration, 1987. Credit: Michael Grey.

26. Bagad de Lann-Bihoué, undated. CC by 3.0 https://creative-commons.org/licenses/by-sa/3.0/

27. Northumbrian smallpipe players, Alwinton Show, Northumberland, 2007. Public domain via flickr.

28. Gordon Duncan, undated.

29. Paddy Keenan, Katharine Cornell Theater, University of Buffalo, late 1990s/early 2000s. Courtesy of Paddy Keenan, photograph by Greg Harcourt.

LIST OF ILLUSTRATIONS

30. Martyn Bennett performing with Cuillin, Buddha Bar, Paris, 1998. Credit: Kenny MacDonald and special thanks to Bj Stewart of The Martyn Bennett Trust.

31. Jack Lee, Glenfiddich Piping Championship, 2017. Credit: Stuart Letford/National Piping Centre.

32. Ally the Piper (Allyson Crowley-Duncan), Dublin Irish Festival, Dublin, Ohio, 2024. Credit: Ally the Piper, photograph by Dominic Marraffa III.

ACKNOWLEDGEMENTS

The origins of this book lie in a very enjoyable lunch with the Managing Director of Hurst, Michael Dwyer, and his wife Rachel in the summer of 2021. I mentioned in passing that I had met my wife, Sabrina, because I wanted to busk with my bagpipes in Cologne, Germany (long story). Michael had not known that I was a piper and, being a true publisher, he instantly enquired if a really accessible cultural history of the instrument had been produced. I was convinced something like that must have been written already, but looking into it, it appeared there was nothing that could quite be described in those terms. A gap in the market! So my first thanks must go to Michael for seeing the opportunity and believing that I could write such a book, and to the rest of the Hurst team for making those hopes a physical reality.

A special place must also go to my friend Donald Mackintosh, to whom this book is dedicated. There were times when I felt my chapters would be ten times better if Donald were writing them, such were his detective powers, enthusiasm, eye for detail and historical prowess. His generosity stretched not just to the time he took in sharing the journey with me, but also in allowing me to publish the fruit of his labours into the early members of the College of Piping and what can only be described as their terrorist activities. This is perhaps the book's greatest scoop, and it is all thanks to Donald.

I would have still struggled to write this book had it not been for a number of other highly knowledgeable people rallying to my cause. Some were especially close to the project—Hugh Cheape and Michael Grey especially—and others helpfully dipped in and out when needed. That list is long, but must include my former piping instructor Colin MacLellan (I count myself unbelievably lucky to have been his pupil), Jenny Hazzard, Dougie Pincock, Allan Hamilton, Joshua Dickson, Gary West, Finlay MacDonald, James

ACKNOWLEDGEMENTS

Burnet, Bill Livingstone, Angus Tulloch, Jamie Forrester, Patrick Gascoigne, David Johnston, Alex Duncan, Andy McCartney, Ross OC Jennings, Sir Charles Fraser and Vivien Williams. For other types of support, Michael Osborne and James Ferguson also deserve a place here. To all these wonderfully helpful people, heartfelt thanks.

Time restrictions sadly kept me from contacting many others who could have made invaluable contributions, and I can think of some piping savants whose encyclopaedic knowledge makes me quiver when I imagine them reading the coming pages. I take full responsibility, of course, for any errors which they, or others, may uncover. Which makes me think with gratitude of copyeditor, Tim Page, who, along with some others mentioned above, saved me from letting a number of howlers through the net.

I would like to thank all those institutions and people who helped to secure the images and permissions for the illustrations, especially Ian Pittaway, Fran Woodrow (East Lothian Council Archives Service), Maggie Wilson (National Museums of Scotland), Iain MacGillivray, Dr John Shaw (University of Edinburgh), Abhimanyu Rathore, Daniel Brambilla-Payne (LSE), John Hunt (irishpiping. com), Karen Rushton (Valence House Museum), John Slavin (Bagpipe News), Jeannie Campbell, Stuart Letford (*Piping Times*), Bob Currie, Michael Grey, Alison Metcalfe (National Library of Scotland), Paddy Keenan, Kenny MacDonald, BJ Stewart (the Martyn Bennett Trust) and Allyson Crowley-Duncan.

Some final, vital words of gratitude. To Jaime Marshall, my agent, for never failing to make time for me, for always fighting my corner, for offering such wise advice. To my parents, Grahame and Rosaly, for giving me the chance to learn the pipes in the first place and, as with all else, providing all I ever needed to pursue my passion. And to my wife, Sabrina, and our boys, Magnus and Arvo, for— now, how do I do this without words starting to fail me—well, I will keep it simple: for your unconditional love, which, I'm tempted to think, is the prerequisite for writing any book which seeks not just to inform, but to inspire. I hope these pages meet that criterion, for that, indeed, has been my ambition.

INTRODUCTION

MORE THAN AN INSTRUMENT

One afternoon in the late autumn of 2022, I sat in my little study in my house just outside Edinburgh and looked over at the set of bagpipes that lay near me—pipes I had played since my tenth year—and felt at one with them. We were both deflated.

The weather outside was grey like my mood, grey like the discoloured woollen cords that held the drones of my pipes together and that had once gleamed white. I was surrounded by open books, charting the history of the bagpipes. They were relatively recent works, written by scholars of impeccable backgrounds, men who'd been steeped in piping culture since their boyhood, who could recite the famous names of the great piping dynasties with all the alacrity of the Twelve Days of Christmas, and whose tweed jackets—I conjectured—must have emanated the sweet perfume of parchment and old leather.

In many ways, their books were marvellous: scholarly, insightful and, for a wannabe piping historian such as myself, invaluable. But the myths were gone. These men had been doing the hard graft of ridding the bagpiping story once and for all of its fantastical elements and its outright lies. Now anyone with a copy of their books would know, to take just a few examples, that there was no clear, linear origins story for the instrument; that the Great Highland Bagpipe in its current form is not especially old; that the pipes weren't really banned after the general purge of Highland life following the Jacobite Uprising of 1745; and that the classic, magnetic stories of how the great tunes came to be composed were often made-up. This was all necessary information. But the connection between myth and romance runs deep. If the romance of the bagpipes is undeniable to thousands of people across the globe, what happens when we sever the instrument from its foundational myths? In that late autumn of 2022, I had begun to question whether there could be any real romance left. A light was ebbing within me. It was a light first kindled when, at around seven years of age, I witnessed in the darkening evening the Lone Piper playing his lament high upon the parapet of Edinburgh Castle during the city's famous Military Tattoo.

I turned back to my desk and lifted the laptop screen. Perhaps an intensive hour with Dr Google would cure my ailment. In a flurry of searches, I landed upon the homepage of dunaber.com, the website of acclaimed Canadian piper Michael Grey, where I was lured in by the title of a recent post: 'Angus MacPherson, Invershin: A 1957 Visit with a Great Tradition-Bearer'. Now the fact is, I was not sufficiently well read in the subject at this stage to recall much about this man MacPherson, but there was enough in the title to get a sensitive-Lowland-Scot-with-Highland-pretentions like me excited. There was the remote sounding Highland place-name; there was the remote (to me) date of the visit; and there was that gravity-laden description, 'great tradition-bearer'. I clicked the title and was pleased to find that there wasn't just text, there was a YouTube freeze-frame image of old Angus, cheeks at maximum extension, showing his pipes who's boss—or, to put it more formally, gie'in it laldy. Always appreciating a visual and audio aid, I clicked the image, and it was then that things started to change for me.

Out through the MacBook speakers, the evocative crackling of a 1950s-recording enveloped the room. The interviewer speaks first, in confident Highland tones. 'You have had a long and interesting life. I would like you to tell me something about your early experience, the early days at your home and what things were like then.' Then comes the quiet, breathy voice of the eighty-year-old Angus MacPherson, lilting beautifully, slowly. It is a voice out of the distant past:

> You've said I've had a long and interesting life. I certainly have had a very interesting life, and in the course of eighty years a man sees many changes, and I certainly have seen many. I was born on the 2nd of July 1877, not in very luxurious circumstances. I was born

near Cluny Castle, Badenoch, the Parish of Laggan. At that time my father was piper to the chief of the Clan MacPherson, Cluny, so that you can well understand that I have had a long connection with piping in particular in my life. I can claim to have had a connection to the great MacCrimmons of Skye. My grandfather, by whom I have been called Angus MacPherson, he had his piping taught to him by the last of the MacCrimmon pipers of Skye, who were pipers to the MacLeods of Dunvegan, John MacCrimmon. My grandfather had lessons from him. So that I can truly claim, without offending anything to the contrary, that I have had a direct line with the MacCrimmons, for now at least five generations. I can remember my grandfather very well, and when I came to the age of starting my piping under my father's care, my old grandfather used to sit by the fireside listening very attentively, watching me as a young lad, and after I did what I could do, he would say very gently and encouragingly, 'That's very good, boy. You'll keep it like that, and your father will see that you become a piper one of these days.' This did give me encouragement, and I followed the art under my father's tuition.[1]

With these words, the muses seemed to resume their song. An alchemy had occurred; MacPherson's sentences pulsed with a sort of mystery. It may have had something to do with the old-fashioned turns of phrase, common to an older generation of players, especially that delightful use of the possessive ('he had *his* piping taught to him', 'when I came to the age of starting *my* piping'). Or perhaps I was just a sucker for Highland sentimentality, enraptured by images of clan chiefs woken for their bacon and eggs by their personal pipers, or seduced by visions of old plaid-clad men sitting by firesides, dispensing wisdom. I admit the allure, but I don't think it was this. There is, to my mind, something genuinely moving and inspiring about Angus's boyhood memories. This is not airy-fairy stuff or the fabrications of a Sir Walter Scott; this is genuine recollection of a lost culture, with traceable roots back into history.[2]

Given the hideous faux-Scottish tourist shops that line Edinburgh's Royal Mile, selling fake bagpipes and blasting rock versions of 'Scotland the Brave', it is no wonder that self-respecting Scots and serious academics make efforts to shed Scottish history of the anachronistic debris accumulated since the time of Scott[3]—not least the common attempts to make a very particular, airbrushed picture of the Highlands synonymous with Scotland, with the Lowlands regularly written out of the picture. I am with those who seek to put matters right.[4] The historian Marinell Ash, in *The Strange Death of Scottish History* (1980), claimed that Scottish historians in the second half of the nineteenth century decided to move away from the 'emotional trappings' of the Scottish past—the romance connected to the tales of Mary, Queen of Scots, or the Jacobites, for instance—and concentrate more on what was considered to be the high seriousness of Anglo-British constitutional history.[5] Even though, with the dismantling of the British Empire, there was a shift back to more specifically Scottish studies,[6] historians of the country's history have remained on heightened alert against any hint of romance in their narratives. This has been especially true for those based in the universities, conscious of a need to prove their rigour in a world increasingly dominated by supposedly hard-headed scientists. When it comes to historians of the bagpipe in Scotland, the romance persisted longer, perhaps because many of them sat at a remove from the seats of learning.[7] But since the 1990s, responding to much of this romance having simply been the result of 'a subjective, often emotional version of history',[8] a justifiable purge has taken place.[9] The question thus arises: can romance, defined as 'a quality or feeling of mystery and excitement', and historical rigour be combined? Hearing Angus speak convinced me it was possible.

This is the task I have set myself for this book: to tell the story of the bagpipes in a historically accurate way but to keep the romance and magic alive. A fine line has to be navigated. When Wilson McLeod, an eminent professor of Gaelic at Edinburgh University, called sternly in 2004 for the excision of romanticism from the practice of Scottish history,[10] we must surely understand that as a rejection of the desire 'to romanticise', meaning 'to think about or describe something as being better or more attractive or interesting than it really is'. This is emphatically not my aim. My aim is to draw attention to those moments, such as we get in listening to MacPherson, when history and romance combine and grant them licence to affect us. If the hairs stand up on the back of our necks, why should we be ashamed of it? He was still speaking of a historical reality. Bagpipe scholar Vivien Williams has said of recent histories of the bagpipe that 'a greater seriousness of approach leaves little room for subjectivity'.[11] This book takes a lighter, though no less historically rigorous approach. Leaving behind the voice of academia, but informed by the best scholarship there is, a space will open up, I hope, where personal emotions can indeed be stirred, with both joy and justification. The pipes are there to entertain; this book should do that too.

I'm aware that everything written above is rather 'Scoto-centric', and that when I speak of 'the pipes', I'm referring to the Great Highland Bagpipe—the type of pipes you see on shortbread tins, with one large bass drone and two smaller tenor drones, all balanced on the shoulder of some kilted gentleman—and thus appear to exclude the vast variety of bagpipes native to other countries and regions. But this is only the introduction. The pages that follow will not turn a blind eye to other forms of the instrument, for the story of the bagpipes is a highly diverse one. In fact, this book will have something of an hourglass figure, starting with a wide international lens as we trace the instrument's origins, narrowing to a more domestic Scottish focus, then re-emerging into a worldwide vision as we follow the reawakening of interest in indigenous piping across the globe. If this book is fairly light on non-Scottish piping between, roughly, the sixteenth and the nineteenth centuries, it is not a result of piping dying out everywhere other than in Scotland, as is sometimes claimed, though it certainly did ebb and in some places vanish. That my insights on international developments are limited over this period has much more to do with the relative disparateness of historical sources from which to create a compelling global narrative for these centuries.[12] If this means that Scotland and the Great Highland Bagpipe loom largest, I hope I will be forgiven by readers from non-Scottish piping communities. Combined with the magic and romance business, this slightly narrower focus will at least mean the book should remain accessible—enticing even—to as wide an audience as possible.

I mentioned this desire for accessibility when I spoke over Zoom to Michael Grey, having reached out to him in excitement about his MacPherson post.[13] His response was enlightening. 'Well you'll have to give your readers a fair dose of Sex, Drugs and Rock n' Roll.' The following pages may struggle to fit that bill entirely, but pipers do seem to be more susceptible than others when it comes to the demon drink, and at least one of them would not have disgraced the cover of a Rolling Stones album. In the main, however, accessibility comes through the very human stories that make vibrant the tapestry of piping history. Avoiding jargon and written pipe music will help too.

Combining historical rigour with the magic of the pipes is one of two ways this book might stand out. The other is the intense focus, in the closing chapters, on recent history and the present day.[14] The bagpipes illuminate contemporary society in remarkable, unexpected ways. To explore the rise of women pipers and to discover what it is to be a woman piper today tells you much about the wider gender issues we face; to investigate the backgrounds of modern-day pipers, and compare them to their predecessors, is to chart a fascinating story about class and privilege; to analyse where money does and does not go within the piping world, in Scotland and beyond, is to understand something of capitalism's two faces, its evils and its benefits, and puts into question the meaning and appreciation of a 'national instrument'. Finally, to look at the vibrancy and inventiveness that can still rise up among the piping enthusiasts of today says a lot about this instrument's continued potency. The pipes may direct us back to history, but they direct us forward too. Or as a piping friend of mine has more appropriately put it: 'Piping might have a ghillie-brogue-wearing foot in the past but points its chanter to the future.'

A final introductory remark. It would be fair to say that the Highland bagpipes look a bit like a decapitated upside-down deer with an inflated tartan stomach. They are also inordinately loud. And yet this almost comic instrument is, depending to whom you speak, the reason for lives changing, for social exclusion turning to inclusion, for bullying, feuds and discontent, for travelling the world, for shifts of culture, and in some cases for love. With the right tune and the right player, its music is, for me and for so many, beautiful beyond words. 'The Lament for the Children' was, according to Yehudi Menuhin, 'the greatest single line of music ever written'.[15] The bagpipes are so much more than just an instrument, and it's in this light that we proceed.

1

ORIGINS

FROM THE PROFANE TO THE SACRED AND BACK AGAIN

A family of instruments that owes its worldwide existence to the fact that shepherds have had a lot of time, and dead sheep, on their hands over the millennia.

YouTube viewer's description of the bagpipes

The above statement is just one of many 'insights' you can find below Kathryn Tickell's video, 'An Introduction to Northumbrian Smallpipes'.[1] Tickell is widely regarded as the foremost exponent of that instrument, making it accessible like never before, having recorded and performed with the likes of Jacob Collier and Sting. Despite this, another viewer of her video seems to have remained in the dark about the instrument. 'I have to admit when I saw "Northumbrian smallpipes" I thought it was something we should all be vaccinated against.' As with the dead sheep and shepherds scenario, it's a classic YouTube comment, something that can be quietly chuckled over then disregarded. And yet both express truths. The second comment, for all its humour, is a reminder of our widespread ignorance about the bagpipes—something this book hopes to redress. The first comment is truthful in more ways than one.

To start with, the first description at least recognises that the bagpipes are a family of instruments, not just the Great Highland Bagpipes that grace the tartan-clad Scots and their imitators. Some say there are over 130 forms of bagpipe.[2] The viewer is also right to think of this family as having a 'worldwide' presence. Bagpipes— the singular and plural are used interchangeably—can be found in

Asia, North Africa, the Middle East and most European countries. Common denominators are the use of reeds to produce the sounds, a bag to supply the air to go through the reeds, a blowpipe or bellows allowing air to enter the bag, a reeded chanter (or two) where fingers can play the tune and, in most cases, one or more drones to offer accompanying notes and harmonies. Chanter, blowpipe and drones usually connect to the bag by means of short pieces of lathe-turned wood called stocks. Differences are found in the design, construction, materials, repertoires and styles of playing. Fixity of form is rarely a key feature in the history of musical instruments.[3]

Our YouTube aficionado highlights one further commonality. Shepherds have long been associated with the instrument, and no wonder, since animals have usually provided the raw materials— sheep included, though goats are probably the most common. This is often reflected in bagpipe names. The *bock* of the Czech Republic—and elsewhere—is likely to come from the German for male goat. The French *chabrette* is a diminutive of goat. If you go to the Metropolitan Museum in New York, you'll find an exquisite figurine of a Harlequin playing the entire animal. It was made in Germany in the 1730s, and though a comic piece, it was common practice for bagpipe makers to use the whole beast, especially in Eastern Europe. Until the end of the nineteenth century, it was still possible to find bagpipes in Hungary that had a chanter emerging from the head of a real goat, and all Hungarian pipes to this day have a carved goat's head as the top stock of the chanter. The Maltese bagpipe, *żaqq*, is composed of the whole goat, minus the head, and is still played today. There is even a man in Sydney, called Risto Todoroski, who has fashioned his own set of Macedonian bagpipes, known as *gaida*, and left the head on—the enormous protruding horns making it a sight to behold as Risto manhandles it into life.[4] It seems, however, that bagpipers are not too fussy about which precise animal they are playing. There are records of the instrument being made out of still-born calves, dogs, large cats, young horses and even the stomach of a grey seal.[5] In Romania, the word for bagpipe is *cimpoi*, which is likely to come from another word meaning 'ruminant stomach'.[6] Russian bagpipes, meanwhile, known as *volynka*, had bags made from ox bladders (*vol* is ox).[7] It's said that when Tsar Peter the Great's pet bear died, he had it made into a form of Polish bagpipe.[8]

It's only natural, then, to ask if this rich variety of bagpipes has a common ancestor and, if so, to wonder when it first appeared.

* * *

The honest answer is we don't really know. Most bagpipe historians writing today are willing to point this out, but even the experts can lead us down unreliable paths in terms of the very first references. Take the claim about the pipe and the dog's anus for instance. I refer to two lines in a Greek play by Aristophanes, of about 425 BCE, which are said to refer to 'pipers from Thebes ... blowing on a pipe with a bag of dogskin and with a chanter of bone'.[9] Most scholars have accepted this as the first written evidence of the bagpipe's existence. But Austrian piper and linguistic historian Michael Peter Vereno, in his ground-breaking book *The Voice of the Wind* (2021)— to which this chapter is much indebted—translates the key line in the Greek as 'On pipes of bone now blow for us the dog's behind!' As Vereno points out, there is no mention of a bag whatsoever. He writes: '[A] bagpipe probably has to be read into the source ... The text seems to be vulgar, abstract and metaphorical.' He further adds this choice observation: '[I]f an animal hide is used for making a bag, the lower half of the body is normally partially or totally lost during the skinning process. The anus would therefore not be fit for being used as a natural tie-in spot for the pipe.'[10]

Vereno's unsettling of the consensus continues as he assesses the various items of material evidence that have been cited as the earliest visual representations of the bagpipe, but in each case there is simply either too much doubt about what exactly is being represented or the date of the artefact.[11] Only when we get to the literature of the first and second centuries CE, with the writings of the Roman biographer Suetonius and the Greek historian Dio Chrysostom, do we find ourselves on surer ground, and we discover that the first named bagpiper in history is the rotund and notorious Roman Emperor Nero (37–68 CE). Chrysostom writes definitively of Nero playing a pipe (Greek: *aulos*) with 'a bag tucked under his armpit'.[12] Some historians, however, have been swift to transfer this fact to the well-known saying about Nero playing a fiddle during the Great Fire of Rome in 64 CE. 'Nero fiddled while Rome burned' has become a go-to description for leaders who appear to do something trivial or irresponsible in the face of an emergency. Given what we know about Nero's ability to play a bagpipe, some scholars have naturally asked whether it was not more likely that he was piping while the city burned.[13]

Yet, once again, a look at the original texts that form the basis of the saying makes the debate seem pointless. They simply mention that Nero was singing about the destruction of Troy, though one of the chroniclers—Cassius Dio—adds that he was wearing a 'cithara player's garb', the cithara being the precursor to the lute, which would eventually lead to the guitar. By the seventeenth century, this brief mention of Nero's costume had morphed into a story about him fiddling away as the city was enveloped in flames. But the point is this: the sources do not mention Nero playing *any* instrument on this occasion.[14] Given the other references to his bagpiping, it's at least nice for us to know that he *could* have piped amid the burning city, had he so wished.

So bagpipes were known in imperial Rome. Contrary to a common belief, there is no evidence they were played in the Roman army.[15] There are only three other references to the instrument in classical times: one by a Latin poet in the late first century CE, one in a piece of graffiti in Pompey and one from a second-century Egyptian papyrus. Given the kinds of words that are used, it's not clear that the bagpipe was actually viewed as a separate instrument from the reeded pipes that are well attested long before this. With these ancient instruments, the air was supplied directly from the mouth, making it difficult to achieve a continuous sound, unless a player could master the art of circular breathing—letting air that has been stored in the cheeks escape into the instrument while breathing in through the nose. Adding a bag may have been viewed simply as an alternative way to achieve continuous sound, the instrument remaining essentially the same to the ear.[16] The words that are used in the classical sources also show that there must have been some connection to Greek culture, but there is no indisputable evidence of the bagpipe's existence in ancient Greek literature or artifacts (though bear in mind, the raw materials of the bagpipe are highly perishable). So, the earliest we can get back to, in terms of concrete proof of the bagpipe's existence, is the first century CE in

Rome and, slightly later, in its eastern provinces. They *may* have been played beyond these regions of course. Indeed, the earlier-mentioned Egyptian papyrus provides names for those it lists as bagpipers; three of the names are of Egyptian origin, two are Greek and one comes from a Latin name.[17] Whether the bagpipe was around earlier remains unconfirmed. Some scholars are convinced their origins lie deeper in the past in western Asia, where melody and drone sound have combined since time immemorial[18]—but with our current knowledge, it's impossible to know.

I appreciate that all this talk of animal innards, dogs' bottoms and historical inaccuracies doesn't quite deliver the romance and magic I promised. Other chapters may have to fulfil that pledge. There is at least some glamour in the fact that the first bagpiper known to history is an emperor, but this shouldn't make us think of the instrument as a means of music making for the elite. That you played the pipe with a bag could have been proof that you were not up to the virtuoso's standards of pipe playing, as such players would have used circular breathing instead. Without a bag, the pipe player could adjust the sound levels of his playing according to the force of his breath and could create stop–start effects with his tongue—a range of musical possibilities denied to the bagpiper. For this reason, Vereno thinks the instrument may have been an object of contempt to the upper classes.[19] Yet the Egyptian papyrus mentioned earlier is a payment roll for a group of musicians, including bagpipers, so it seems it was still possible to make money by playing the instrument. The question of where the pipes sat within the class system would come to be one of the most interesting questions in its later history, as we'll see. Playing the bagpipes, and the level to which they were played, said a lot about the player's standing—or lack of it—in the community.

* * *

After these early references, the lights go off and the Dark Ages set in, as Western Europe goes into meltdown after the fall of the Roman Empire. A hiatus of about 700 years intervenes between these first references and the next, when the bagpipes, under the names of *chorus*—a bagpipe without drones—and *tympanum*, reappear in monastic texts—possibly as a result of the growing influence on Europe at this time of Islamic culture, a culture that seems to have had reeded pipes, with drone accompaniment, since early times.[20] In these monastic texts, the bodies of dead animals are once again subjected to all sorts of indignities. A ninth-century psalter defines a 'tympanum' as 'an inflated cat skin, which has two pipes in its legs and one in its neck'.[21] By the thirteenth century, monks started to liberate animals—imaginatively at least—from their oppression. Illuminated manuscripts now begin to show a wide variety of bagpipes, and often they are being mastered by animals themselves.[22] In many cases, they are not considered as playing to the glory of God. The influential bagpipe historian Hugh Cheape writes: '[A]nimals which were associated with the lower passions of lust and avarice [e.g., sows and monkeys respectively], and therefore with Satan, were offered as visual precept and distraction towards higher passions.'[23] Frankly, the bagpipe was a phallic symbol and often used as an identifier for the sins of gluttony and lechery;[24] its potency was only enhanced in the hands of a lusty pig. That the instrument was also held by some to be rather unpleasant to the ear adds a further dimension. Scholar Kathleen Scott puts it bluntly: '[M]edieval iconography took a direct means of communicating its distaste: it represented the ugly-sounding pipes in the arms of an ugly-sounding animal.'[25]

Some push the sexual aspect further. In a manuscript of 1487, *De Caelo, De anima*, now housed in the British Library, there is a marginal doodle of a pig playing a pig's bladder as a bagpipe. A jester dances behind the pig mimicking the animal as he pushes one hand to his chest—housing his own air—while the other hand grasps his own penis and testicles. A scholar of medieval queer history states:

> Playing the medieval bagpipes was an intimate contact with (animal) skin, and when the player was imagined to be an animal, it bordered on cannibalism. But what if the bagpipe was human skin? What if the bagpipe stands for the human body, with baggy glands and dangly appendages? The pig plays the pig-bladder. It handles the hard shaft and makes noises. The hairy or stretchy exterior moistens with the player's breath and saliva. The jester plays his own body, that makes noises and secretes bodily fluids. These 'instruments' attend

to their materiality. So animals playing bagpipes could remind one of human masturbation.[26]

This is probably making too much of one image—generalising the exception, as it were—but there may be something in it. Certainly, the medieval artist did not suffer from prudery. Hieronymus Bosch, in his triptych *Garden of Earthly Delights* (1490–1510), seems to luxuriate in the pleasures of the flesh, even if he is ultimately condemning them. In the painting's central panel, the penetration of orifices, human and animal, is clearly depicted, and bestiality is blatant. Fruits of outrageous size are sucked and devoured with abandon. The symbolism is so bizarre and extensive that Bosch makes Dalí look like a realist. But it is in the right-hand panel, depicting judgement and hell—the panel that viewers spend most time looking at[27]—that the bagpipes come in. A huge bagpipe, made to look like a scrotum and penis, seemingly blasting a single note, stands in the middle of a disc, around which demons and 'sinners' parade. That an enormous pair of severed ears stands next to this image, with a giant knife between, suggests the physical pain inflicted by the instrument. Another bagpipe appears to be a monster that plays itself, with smoke and fire emerging from the chanter—a symbol of masturbation again, perhaps? But we shouldn't take this as a sign that bagpipes were selected for special, derogatory treatment. Instruments of all kinds bedevil the poor inhabitants of this noisy hell. Highlights include a crucified harpist, strung up upon his harp, with the strings piercing his spine, neck and anus, and a wind player borne down by a supersized bombard or shawm, while a recorder penetrates his behind. Still, the bagpipes did seem to have a special place in the medieval artist's mind when it came to the horned ruler of hell. The instrument is found again and again in the hands of the devil.[28] This is hardly surprising when we remember that the animal most commonly associated with the Evil One was the goat. This demonic connection would of course become immortalised centuries later in Robert Burns' classic poem 'Tam O'Shanter'. There, 'Auld Nick ... screw'd the pipes and gart them skirl'.[29]

Bosch evidently had a strong distaste for music, mixed with an obsessive fascination. His works are saturated with the theme. This reflected the church's complex and ambiguous attitude towards music. Minstrels, the main performers of secular music, were particularly suspect, their shades of bawdiness giving rise to clerical accusations of all sorts: igniting carnal desire, vanity, idleness, lechery. Their willingness to sing openly about the shortcomings of the clergy didn't do them any favours, nor did their readiness to sing the praises of whoever paid them to render praise. John of Salisbury, the twelfth-century bishop of Chartres, so disliked minstrels that he called for their mass extermination.[30] Though things never went that far, instrumentalists in general came to be a legally oppressed minority. As Ian Bostridge, Britain's greatest performer of German Lieder, has written:

> During the Middle Ages, instrumentalists had been viewed as incompetent in many legal matters: unable to be judges, witnesses, or jurors; ineligible for land tenure; unable to serve as guardians or to hold civic office; not accepted by the trade guilds; with no right to normal damages as plaintiffs in a civil case.[31]

No wonder the church repeatedly stated that it would only countenance voice and organ during the liturgy.

And yet the volume of a bagpipe makes it an ideal instrument for a procession, and there is evidence of pipers playing on pilgrimages and at church festivals and feasts across medieval Britain and Europe—indeed, it continues to this day with the Le Pardons festival in Brittany. (That is not to suggest that these 'pious' occasions couldn't be bawdy affairs. Twelfth Night celebrations, observed one commentator, 'became so boisterous that it was necessary to appoint a Lord of Misrule to govern the festivities').[32] Suspicion of instrumentalists didn't stop monks populating their manuscripts with instruments and musicians of every kind, playing in praise of holy figures, especially paintings of the Virgin Mary and the infant Jesus. Despite all we've seen about Bosch and licentious pipe-wielding pigs, bagpipes are often found in such devotional settings. This is largely due to the ancient connection between bagpipes and shepherds—that band of lowly men who rushed to the crib in Bethlehem. There are numerous *Annunciations to the Shepherds* in which a piper is either puffing away or, seconds after detaching from his blowpipe, looking up in astonishment at the angel announcing news of Jesus' birth. In the exquisite Belles Heures created for Jean de France, duc de Berry, in the first decade of the fifteenth century, there is a crib-side image in which a bagpiper falls before the Mother and Child, his bag still inflated and thus presumably still wailing away. Joseph holds his head in his hand. The duke's meditations, which accompany the paintings, refer to Joseph as sitting 'quite dejected because he was unable to provide the Virgin Mary with everything necessary'.[33] But perhaps this was to miss the mark. Perhaps Joseph's pained posture was a response to the sound of the wailing bagpipe.

The web of meanings attached to the bagpipes—sexual, sinful, sacred—could, on occasion, coalesce in a single image. The famous sixteenth-century fresco at Saronno by Gaudenzio Ferrari has a female angel playing a bagpipe with two one-hand chanters, which protrude from a bag with two large, curvaceous bulges, held precisely at chest height. It's as if she is playing with her breasts, just as much as she's playing the phallic pipes.

* * *

But as we enter the sixteenth century, and the first rumblings of the Reformation are heard, bagpipes start to break free from their sacred settings and find another type of immortality in the hands of great secular artists. Albrecht Dürer's peasant engravings (1514–19), with their famous bagpiper reclining against a tree and the dancing couple (the two images are probably intended as a pair), show an altogether less holy scene. This was not intended as a critique of earlier religious art, but it may have represented Dürer's backlash against his Italian critics, who thought him incapable of working within a classical idiom. As art historian Jürgen Müller has convincingly argued through a close analysis of the structures and shapes of the images, the bagpiper is Dürer's ironic take on the ancient *Piping Faun* of Praxiteles, while the dancing couple are his response to *Laocoön and His Sons*, the magnificent sculpture that had only just been excavated in Rome in 1506.[34] In choosing a 'vulgar' bagpiper and rustic, ungainly dancers as the focus of his craft, and yet using all the skill that any Italian could hope to muster, the German Dürer was giving a veiled two fingers to his Southern contemporaries.[35] Along with Dürer, Pieter Bruegel the Elder (d. 1569) would ensure that, henceforth, the bagpipes were to be closely linked in the European imagination with peasants, jollity and all things frivolous.[36] Crucially, Bruegel would also cement the idea that piping was closely linked to dancing.

They could have dark connotations too, as dancing, fools and bagpipes all combined into one new artistic exercise: the depiction of the 'Danse Macabre', or Dance of Death. These paintings or murals, produced in the wake of the Black Death, were intended to remind viewers of the shortness of life and the nearness of death and combined the frivolous with the terrifying. Typically, a personification of death in skeletal form dances a mortal to the grave. Death provides the music. Very often, it is the music of the bagpipe—an echo, perhaps, of the old German legend, stretching back to around 1300, of the Pied Piper, who led the children of Hamelin to their deaths with the sound of his pipe. Hans Holbein the Younger (1497–1543) followed the tradition, and again it is the phallic that seems to provide the rationale for the presence of the pipes. In his image of the Fool being danced away, the Fool is about to hit Death with an air-filled bladder or sack, as Death exposes the Fool's dangling privates. In a welter of phallic imagery, Death's bagpipes act as the correlative sack and appendage. It's unclear how we are to unpack all this, but one thing is for sure: the bagpipes are not an accidental choice; they are not just 'any old instrument'.

That sense of the pipes as a generative force for wide-ranging meanings has underpinned much of the story in this chapter. If an instrument is needed to evoke the highs and lows of human nature, there is no better choice than the bagpipes. And that's not just noticeable in the early history we've covered so far. We'll see it recur again and again, though the setting will shift to some extent. Which brings us to Scotland—that strangely absent land from our opening survey. But having got to the lifetime of Holbein the Younger, that country has well and truly entered the story. The question becomes: how did the pipes get there? The answer will surprise some, for England might have a lot to do with it.

2

GETTING TO SCOTLAND

RESISTING NATIONAL BOUNDARIES

You don't have to look like an ancient prophet or a Marxist revolutionary to speak authoritatively on the folk traditions of Eastern Europe, but it helps. Just take a look at the legendary Czech ethnographer and bagpipe-reviver Josef Režný (1924–2012). You can't but listen to the man when you see such a combination of hair and beard. If the Angus MacPherson of our Introduction was a 'great tradition-bearer' in Scotland, Režný was certainly that in his own country. The 1950s footage of him sitting in a field with an aged countryman, who intones a traditional song while a youthful Režný feverishly scribbles down the notes and lyrics for posterity, shows the kind of man we're dealing with.[1] Across his lifetime, he collected over 1,000 folk songs and seventy-six different dances. It was Režný, moreover, who founded, in 1955, the precursor to the International Bagpipe Festival in Strakonice, where you can still go to see and hear the rich diversity of piping traditions hinted at in the previous chapter and that the festival helped to reignite.

In an interview of 2004, Režný put his finger on a problem that faces any historian of the bagpipe when he said that there was 'no such thing' as a 'Czech' bagpipe. His interviewer, Mark Patterson, reflected that Režný thought 'in cultural not political terms'. Referring to what he called the 'middle European piping zone', Režný claimed that 'the same kind of compound-reed instrument is played in all of these regions, in similar ensembles with instruments such as clarinets or fiddles, and similar styles of music are performed'. He continued:

Very similar bagpipes are played in Bohemia, Germany and Poland; and in Bohemia and Moravia, bellows-blown instruments are the norm. So there is no 'Czech bagpipe' … this expression is nonsense. Every region of our country is different and they can still be distinguished by their dance and song repertoires. There is no 'national' folklore.

Režný traced his own Prachen bagpipe tradition to the thirteenth century but recognised that it seemed to be in decline, with only about 300 contemporary players—nothing compared to what he saw in Galicia, Brittany, Ireland and Scotland. Having denied, initially, the importance of national boundaries, Režný's words soon took on political overtones:

In general, the culture is weakening, because the bearers of it have been dying out. It is very rare to find a family where the tradition is passed on from the older generation to the younger ones. It corresponds with general changes in today's society; what is 'normal' and what is not? But in our country there is still something like a 'hidden patriotism'—a feeling of ethnic integrity—and that is why some features of the tradition can be preserved.[2]

The interview is illuminating on two fronts. On the one hand, it suggests something of the fluidity of bagpiping culture, a culture where boundaries cannot be easily drawn. Just as importantly, and almost paradoxically, it also shows how the bagpipes find themselves so immediately and intimately attached to the identity of a people and a place: it is 'patriotism' and 'ethnic integrity' that ensure the survival of Režný's native Prachen tradition. The whole topic is *charged* with political and cultural significance.

Shifting our gaze southwards, the history of piping in Austria reinforces both points. Vereno, much quoted in the previous chapter, has written of his native country:

The Austria the world knows today is actually a quite young country and consists of only a small part of what was once the Habsburg Empire (which throughout history was commonly labelled as 'Austria') and thus part of the greater Holy Roman Empire … Most of the bagpipe's history in this region features a constant flow of cultures from West to East and North to South, and Austria never was home to only one nation with one language, but always a meeting point of diverse peoples, tongues and cultures.

Vereno adds: 'Therefore, the beginnings of piping in Austria cannot be investigated in seclusion from neighbouring cultures and regions.' Good luck, in other words, to the historian who, scholarly tweezers in hand, tries to lay bare the sinews of its history as distinct from the history of the nation itself and its wider European context. And yet, once again, for all the flux, the bagpipes assert themselves as cultural icons for specific places *and* as markers of identity capable of transcending geographic boundaries:

> [T]he Germans of Egerland in Bohemia (belonging to Austria until 1918) kept their piping tradition vividly present until their expulsion from Czechoslovakia in 1946 … After the forced resettlement, most pipers did not continue their tradition in their new homes in Germany, since the rural piping was not suitable for the big cities anymore. When the interest in piping in Germany grew again in the 1970s, the line of tradition to the Egerland pipers had been broken for almost twenty years. Little did the new pipers know then, that indeed a German/Austrian piping tradition continues to exist with no interruption in the New Zealand community of Puhoi, which was founded by Bohemians in the 1860s. Although the German language has mostly vanished, the interest in Bohemian piping is still going strong there.[3]

This perfectly highlights some of the paradoxes and tensions at play when it comes to the nature and history of the instrument. The bagpipes can speak so intensely of a particular place and people. Yet, at the same time, they are one of the most transferable, most malleable, most travelled instruments ever to have blasted their way around the globe.

* * *

So much of this is relevant to Scotland's story. Here, too, we have a 'constant flow of cultures' contributing to the nation's character. It is probably not relevant, for our purposes, to delve into times much before the fourteenth century, because it is only then that evidence for the existence of the bagpipe in Scotland begins to appear[4]—hence the omission of Scotland as a player in our opening chapter. Tellingly, the nature of the earliest architectural evidence is clearly linked to Scotland's strong bonds with the continent prior to the Union of the Crowns in 1603. I'm referring to the stone carvings of single drone bagpipes on the masonry of Melrose Abbey (where the piper is a pig), Rosslyn Chapel (where the piper is an angel) and a cottage in the aptly named village of Skirling, Peeblesshire (though the date of this last example is contested).[5] Each of these follow the dominant early European tradition, that is, they play conical chanters, and there's a single drone and a blow-pipe, a set-up not far from what one finds today in the *gaita* played across the Iberian Peninsula, most famously in Galicia.[6] In every cultural respect, not just architecturally, the flow of influence to and from Europe could be felt over this period. As the renowned historian of Scotland Jenny Wormald wrote:

> Scotland in the late fifteenth and sixteenth centuries had been intensely outward-looking, self-consciously aware, indeed proud, of her receptiveness and contribution to the political, economic, religious, and intellectual life of Europe. The personal union of the crowns [in 1603] meant that her frontiers narrowed, as English interests began to restrict her freedom of action.[7]

This connection with Europe was of long-standing, and often it seemed to bypass England rather than use it as a conduit. Cultural historian Kylie Murray has pointed out how the post-Brexit scenario of the Scots seeking out a figurehead of a European political and economic union, in the hope of an intervention to quash England's claim to constitutional jurisdiction over Scotland, has close parallels to what had already happened in the late 1100s. At that time, the archbishop of York was presumptuous enough to claim that the Scottish Church fell under his authority. Scotland saw the matter differently and approached Pope Celestine III, whose subsequent bull, *Cum universi*, stated that the archbishop was wrong in his assumption and that the Scottish Church was in fact a 'special daughter' of Rome. There was to be no intermediary. As Murray observes: 'The Scottish Church was deemed an independent entity from that of England's, but equally a member of a larger European community and subject only to the Pope.'[8]

Musically, that connection to Europe was clearly evident in the centuries to come in the relationships Scotland developed with the Netherlands, which has been called 'the Vienna or Berlin of the fifteenth and early sixteenth centuries'.[9] There are numerous examples of Scots travelling across the channel and returning with a wealth of musical skills and practices, which soon filtered into the wider Scottish culture: five-fingered organ playing is one example. The appearance in Scotland of the professional musician and the salaried singer is also linked to earlier Dutch practices.[10] Musicologist Joan Rimmer, in her Cramb Lecture of 1990 at the University of Glasgow, certainly felt there was a strong case for arguing that the compositional characteristics of much traditional Scottish music, including that belonging to the Great Highland Bagpipe, were rooted in an older approach that was widespread across Europe.[11]

To add to this flow of communication with Europe, there was also an internal flow between the Highlands and Lowlands. In fact, the idea of a Highland line dividing the two regions was not one of significant antiquity. It was only with the priest and chronicler John of Fordun, writing in the 1370s, that this notion entered the national consciousness.[12] If you look at the material culture from this time— its tangible relics—the country was much the same from north to south, from east to west, in its agricultural practices especially. Wormald again:

> The later history of the highlands, the popular images of Glencoe ... and the Forty-Five, and Walter Scott's romantic domestication of the noble savage and invention of modern tartan, all combine to create the idea of a gulf [between Lowlands and Highlands] which had always existed. In the early sixteenth century the gulf was beginning to open; but there were still many bridges across it.[13]

Nonetheless, it is especially true of pre-1603 Scotland that an outward-looking perspective achieves—in the words of Sir Tom Devine—a 'richer and more intellectually convincing explanation of the nation's development'.[14] When it comes to trying to account for the bagpipes' appearance in Scotland, just take Scotland's relationship with Ireland.

It's generally acknowledged that, for much of Gaelic Scotland's past—perhaps until as late as the eighteenth century—there was a very close cultural correspondence with Ireland. The way their musicians, poets and scholars were trained and organised bore significant similarities, and often what appeared in Scotland was the result of Irish initiative.[15] It's no surprise that Ireland was known as the *maior scotia* or 'greater Scotia', with poor old Scotland as *scotia minor*, 'lesser Scotia'. The relationship between the two is now seen as critical to the story of the bagpipe's early presence in Gaelic Scotland and how the instrument functioned within that society.[16] A look at those families who are regarded as the 'piping dynasties' from this time—the MacCrimmons, MacArthurs, Rankins and MacGregors, for example—is especially enlightening on this front.

These dynasties served the families of particular clan chiefs for generation after generation as hereditary pipers, some of them even having their own colleges of piping on land that had been granted to them by the chief for their services. Other perks were included. One family, for instance, enjoyed the special privilege of being entitled to a portion of any cow slaughtered for the chief's household; the only downside being that that portion was the udder![17] When Dr Johnson toured the Western Isles in 1773, he encountered the last remnants of these piping dynasties, and with regard to the most famous of all, the MacCrimmons, he was assured they had a presence on Skye, as hereditary pipers to the MacLeod chieftains, 'beyond all time of memory'.[18] That antiquity is not necessarily provable from the evidence we have, but they and other families were certainly present from at least the sixteenth century. The harpist and bard had been features of a chieftain's court long before the arrival of the piper, but gradually it was the latter who took on the task of composing tunes for his master, be they salutes, eulogies or laments, and performing for great occasions. This practice, and the practice of handing on their compositions and techniques, clearly formed part of a wider musical and poetic tradition within a Gaelic culture zone that spanned both Scotland and Ireland, with Ireland acknowledged as its 'wellspring'.[19]

A supporting piece of evidence is worth quoting here for its similarity of tone to that magical MacPherson recording quoted in our Introduction. It is taken from a letter of 1763 from the Reverend John MacPherson (those MacPhersons!), minister of Sleat, recollecting a visit to Uist about twenty years earlier:

[T]here was an ancient little family, the head of which united the professions of the bard, genealogist and shennachy [storyteller]. The bard of that family whom I had occasion to know, was a man of some letters, that is to say, he and his ancestors, for many ages, had received their education in Irish Colleges of poetry and history, and understood the Latin tolerably well.[20]

Without getting too diverted from the main point—that you can't think of Scotland, and the bagpipes in Scotland, in isolation—such a quote (and there are many like it) stands as a form of rebuttal to the famous British historian Hugh Trevor-Roper's claims around Scotland's propensity to invent traditions for itself, claims first formulated in 1977.[21] Such claims, in the words of one knowledgeable though offended Scottish commentator, take Scotland to be 'a sham nation kept going for centuries by inventive trickery' and seek to demonstrate that 'mythopoeia is a Celtic disease from which hardheaded Anglo-Saxons have never suffered'.[22] Although Trevor-Roper's account is itself now largely 'discredited',[23] the after-effects can still be felt and familiar Scottish history too readily consigned, in one indiscriminating sweep, to the realms of fantasy.

What a quote like the one from the Reverend MacPherson does is remind us that—while there are undoubtedly mythologising forces at play in the centuries-long narrative-making of any ancient country—there remain concrete pieces of evidence that can still excite our emotions and heighten our sense of mystery. The world of bards, shennachies and colleges of poetry was a *real* world. Trevor-Roper, writing in a decade when UK unionists such as himself were fearful of a rising tide of political nationalism in Scotland, attacked a particular version of Scotland in order, as one of his editors puts it, to counter 'the attempt by Scottish nationalists to rouse atavistic tribal loyalties in support of their cause through appeal to a fraudulent romantic version of the country's history'.[24] In the case of MacPherson, there is surely a touch of romance to the picture he paints of 'the ancient little family'. But there is nothing to justify, in this case, the accusation of fraudulence. Moreover, MacPherson's words remind us that the so-called barbarism of the Highlands, oft repeated by the historical enemies of its people, requires serious qualification. This is an account of a *civilised* family. It reminds me of what the seasoned, much-travelled scholar Adam Ferguson (1723–1816), professor of moral philosophy at Edinburgh, said of the Gaelic people from which he himself sprung: 'Had I not been in the Highlands of Scotland I might be of their mind who think the inhabitants of Paris and Versailles the only polite people in the world.'[25]

But before we get too dewy-eyed at these recollections, here are the sobering words of Cheape to remind us of why a quote such as MacPherson's matters in the first place: 'The centrality of Ireland in a medieval western European context has been firmly and consistently written out of the Scottish historical tradition ... [F]or the under-standing of Highland piping, its historical context, as well as broader issues of cultural roots and mores, we ignore Ireland at our peril.'[26]

In light of the Euro-focused reflections at the beginning of this chapter, it's important to note what Cheape goes on to add: 'Ireland also may have been a source and conduit by which European learn-ing and musical traditions (such as hymn metres and ballads) reached the *Gàidhealtachd* [i.e., Gaelic-speaking regions] of Scotland, although such a proposal needs more examination.'[27] It's possible, in other words, that the bagpipes reached Gaelic Scotland from Europe via Ireland along what Cheape calls an 'Atlantic corridor', but there is as yet no proof of this.[28] There is, in fact, a long tradi-tion of belief in Ireland that the bagpipes were invented there inde-pendently of Europe.[29] Teasingly, there are references to pipers in the Book of Leinster (c. 1160) and the Statutes of Kilkenny (1367), but it's unclear exactly what a 'piper' was in this context.[30] No additional bag needs to be assumed. Bags only become evident in the Irish evidence from the fifteenth century at the earliest.[31] The hard Scottish evidence thus predates the Irish, though nothing con-clusive can be drawn from this.

We'll have more to say on bagpipes in their Gaelic context in later chapters. For now, it's enough to note the resonances between the fluidity we find in Central Europe and what we find between Scotland and Ireland. In both cases, the culture out of which the bagpipe emerges refuses to conform to national boundaries, and yet the instrument quickly becomes emblematic of a particular place and people. The same is true again if we look to Scotland's relation-ship to England.

* * *

It will surprise some readers to learn that, in all likelihood, the bagpipes in England pre-date the bagpipes in Scotland. While we can get back to the fourteenth century north of the border, in the south we can get back—possibly—to the time of Leofric, bishop of Exeter, who died in 1072. It is to Leofric that the *Codex Exoniensis* or *Exeter Riddles* are attributed, and among the many Anglo-Saxon riddles collected there you can find one that seems to point to the answer—bagpipes:

> I saw a strange thing singing in a house;
> Its shape was more wonderful than aught among men.
> Its beak was underneath, its feet and hands birdlike;
> Yet fly it cannot nor walk at all ...
> Brave, eager for glory it remains dumb,
> Yet it has in its foot beautiful sounds,
> A glorious gift of song. Wondrous it seems to me
> How this very thing can play with words
> Through its foot beneath adorned with trappings.
> It has on its neck when it guards its treasure,
> Bare, proud with rings, its two companions,
> Brother and sister ...[32]

If this isn't concrete enough evidence of the bagpipe's presence in England, the next mention is still earlier than anything known in Scotland. This is the 1288 reference to 'a certain servant with a bagpipe who piped before the king',[33] as recorded by the treasurer to Edward I. His payment of 2 shillings was roughly equivalent to a week's wages for an agricultural labourer, so it was no mean job.[34] That the pipes had a place in the noble households of England at this time is suggested by a piece of archaeological evidence too. What appears to be a boxwood drone, conforming in style and size to early manuscript images of bagpipes with a drone, has been unearthed at Weoley Castle in Birmingham and dated to the late thirteenth or fourteenth century.[35]

Yet, at the same time, the instrument could conjure up the very opposite of nobility. Nowhere is this clearer than in the famous reference in Chaucer's *Canterbury Tales* (1387–1400), where in the Prologue it is said of Robin the Miller: 'A baggepipe wel koude he blowe and sowne, / And therwithal he broghte us out of towne.'[36]

Given the highly uncomplimentary depiction of the Miller as a drunkard and a moral degenerate—he is a 'a janglere and a goliardeys / And that was moost of synne and harlotries' (a buffoon and teller of dirty stories, mostly about sin and deeds of harlotry)[37]—the agreed medieval symbolism of the bagpipes, as discussed in our previous chapter, was on hand for Chaucer to plug into. Kathleen Scott explains: '[B]y giving the Miller a set of bagpipes, Chaucer was symbolizing not only the general moral nature of the Miller but also one of the immediate physical effects of his over-indulgence. He was comparing the whining sound of the pipes to the wheezing sound of the Miller.'[38] For added impact, Chaucer also likens the Miller to that animal most commonly connected to the bagpipes in medieval imagery, the sow: the animal of lechery. 'His berd as any sowe or fox was reed / ... Upon the cop right of his nose he hade / A werte, and theron stood a toft of herys, / Reed as the brustles of a sowes erys.'[39] Connected to such a man, with his bristly wart, you might say the pipes had a bit of an image problem.

Church carvings across England play heavily on the sow/pipes theme. In Yorkshire alone, puffing pigs of one form or another are to be found in at least five medieval churches. In Beverley Minster, the torso of a man, dated to around 1340, can be found on a bracket. He is playing an instrument that is half pig, half bagpipes, which is only suggestive of one thing when it comes to the sound of the pipes. Given the date, and the other early English references, it's under-standable that some historians conjecture that the pipes arrived in Scotland *from* England: horror of horrors![40]

If we compare what was happening in the royal courts north and south of the border, the evidence would suggest that the pipes played a more central role to entertainment in London than they did in the palaces of Scotland. From at least the reign of Henry VII in the late fifteenth century, until 1570 in the reign of Elizabeth I, the English monarchs all had pipers among their court musicians. These men were well paid and bedecked in fine livery. After the death of Henry VIII in 1547, an inventory of his possessions was drawn up, and among the myriad musical instruments listed, five of them were bagpipes, one of which is described as having 'pipes of Ivorie, the bagge covered with purple vellat'.[41] This doesn't prove Henry played the pipes himself—and there is no proof behind the legend that he wrote the tune 'Greensleeves'—but it does show the esteem in which the instrument was held in this royal setting.

Pipes remained popular across sixteenth-century England more widely, though they could on occasion be the cause of official displeasure. In 1592, a man in West Somerset was called before the local magistrates and upbraided for disturbing a church service by 'causing the bells to be rung, and dyvers baggepipes to be blown, to the grete dishonor of Almighty God'.[42] It is tempting to think that 'dyvers' here refers to the number of different forms the instrument took at that time, so that there was no set 'English bagpipe'. Certainly, English church carvings and art of the sixteenth century show that twin chanter bagpipes were just as well known as single chanter pipes were.[43]

The earliest reference to the pipes at the Scottish court is a payment in 1362 of 40 shillings to pipers who played for David II—though, as is so often the case, we cannot be utterly certain that *bag*pipes were played, perhaps they were playing the shawm or fife, and we must bear this in mind whenever the records simply state 'pipes' or 'pipers';[44] it's not until the publication of the brilliantly irreverent *Colkelbie's Sow* (c. 1460–70) that we get the first explicit reference to a 'bag pype' in Scotland.[45] Rewinding from there a moment, it's said that James I of Scotland (reigned 1424–37) was a multi-instrumentalist and that one of his skills was playing the bagpipes—but the translation of the original Latin word used (*choro*) has been disputed, and some believe it should be rendered 'fiddle'.[46] In 1489, under James IV, we hear for the first time of the nationality of the pipers who played for the sovereign, and these are described as 'Inglis pypars, that com to the Castell yet [gate] and playt to the King.' They were evidently held in high regard for they received the princely sum of £8, 8s. 'Inglis pyparis' played again at Linlithgow in 1491 for £7, 4s. It is only in 1497 that native Scots pipers are mentioned, in the form of the 'comoune pyparis of Abirdene' and a 'pypar of Dunbertane'[47]—perhaps some of the earliest references to 'town pipers' that we have (see Chapter 3).[48]

Notably, the Scottish monarchs, unlike their English counterparts, did not provide salaried positions to bagpipers. Ironically, when James VI of Scotland ascended the English throne as James I in 1603, he appointed a man to take up the vacant place left by

Richard Woodward, the last of the English sovereign's bagpipers, who had died thirty-three years earlier in 1570. But instead of appointing a bagpiper he appointed a bass viol player instead![49] The role of Sovereign's Piper—with one brief exception for a 'bag-piper in ordinary' in 1663—would not return until the reign of Queen Victoria, when Angus Mackay arrived on the scene in 1843.[50]

If we might zoom out for a moment, it's interesting to note that courtly interest in the bagpipes was not limited to England and Scotland. We have documentary proof of the use of the small French bagpipe known as a *musette*, both mouth-blown and bellows-blown (the first bellow-blown pipe can be dated to 1536, on an Italian type of bagpipe known as the *phagotum*),[51] from the courts of François I (reigned 1515–47) all the way through to Louis XIV (reigned 1643–1715).[52] The popularity of the smaller forms of the instrument was mirrored elsewhere across Europe, as many other countries developed their own 'pastoral' bagpipes: the Italian *sordellina*, for instance, or the Central European smallpipe known as the *Dudey*. (There is an irony in these being referred to as 'pastoral' pipes. They seemed to have developed in response to the process of urbanisation—in other words, they were for indoor rather than outdoor playing.) These instruments would come to influence English, Scottish and Irish bagpiping, as we'll see.[53]

But before these rather delicate bagpipes reached Scotland, it would seem the Scots and the Irish had developed a more robust approach. There are accounts of the Scots using the pipes in battle from as early as the Battle of Flodden in 1513,[54] and there's an illustration of Irish troops being led into battle at the Siege of Boulogne in 1544.[55] Most interestingly, in 1549 a French military officer, reporting on the Scottish response to Henry VIII's series of Scottish invasions known as the 'Rough Wooing' (1543–51), states that 'the savage Scots incited themselves into battle with the sound of their bagpipes' (*Les Ecossois sauvages se provocquoyent aux armes par les sons de leurs cornemeuses*).[56] Two words in particular ought to be noted here: *sauvages*, which in a 1707 English translation of the text is rendered 'Highlanders',[57] and the possessive adjective *leurs*, which Williams has described as 'particularly telling: they are not described simply as "bagpipes", but rather as an instrument which belongs to a country'.[58] Had the Highlanders developed a national instrument already?

* * *

All this leaves us with a pretty muddied image of how the pipes reached Scotland. Did they come direct from Europe, just one cultural import among many? Was the shared cultural heritage with Ireland to account for it? Or did England, with its older piping tradition, act as a conduit, receiving the instrument at first from the Continent and then allowing a northwardly osmosis to occur? It would seem wise not to discount any of these influences. They were probably all at play. As in the Czech Republic, as in Austria, the fluidity of national boundaries and the fluidity of the instrument asserts itself upon us. But if there is no such thing as a 'Czech' bagpipe, there very much is a Great Highland Bagpipe, and judging from the previous paragraph, it could have already 'belonged' to the Highlanders by the mid-sixteenth century. Can we really talk in such reductive terms? And did this bagpipe speak for the entirety of Scotland? These are questions for Chapter 3.

3

YOU'LL TAKE THE HIGH ROAD
AND I'LL TAKE THE LOW ROAD

A DIVERSE AND FLUCTUATING CULTURE: 1500–1700

'Are we aloon? I wish to tick to you.' So speaks the Englishman Crabtree in the BBC's classic comedy series *'Allo 'Allo!* Crabtree's famous malapropisms, uttered while working as an inept undercover policeman in occupied France, were not what I was expecting to recall as I sat quietly deciphering the Burgh Records of Dunfermline from 1503. But when I read of one Andro Piper accusing one Rob Purrok for the 'brekkin of his pip',[1] my mind was immediately transported to the man famous for such lines as 'I was pissing by the door, and I thought I would drip in.' Such are the unexpected pleasures of historical research!

But this reference to poor old Andro and his broken pipe has more than just comedic value. It's a reminder that the role of the piper—though we note with caution that we have to assume the addition of a bag—in society was sufficiently settled by the early 1500s that it could act as a surname just at the time that surnames based on professions were beginning to come into being. Yet, this was Dunfermline, far below the Highland Boundary Fault Line. Despite all we heard in the last chapter about Irish imports into the Highlands and hereditary pipers to clan chiefs, we find just as much evidence of a thriving piping culture—and yes, the bag is often explicit—in the Lowlands as we do in the Highlands over the course of the fifteenth and sixteenth centuries.[2] This Lowland culture includes hereditary pipers showered, like their northern counterparts, with benefits for their labours. And while Highland pipers were sometimes bards too,[3] we're told by Sir Walter Scott—who, in this respect, might be considered a fairly reliable source[4]—that the Border pipers were also 'great depositories of oral and particularly poetical tradition'.[5]

These Lowland pipers, instead of serving a chieftain as happened in the north, served and earned a livelihood through the people of the town, often with a drummer, known as a 'swasher', in tow. Commonly referred to as town 'waits'—from the Anglo-Saxon *wacian*, to watch or guard—they were tasked with waking the inhabitants in the morning, getting them home in the evening and cheering them in festivity, not least through providing music for dancing (a key function of Highland pipers too until the nineteenth century).[6] Like Highland pipers, they were also said to accompany the harvesters in the field and during other forms of work.[7] The ubiquity of the town pipers within the everyday life of the people is captured wonderfully well in the famous, trend-setting 'Life and Death of the Piper of Kilbarchan' by Robert Sempill the Younger (c. 1595–c. 1663) commemorating the great Habbie Simpson (1550–1620). This stanza weaves within it some of the tunes he would have been known to play: 'Now who shall play the day it daws / Or hunts up when the Cock he craws / Or who can for our Kirk Town Cause, / stand us in stead? / On Bag-pipes now no body blaws, / Sen Habbie's dead.'

Such characters weren't unique to Scotland, and the evidence seems to suggest that the Lowlands and Border regions shared a cohesive musical 'culture-province' with the north of England.[8] Sheffield, Newcastle and Liverpool all had their own town pipers, as did many other English towns, but it's not clear they all played the *bag*pipe.[9] These men weren't always as reliable as old Habbie. Henry Halewood, town piper of Liverpool on and off between 1571 and 1589, was repeatedly arrested and fined for bad behaviour, including 'lewdnes'.[10] European towns were also known to have pipers attached to them, though again we must be cautious about how many of these musicians were specifically bagpipers.[11]

Europe remained key to what was going on in England and Scotland. The most obvious European revolution that we might think of at this time, namely the Reformation, strangely did not affect pipe music, or Scottish music in general, as one might expect.

People tend to think the Reformation brought a near-instantaneous axe upon cultural endeavour. That is not the case.

In fact, it was during the first sixty years of the new Scottish Kirk, from 1560 onwards, that some of the most energetic Scottish ballads were written, such as 'The Laird o'Logie' and 'Kinmont Willie'.[12] Though records of the church courts show that bagpipers were frequently found guilty of inciting drunkenness and dancing on the Sabbath, such censure was not done out of a general distrust of music.[13] Piping remained central to the local community, just as it did in the Lutheran regions on the Continent, probably because of Luther's more-worldly stance on music. Thus, as late as 1742, we find Bach ending his well-known 'Cantate burlesque', popularly known as the *Peasant Cantata*, with the chorus *Wir gehn nun, wo der Dudelsack / In unsrer Schenke brummt*—'We're going now, where the bagpipe / Whines away in our pub.' Of Scotland, Wormald has written: 'It is the church of the seventeenth century, not the sixteenth, that created the image of harsh antagonism to enjoyment of the things of the world, including the cultural things.'[14] Even this later antagonism seems to have largely bypassed the playing of the pipes, and it was only with an upsurge in evangelicalism in the 1800s that one can detect a 'puritanical frown on music and dance'.[15] The decline of pipe music in the Lowlands during that century—to which we'll come in Chapter 5—probably had less to do with religious matters than it did with socio-economic issues, as the urban environments of the Lowlands changed.[16]

But prior to this there was no sense that Highland piping dominated over Lowland. Staying with the theme of the importance of Europe, it was thanks to trade with the continent that the burghs were prospering in the late fifteenth and sixteenth century. The wealth that was generated allowed the burgesses to emulate the traditions and opulence of aristocratic and royal courts, and the employment of town musicians was part of that. They were treated with respect, housed and clothed out of the townspeople's purse. In my own town of Haddington—which had its own piper from at least 1542—we know that John Reid, appointed in 1662, was provided with 'ane doublet of Lyonis cameis, ane pair of blue breeks and schooner' (a camel coat, a pair of blue trousers and shoes).[17] In Jedburgh, further south, the Piper's House is still detectable from the little stone statue of a piper on the gable. The family who lived there, the Hasties, are said to have held the office of town pipers from the beginning of the sixteenth century until the end of the eighteenth, a longevity of service that, if true, outstrips anything we find from authentic Highland examples.

Any neat Highland/Lowland distinctions are very hard to draw until the eighteenth century. The Scottish borderer and polymath John Leyden (1775–1811), who edited the remarkable sixteenth-century tract *The Complaynt of Scotland*, tells us in his introductory essay of 1801:

> The instrument of Habbie Simson, the piper of Kilbarchan [west of Paisley, and thus in the Lowlands] ... was undoubtedly the Highland bagpipe. In the middle counties of Scotland, the Highland bagpipe has always been more popular than on the Border. But the instrument of John Hastie, town piper of Jedburgh, about the same period, was undeniably the Lowland bagpipe, and, within these [last] ten years, was seen by the editor, in the possession of his descendant.[18]

Leyden continues:

> The original airs of the *Gathering songs* and Historical ballads [that one finds played by the Border pipers] have no inconsiderable resemblance to the martial tunes of the Welch, Irish, and the Scotish [sic] Highlanders, and formed the favourite music of the Border pipers; among whom, the perfection of the art was supposed to consist in being able to sing, dance, and play on the bagpipe, at the same time ... With the town pipers, there is the utmost reason to believe, that many ancient airs have perished ... I only recollect *the Hunting of the Fox* which, from its uncommon expression, and the irregularity of its modulation, seemed to have a strong resemblance to a Highland pibrach [sic, more on pibroch/piobaireachd later].[19]

Part of the challenge here is that we don't really know what precisely is meant by a 'Highland bagpipe' and a 'Lowland bagpipe' until the late seventeenth century.[20] Given what Leyden says about Lowland pipers singing and playing at the same time, he clearly thought the Lowland form was distinguishable by the presence of bellows and the absence of a blowpipe. But according to the man who has done most to delve into the history of Lowland pipes, Pete Stewart, it's probably more accurate, when imagining early forms of this instrument, to think about what we find at Melrose and Rosslyn—a single drone, a conical chanter and, critically, a blow-pipe, just as we find in the earlier European tradition. There is an oak bookcase, thought to be originally from a bedstead in Threave Castle, Kirkcudbrightshire (in the Lowlands), upon which a carving of a bagpiper can be found (c. 1600), and here the European model is followed. It's the same again on the statuette on the Piper's House at Jedburgh (Hastie's own house remember), though the date of the statue is uncertain, with the house first built in the seventeenth century but much altered over the years. A very similar statuette at Craigievar Castle in Aberdeenshire—which could still be considered Lowlands—can be more accurately dated to when the castle was built between 1610 and 1626. The man who built the house, William Forbes, was known as 'Danzig Willie', making his fortune in the Baltic trade as a merchant. It has been suggested that this is one of the first images of the imported *Dudey*, a form of bagpipe from Central Europe.[21] Interestingly, both the Jedburgh and Craigievar carvings show the bag held in the European style, with an almost vertical positioning under the arm.

As these remarks show, the evidence is all rather piecemeal. As one reviewer of Stewart's book, *The Day it Daws*, puts it, 'the information he would have liked to give us, which would have joined everything neatly together, is not available.'[22]

If we can't be certain about the precise timings around the bellows/blowpipe question, what about drones? The earliest representation of pipes with two drones in Scotland can be found in a psalter belonging to Thomas Wood of Dunbar (again, Lowlands), dated to 1562–6, where the inevitable pig is happily piping away. For clear evidence of three drones, we have to wait for the luscious portrait, this time in a Highland setting, of the piper to the laird of Grant, dated 1714—the earliest known painting, though probably not entirely accurate, of the bagpipes in Scotland. The instrument there is not that far from what we know today as the Great Highland Bagpipes, with three drones and a blowpipe, though the tenor drones are held in a common stock, and the chanter is not a plausible representation of what was actually played.[23] Interestingly, the instrument is held under the right arm, with the right hand highest on the chanter, neither of which is standard today. But the idea of 'the wrong shoulder' is one that only came in late to piping as a result of its more formalised military use, when the practice of close order 'counter-marching' in ranks could lead to clashes of drones unless everyone held the bag on the same side.[24]

This leaves us with the question: did these Highland pipes develop quite independently of what was developing in the Lowlands, or were they just different branches of the same blossoming tree out of Europe? Stewart has his own inclinations on this question but remains ambivalent: 'The instrument which I believe was the instrument of the Lowlands may well have had a quite different history from the Highland pipes. There was clearly overlap between the musical traditions but, by the 18th century, there was a separate Lowlands tradition.'[25]

* * *

Separate, but perhaps not radically so. In an essay of 1784, probably by John Ramsay of Ochtertyre—an essay that has its faults, as we'll see in Chapter 5—there is this claim: 'The large bagpipe is their [the Highlanders'] instrument for war, for marriage, for funeral processions, and for other great occasions. They have also a smaller kind, on which dancing tunes are played.'[26]

If accurate, these smaller pipes may be the pipes with two tenor drones that we'll encounter in our next chapter or the three-quarters sized pipes with three drones mentioned there too. Or they may have been bellows-blown pipes, now known as the Lowland or Border pipes, which probably arrived in Scotland less than 100 years before Ramsay was writing (again, these will be dealt with more fully in the following chapters). It's hard to know how far back into the past this co-existence of large and smallpipe went in Highland culture, but it's clear from the earliest Gaelic terms, which start appearing in the late sixteenth century, that they are referring to the Piob Mhòr, the Great Pipe: *sgal* (blast, yelp, shriek, yell, skirl); *gàirich* (shouting, roaring, raging); *nuallanach* (howling, roaring, lowing, loud). As Cheape observes: 'Various readings can be taken from these Gaelic terms and "carrying sound" can easily become "noise". Many considered the bagpipe a vulgar incomer and nuisance.'[27] From as early as 1500, we find Gaelic poems praising and dispraising pipers with equal measure, with the pipe's loud noise a particular target for invective.[28]

Small wonder that, in addition to their role in the court of the clan chief, the Great Pipes became associated with military exploits. We have already heard of reports of the pipes being used before battle in 1513, 1544 and 1549. Another sixteenth-century reference to the bagpipes in battle comes from one of Scotland's most famous scholars, George Buchanan, who says of the Highlanders, 'instead of the trumpet, they use a bagpipe' (*Loco tubae, tibia utuntur utriculari*). Most interestingly, the cultured clergyman Alexander Hume writes in his poem, *The Triumph of the Lord, after the Manner of Men* (1599), of 'hieland pypes Scots, and Hibernik' being used in sea battle against the Spanish Armada in 1588.[29] Bagpipe historian Francis Collinson makes much of this reference, but he unfortunately took it down second hand and thus misprints the line as 'hieland pipes, Scottes and Hybernicke', which allows him to think that Hume was differentiating between three forms of bagpipe: the Highland, the Scottish (i.e., Lowland) and the Irish, Hibernia being another name for Ireland.[30] With the comma only after 'Scots', the inference is in fact that there were two forms of 'Highland pipes', one Scots and one Irish. Whatever the case, it's clear that by the sixteenth century bagpipes were an established instrument of war for the Scots.

The bagpipes' capacity 'to entertain the clansmen on their march to the battlefield and ... to encourage them during the prelude to battle' was part of the reason for their gradual rise to pre-eminence over the bard and the harp, which had long held the high ground in the social world of the Highlanders.[31] The bards' and harpists' heyday had been sustained by the relative stability that had been afforded to much of the Gaelic-speaking regions through the Lordship of the Isles—that is, the cultural and political unit overseen by Clan Donald (the MacDonalds) from the early twelfth century until at least the late fifteenth century, stretching from Kintyre in the south to Ross in the north and including the Hebrides. With the Lordship breaking apart after its forfeiture to the crown in 1493, the following two centuries were a time of federation and fragmentation among the clans of the Gaels as they sought new political alignments to provide economic and geographic security. It's no surprise, then, that that most powerful of instruments—the bagpipes—rose to prominence in a time of clan feuding and struggle.

* * *

Before we say more on the instrument's connection with combat, we should not underestimate the musicality of the Great Pipe at this time. Some of the earliest bagpipe tunes that we have are known as *piobaireachd* (pronounced pee-broch, meaning simply pipe playing or pipe music in Gaelic, and usually spelt in English as pibroch) or *ceòl mòr* (big music). Although—or perhaps because—the Highland bagpipe has only nine notes,[32] and many of the most famous piobaireachd were composed using the pentatonic scale (i.e., drawing on just five notes from the seven-note major scale), piobaireachd can create an astonishingly mesmeric effect. It is the melody, the unfolding structure with its theme and variations, and the finger embellishments placed upon the notes, rising to greater and greater complexity, that combine to beguile the listener. And that is to say nothing of a piobaireachd's length! It is known therefore as the classical music of the Great Highland Bagpipe. Before proceeding, if you're new to this branch of pipe music, I recommend searching online for a recent piobaireachd performance from the Glenfiddich championship, where you will hear one of the top ten contemporary players on the competition circuit performing this remarkable music.

Having familiarised yourself with the art form as it sounds today, a word of caution. Piobaireachd was originally taught—and to a limited extent still is taught—by singing the music: *canntaireachd* in Gaelic, meaning 'chanting'.[33] Written pipe music only appeared in the late eighteenth century, and even after that tunes were written in different ways by different people.[34] To play any of these today will also involve the player's interpretation. We simply do not have direct access to what this music originally sounded like. Certainly, the very first references to piobaireachd suggest that it did not conform to the uniform style of playing that we now know; even perhaps that piobaireachd, with the Gaelic meaning taken quite literally, was used by some simply to mean pipe playing in general, thus encompassing music for dancing too.[35] Indeed, dance music—or light music (ceòl beag)—with its reels, jigs and other forms, was clearly a central part of Highland piping culture from its earliest days, and many players of this music were simply 'community pipers', quite ordinary men free from the trappings of the grand hereditary pipers.[36]

It's important to remember this and not let the evident gravity of piobaireachd for the Gaelic peoples eclipse the importance of light music within Highland culture.

There have been other warnings not to equate what we know today of piobaireachd with what was originally performed. The highly regarded Piper Major Robert Reid (1876–1964) is claimed to have repeatedly said that piobaireachd playing was perfected in Glasgow at the end of the nineteenth century. To support this, journalist Alistair Campsie published evidence to suggest that in the eighteenth century piobaireachd was played without grace notes[37]—a feature the art's practitioners would now view as all important. That claim, however, quickly evaporates, or at least must be seriously qualified, when one looks at the earliest systematic account of piobaireachd ever to be published, Joseph MacDonald's *A Compleat Theory of the Scots Highland Bagpipe*, which was written around 1760 though not printed until 1803.[38] There, grace notes are very much in evidence.

If Campsie's claim can be discounted, the celebrated contemporary folk artist and piper Allan MacDonald has nonetheless done excellent work to demonstrate the variety of past styles. If you hear a piobaireachd today, the words 'slow' and 'stately' may spring to mind, but MacDonald writes:

> There are eighteenth century references to pibroch spelled in various ways in the Dictionary of the Older Scottish Tongue and the impression is clearly that the style of music meant by this genre was lively ... There is further evidence to show that the demarcation between the pibroch ùrlar [the opening statement or ground, which all subsequent variations in the piece play on] and light music was not as clear as at the present day.[39]

In line with this, one knowledgeable commentator, after close examination of MacDonald's *Compleat Theory*, has argued that 'light music and piobaireachd formed part of a single progressively more complex system of ornamentation'.[40] There is thus not much ground to support the claims, which are sometimes voiced, either that the music of the Great Pipe was originally solely piobaireachd[41] or that the great players of the past felt only disdain for light music.[42] When Seumas MacNeill, creator of the College of Piping in Glasgow, wrote in 1968 that piobaireachd 'is as far removed from the other branches of pipe music as a sonata is from a pop song',[43] we have to be aware that, historically, this is not likely to be true. (Saying all this, I'm reminded of a story put into print by the great Canadian piper, William 'Bill' Livingstone. As a young lad, he played for his father a slow air 'at dirge speed'. His father's response was priceless: 'Bill, come on, even grief has a tempo').[44]

With these cautions in mind, we must remember that the earliest piobaireachd arose within a culture heavily influenced by Ireland, as previously noted. Within that shared culture, the poetic practice of the bard was taken with great seriousness. Their poetry was strict, formal and dignified, with an elaborate system of metres. Piobaireachd, in its compositional structures, can be seen as the musical extension of that poetry[45]—though that should by no means rule out other influencing factors: medieval Gaelic song as well as harp music have, in all likelihood, played a shaping role, and it has even been suggested that the ancient Norse tradition of skaldic poetry shows similarities in compositional approach.[46] Though we may never know which of these played the greatest role, MacDonald's *Compleat Theory* was intent on showing that piobaireachd was 'a highly organised, systematic and rule-bound music'.[47] MacDonald's aim was 'to demonstrate the elegance and coherence of its underlying structures'.[48]

Just as bards were sent to colleges of poetry in Ireland, so too were pipers sent to colleges of piping, of which there were a number in Scotland (and Ireland too).[49] The MacCrimmons' college at Boreraig on Skye has become the most well known to piping enthusiasts, though its fame may be largely due to the possible inflation of the MacCrimmons' reputation by nineteenth-century commentators,[50] and more recently some doubt has grown up about whether or not the college really did exist as a fixed establishment.[51] But we certainly know of colleges elsewhere under the care of other clans, such as the MacArthurs, the Rankins and the MacGregors.[52] These were cultural centres, and the men that came through them went on to serve clan chieftains with anything but barbaric tastes. As Cheape reminds us: 'The Highland chieftains [of the sixteenth and seventeenth centuries] consumed the best of foreign culture and their taste is endlessly praised in Gaelic song.'[53] So much so that this might justly be termed a 'golden age' for Gaelic culture.[54]

Inevitably, much myth has grown up around the origins of particular pieces of piobaireachd. Usually, origin stories are an amalgam of various authentic oral memories along with the smoothing out of contradictions by later editors. But there are exceptions. One story especially stands out. It concerns the piobaireachd 'I Got a Kiss of the King's Hand'. Scholar Roderick Cannon has written of it as being in 'complete contrast' to other origin stories.[55] The key element is the very early date in which the story was written: the 1680s. This is when James Fraser, minister of Kirkhill of Wardlaw near Inverness, reported on the gathering of Charles II's Royalist forces at Stirling in May 1651. Crucially, many pipers were present.

Fraser's account also contains a number of little details that suggest he had spoken to an eyewitness. He writes that, during the Stirling assembly, there was a great competition among the pipers, and that '[a]ll the pipers in the army gave John Macgurmen [MacCrimmon] the van, and acknowledged him for their patron in chiefe'. Then, early one morning, while reviewing his troops, the king 'saw no less then 80 pipers' standing in a crowd bareheaded. In the middle of them stood John MacCrimmon, with his head covered. Charles asked his attendants who this man in the middle was. He was told: 'Sir, yow are our King, and yonder old man in the midle [sic] is the Prince of Pipers.' Fraser tells us that the king then called MacCrimmon to him by name. The famous piper approached and knelt before his sovereign, at which point 'his Majesty reacht him his hand to kiss'. The delighted MacCrimmon, we're told, 'instantly played' an extemporary tune that he called 'Fuoris Pòòge i spoge i Rhi' or 'I got a kiss of the king's hand'.[56] According to Fraser, the king and everyone present were in envy of him.[57]

Of course, there is still much that could be exaggeration. One listen to the majestic tune itself and the idea that it could have been produced off the cuff becomes unthinkable. Nonetheless, Fraser's account no doubt reflects authentic truths about the culture of

Highland piping in the mid-seventeenth century—that a bond existed between pipers, that there could be a sense of hierarchy among them and that the music that was being composed was not necessarily always martial in character.

* * *

We should be careful, then, not to reduce early pipe tunes to the kinds of things that might have been played going into battle. The links to the formal structures of poetry also remind us that the music was anything but primitive.[58] As piping authority William Donaldson has so powerfully argued: ever since the publication of the poetry of 'Ossian' by James Macpherson in the eighteenth century, which took Europe by storm and altered forever the way the Highlands were viewed, there has been a tendency to equate Highland art forms with noble barbarism, with wildness and irregularity.[59] Thus can Lord Byron write in the third canto of *Childe Harold's Pilgrimage* (1812–18): 'How in the noon of night that pibroch thrills / Savage and shrill!'[60] Seen in the light of the bardic tradition, however, pio-baireachd speaks rather of refinement and the heights of culture.

This doesn't mean that other aspects of life in the Highlands, and elsewhere in Scotland, weren't violent. While everyday life in England, Wales and Ireland was becoming increasingly pacified, Highland clan feuding and raiding, as well as Lowland border reiving, continued well on into the seventeenth century.[61] Devine, speaking on that great treasure of British radio *In Our Time*, has put the matter succinctly—'the clan [was] essentially a martial society'.[62] This spirit was not geographically limited to Scotland alone. Across the early modern period, Scots were to be found fighting in France, Sweden, Russia, Prussia, Denmark and the Netherlands.[63] Such was their ubiquity that 'rats, lice and Scotchmen' were said to be present across the globe.[64] This military reputation would come to have a profound impact on the perception of bagpiping.

Another key scene-setter for the piping story is what would happen after the Union of the Crowns in 1603, for it is then that a British, Anglo-Scots military identity began to appear.[65] This was very much part of the wider changes that were happening in the 'military revolution' of Western Europe between 1590 and 1640, when governments, mainly through pay, were turning warriors into soldiers.[66] Prior to the union, James VI had managed to bring the south and east of Scotland into subjection to the Scottish crown, but the north and west remained laws unto themselves. The union provided a catalyst for a strong centralising push into these untamed regions. As a result, Independent Highland Companies were formed from among clans loyal to James, with warrant to police and enforce the law (the name and origins of the Scottish regiment the Black Watch can be linked to this past). Though numerically small and weak in terms of their composition,[67] their very presence marked the beginning of an internal division within the Highlands between warriors-turned-crown-soldiers and warriors loyal solely to their chief. Critically, there were pipers among both.[68] It has been estimated that, in the companies, there was one piper to every fifty men.[69]

By 1627, during the war with France, we know for sure that some bagpipers were in the service of the crown.[70] One of them, Allester Caddell, had a ghillie to carry his pipes for him, which, we are told, was the custom of the time.[71] Evidently, pipers were of some status. A ranking list of one regiment in 1637 places the piper in a middle position between the officers and the men.[72] It's fascinating to note, incidentally, that this military role for the pipes was not the sole preserve of the Scots in the seventeenth century. James Turner's *Pallas armata* of 1683 has pipers in English and German regiments. Of the latter, Turner writes: 'I look upon their Pipe as a Warlike Instrument.'[73]

To speak of the pipes as a martial instrument for the Highlanders we therefore have to be conscious that we cannot speak in uniform terms about Highland martial culture, certainly not after 1603. In fact, Scotland was to be repeatedly torn apart by religiously or politically motivated civil war for the next century and a half. So we ought not to think of the Highland bagpiper during this period as if he were clearly representative of a homogenous, victoriously heroic demographic. Nor can we speak of Scotland simply as if it were a unified political entity, of which the bagpipe can speak. And it wasn't just the Highlanders themselves who experienced a lack of unity. Wormald observes: 'As the prospect and then the reality of the English succession affected him, the lowlander found his contact with the different culture of the west an increasing embarrassment. Thus the gulf widened, to the detriment of both lowland and highland society.'[74] In other words, the question of the union with England put into question the union of Scotland itself—a feeling that feels all too familiar today. Then as now, the picture of the nation is a decidedly messy one.

* * *

You might have thought that by focusing on the pipes, the mess would clear a bit. Surely this instrument, having become embedded within society, could act as a sort of unifying element. Not a bit of it. Our dive into Lowland and Highland piping culture has only reinforced the sense of turbulence during the period. The bagpipes were not a fixed instrument, and their different forms leave behind them a scattered range of evidence that is, at times, conducive to a headache. But perhaps, for that very reason, they do in fact shine a revealing, dare I say unifying light on the nation itself. Their very differences—their varying number of drones, their 'small' or 'great' nature, their blowpipes or lack of them—are reflective of the diverse and fluctuating culture that was Scotland between the fifteenth and seventeenth centuries.

One might hope that by the time the eighteenth century comes around, with the Jacobites becoming ever more prominent, the picture would become a little less blurry. After all, in the English press, the bagpipes were practically synonymous with Jacobitism. It is the purpose of Chapter 4 to see if the picture does indeed clear, and if the English were right to be so confident in their conflations.

4

PIPING IN JACOBITE TIMES

THE SOUND OF DIVIDED LOYALTIES: 1700–46

On the face of it, every effort was made to get the history right in the televised adaptations of Diana Gabaldon's *Outlander* books. Gaelic was used, filming took place in Scotland itself and the costume department was faithful to the period. The producers even employed a well-respected historical expert from the University of Glasgow to guide them on their way. But when you see the rippling muscles of the central male character, Jamie Fraser (played by actor Sam Heughan), it's hard not to feel a little sceptical about his physical appearance. Did Highland gentleman of the mid-eighteenth century possess gym memberships?

Fraser's fictional character has become the quintessential image for the Jacobite Highlander. Apparently, he had received early training in swordsmanship, so that might be a way of accounting for the pronounced abs and bulging pecs. But, really, we all know that Fraser's/Heughan's chiselled body, coupled with his scintillating onscreen chemistry with Claire Beauchamp (actress Caitríona Balfe), is really there because, let's be frank, sex sells.

The uilleann pipes (pronounced ill-yin) sell too, it would seem. Strange as this might sound, most films depicting Highland Scotland are accompanied by the tones not of the Great Highland Bagpipes but of the bellows-blown pipes most commonly associated with Ireland. *Braveheart* is the obvious example. The man who performed on the score, the American piper Eric Rigler, is perfectly capable of playing the Great Highland Bagpipe, but as he explained, 'James Horner, the composer, said he knew exactly what he was doing and that he wanted the uilleann pipes because they fitted into an orchestra better than the Scottish pipes. They're not so loud and commanding, and have a greater range of notes.'[1] It was thus with joy that devotees of the Great Highland Bagpipe, on first encountering the *Outlander* theme tune, heard the dulcet strains of the Highland pipes singing back to them (the piper behind the microphone was once again our man Rigler). And yet, for viewers of the first series at least, that initial pleasure quickly disappeared if they watched on beyond the opening credits. As one commentator on the Pipes|Drums website put it in an article entitled 'Outlandish':

> 'Finally!' I thought. 'The Highland pipes will be used throughout this series that celebrates Highland stuff.' What a disappointment … There is hardly a Highland pipe to be heard or seen in the actual episodes. When they chase across the Scottish hills, it's to the thrumming register of the bellows-blown Irish pipes. When the evil redcoat is dispatched, it's to the soft tones of Ireland's national bagpipe.[2]

Funnily enough, the issue with this use of the uilleann pipes is not so much their Irish connection but a question of dates and geography. As we'll see in our next chapter, the instruments from which the uilleann pipes are descended—namely the pastoral or union pipes—are as native to England and Scotland as they are to Ireland. But these were very new to Britain at the time in which the early *Outlander* series are set. In the very year that Claire Beauchamp arrives in the eighteenth century, 1743 (travelling back in time from 1945), the very first book of bagpipe music ever printed in Britain or Ireland appeared.[3] Its title is telling. This was John Geoghegan's *The Compleat Tutor for the Pastoral or New Bagpipe*—note the penultimate word. This 'new' instrument was also not commonly, if at all, played in the Highlands. In 1743, the established bagpipes in the regions through which Jamie Fraser and Claire Beauchamp romp were undoubtedly the Highland Great Pipes precursors of the Great Highland Bagpipes we know today.[4]

There are times in the series where the Great Highland Bagpipe does appear but, as the last sentence shows, even that instrument is somewhat anachronistic in the context. In reality, there was no settled form for the Highland pipes until the nineteenth century.

The few surviving sets from the eighteenth century, even some reputed to have been played at the Battle of Culloden—a focal event in *Outlander*, as it was for the age itself—are a testimony to the continued diversity of bagpipes in Scotland at the time.

* * *

Before we hear more about that diversity, a bit of clarification. The Battle of Culloden was fought on 16 April 1746 and was the last pitched battle on British soil. It brought a decisive end to the Jacobite Rebellion of 1745 (often referred to simply as 'the '45'), through which Prince Charles Edward Stuart—otherwise known as Bonnie Prince Charlie—had sought to restore the House of Stuart to the British throne. Charles' supporters were known as Jacobites for their allegiance to the continued line of Charles' grandfather, James VII of Scotland and II of England—Jacobus is the Latin rendering of James—whose reign was ingloriously brought to an end in the Glorious Revolution of 1688. Though we must remember that the Jacobites were composed of 'loosely-knit, faction-ridden, internationally dispersed promoters',[5] and though we must recognise that 'there is no consensus among historians about the precise nature of the movement',[6] we can at least simplify things by saying that the Jacobites who fought for their cause (many didn't), did so against government forces, representing the British crown. In other words—though most historians don't like to use the words—the Jacobites fought against the British Army.

At the time of Culloden, the monarch was George II. George was born and raised in Hanover, northern Germany, but through the Act of Settlement and the Acts of Union at the start of the eighteenth century, his father had become king of Great Britain and Ireland in 1714 as George I. The Georges were descendants of the Stuarts too, as George I's mother was the granddaughter of James VI and I, but they represented the Protestant line of the family, which was the preferred line in the political circles of England and Lowland Scotland, hence its rise to power. The senior line of the House of Stuart, on the other hand, retained the older Catholic tradition, which sat more comfortably with the mainly Episcopalian allegiances of the Highlands (only about 2 per cent of the Scottish population was Catholic by this stage).[7] But even within the Highlands, allegiances were torn, as we'll see.

* * *

Which takes us back to Highland diversity at the time, particularly the diversity of the Highland bagpipes. The first thing that will strike you if you visit the museum at the National Piping Centre in Glasgow and look at their 'Culloden pipes' will be the fact that they only have two tenor drones. The museum's other pre-1800 sets are different yet again. One of them was originally gifted to the College of Piping in 2012 by piping enthusiast Norman Welz of Baden-Baden. These had been in his family for generations and bear the date 1749, just three years after Culloden. They were known to have belonged to a soldier with the exceptionally Scottish name of Hamish Wallace. He was in the service of the duke of Atholl and was sent to Austria to fight for the Habsburgs during the second half of the eighteenth century. There he married, and eventually settled in Germany. The pipes had been in that country ever since.

These, however, do have a bass drone. That doesn't mean they're just like a modern set of Highland pipes. In fact, they are only three-quarters of the size. We might account for the variation in the number of drones by the reason provided in a note inserted into MacDonald's *A Compleat Theory* by his brother, Patrick. In this, Patrick observed that bass drones were used by pipers in the north Highlands but that, in the west, pipers had laid aside the bass drone because, in their estimation—with which Patrick vigorously disagrees—'the loudness of it drowned the sound of the Chanter music'.[8] They thus retained just the two tenors. We know that two drone bagpipes were being played at the first formal piobaireachd competitions organised by the Highland Societies of London and Edinburgh in the late eighteenth century—we know this because they were banned from competition in 1821 as representing an unfair advantage.[9] Moreover, the esteemed piper John Bàn MacKenzie (1796–1864) is said to have told a fellow piper that when he was learning piobaireachd as a young lad on the Isle of Raasay, pipers there only had two drones on their pipes.[10]

We also know from our previous chapter that some Highland pipers had two sets of pipes—one large, one small—but that it remains unclear precisely what the large and smallpipes looked like. Whatever the truth may be, the point is that significant variation was part of the bagpipe culture of the time.[11] In fact, it's said that individual pipers would supervise a wood turner (i.e., a skilled lathe-worker) while he made a set of pipes and could thus dictate the design and style of decoration. It was only as demand for instruments increased in later centuries, and as competitions took hold of solo piping culture and their governing bodies attempted to level the playing field, that turners imposed a greater degree of standardisation on their products.[12]

Reading about another set of pipes that may have been played at Culloden reveals a further aspect of Highland diversity. These are known as the Tain pipes, having been found behind a stone fireplace in that town (35 miles north of Culloden), perfectly preserved due to a protective varnish that had been applied before they were hidden; so perfectly in fact that the pipes were played—once more?—on Culloden Moor in 2019. To those steeped in the old 'Jacobite equals Scottish' equation, it will come as a surprise to find a writer in a 2019 edition of the *Piping Times* asking about these pipes, 'who was the piper and [if they were played at Culloden] which side was he on?'[13] Yes, that's right, a British Army soldier—not a Jacobite—could have been playing these pipes. A trip to the Culloden museum to see the Great Pipes of Baleshare, also said to have been played at the battle and again with just two tenor drones, will unsettle our assumptions yet again. According to the family that gifted the set, their ancestor from North Uist fought, as a clansman loyal to the MacDonalds, for King George II, *not* the Young Pretender, Prince Charles.[14]

We could do worse than turn to the historical advisor for *Outlander*, Tony Pollard, to get some clarity on the matter. He is professor of conflict history and archaeology at the University of Glasgow, and although he was unable to keep uilleann piping out of the background music, he was able to remind the show's producers that the political scene in eighteenth-century Scotland was remarkably complex. In an interview with British Heritage Travel in 2022, Pollard was asked: 'What's the hardest part to get right about 1700s

Scotland? The thing most people don't usually consider?' Pollard's answer takes us to the heart of things:

> I think it's breaking down the popular misconception that the Jacobite Wars, and in this case the '45, was a straightforward battle between Scotland and England and that all Jacobites were Catholics (in the '45 most were Episcopalian). As ever with history, the reality is a lot more complicated and the edges are blurred. The Jacobite wars were in many ways Scottish civil wars and wars between the Highlands and Lowlands. There obviously was an England versus Scotland element, and some historians regard the Jacobites as a nationalist movement, but this is only a part of the story.[15]

In fact, it's even more complicated than that. When Charles first arrived in Scotland from France on 25 July 1745, he found there was very little support for his cause in terms of manpower (despite a widespread residual loyalty to the Stuart dynasty in spirit). It was only after the powerful chief of the Camerons of Lochiel decided to join the Jacobite cause at the beginning of August that many other Highland clans decided to follow suit. Note the word 'many'. It was not all the clans. As we've already sensed, even within the Highlands there were deep fissures of allegiance. A look at the MacCrimmons of the eighteenth century brings these complexities alive like nothing else.

* * *

The MacCrimmons were the hereditary pipers to the clan chiefs of the MacLeods of Dunvegan, Skye. They have come to represent—sometimes at the expense of other dazzling bagpiping families—the summit of Highland piping. You might think, then, that they fought on the side of the prince. Wrong. Their allegiance to the MacLeods meant their fate lay elsewhere.

The principal chief of the clan, Norman MacLeod, developed a nickname within his own lifetime that tells you something about his character. He was known as *An Droch Dhuine*, which means the Wicked Man in Gaelic. At least two incidents appear to justify the name, and though not piping-related, are well worth telling, not only for the light they throw on the brutality of the times but more importantly for the light they throw on the kind of man that the most lauded of all piping families, the MacCrimmons, had to follow.

The first incident was the abduction of Rachel Erskine, Lady Grange, orchestrated by her husband the Hon. James Erskine, Lord Grange, a Scottish judge serving the British government. Among a host of marital difficulties, Grange was afraid, so people have conjectured, that his wife would expose him as a Jacobite sympathiser. Norman MacLeod was known to have been complicit in the act; and in fact, it was a laird and lawyer by the name of Roderick MacLeod who, together with a MacDonald laird, led the band of men who took Lady Grange by force from her Edinburgh home in the middle of the night in January 1732.[16]

The story entered Scottish folklore because of the continued tragedy of Lady Grange's life. Taken from island to island, she was eventually brought to the most remote of all Scottish islands, St Kilda, some 100 miles from the Scottish mainland, from where she wrote in a smuggled letter to Edinburgh: '[I]t is impossible for me to write or for you to imagine all the miserie and sorrow and hunger and cold and hardships of all kindes that I have suffer'd since I was stolen.'[17] Her hoped for release never came, though she was taken off St Kilda in 1740. Lady Grange died in Waternish, Skye, in 1745, still imprisoned and in hiding. Her body was buried there, though her husband had allegedly already carried out a sham funeral in Edinburgh after her disappearance. Stranger still, yet another fake burial took place—of a coffin filled with earth—after she died, this time at Duirinish Churchyard, also on Skye; more specifically, in Dunvegan, next to the home of Norman MacLeod.

As the sorry tale of Lady Grange unfolded, MacLeod had no intention of keeping himself out of trouble. Atrocious with his money, he amassed huge debts, and one way of seeking to make them good, alongside selling vast tracts of his ancestral land, became known as the 'Ship of the People' plan of 1739, which he devised together with Sir Alexander MacDonald of Sleat. The two men arranged to have nearly 100 of their tenants in Skye and Harris, some of them children as young as five, kidnapped and sold into slavery in the American colonies, reporting them as petty criminals. Thankfully, when the ship stopped for supplies in Donaghadee, Ireland, a number of the captives tried to make an escape, and local authorities became aware of what was happening. Though the case eventually came before the British government, MacLeod and

MacDonald escaped prosecution, perhaps due to the favourable machinations of the head of the judiciary in Scotland, Duncan Forbes of Culloden. The leniency shown may account for MacLeod's decision to join the government forces against the Jacobites at the time of the rising six years later. And thus we return to the MacCrimmons.

There were at this time two notable MacCrimmon pipers serving the MacLeods, namely the brothers Malcolm and Donald Bàn, the former serving Norman MacLeod and the latter serving another MacLeod chieftain on Harris. Despite the web of myths surrounding the MacCrimmons,[18] not least Donald Bàn, there is one remarkable tale rooted in fact. This is the story of the Rout of Moy on 16 February 1746, exactly two months before the Battle of Culloden. At that time, the Jacobite army under Bonnie Prince Charlie was on its way north to Inverness after its abortive attempt to march on London, and from there they hoped to plan a new campaign southward. In early February, the prince travelled northward from Crieff in Perthshire and eventually arrived on the 16th at Moy Hall, 8 miles south of Inverness, the home of Aeneas Mackintosh, chief of his clan. Aeneas, however, was in Inverness serving as a government soldier! Aeneas' wife, on the other hand, Lady Anne Mackintosh, was loyal to the prince, so loyal that she earned the title 'Colonel Anne' for her work in raising her husband's clansmen to fight for the Jacobite cause. The French ambassador to the prince described her thus: 'The intrepid lady, a pistol in one hand and money in the other, traversed the country; menaced, gave, promised, and, within fifteen days brought together 600 men.'[19] Apparently, Prince Charles called her *La Belle Rebelle*, the beautiful rebel.

But Aeneas Mackintosh's presence in Inverness was a sign of the present danger that Charles faced in staying so close by. Mackintosh was serving under John Campbell, earl of Loudoun, who was in command of a large body of government men—his own 64th Highland Regiment and the Independent Highland Companies. Norman MacLeod of Dunvegan (a cousin, would you believe, of Lady Anne) was also in Inverness at the time with his own companies. Present, too, was his son John MacLeod, representing the branch of the family that lived on the Isle of Harris and now in command of one of the companies in Loudoun's regiment. His piper was Donald Bàn MacCrimmon. Donald Bàn's brother Malcolm was not present, having been taken prisoner the previous December at the Battle of Inverurie. One story has it that the pipers serving under the prince refused to play the morning after the victory, stating, 'whilst McRimman was in captivity, their pipes were *dumb*; and nothing, but the release of their master, could make them return to their duty'.[20] If true, the bond of pipers, for a short moment, showed itself more powerful than the political disunity that was tearing the country apart.[21]

But back to Charles at Moy Hall. When it was discovered that he was lodging with Anne, Loudoun (seemingly at the insistence of Norman MacLeod)[22] set out that night with his troops, 1,500 of them, intending capture—notwithstanding the affair that Loudoun seems to have been having with Lady Anne herself![23] Loudoun's intentions became known, and word was sent ahead to warn the prince. Charles fled to a nearby wood, while Lady Anne sent a handful of her men—five according to strong local tradition—led by the local blacksmith Donald Fraser, towards the government troops and ordered them to keep a look out, hidden in the surrounding moor.[24] Seeing Loudoun's men approach up the road, these few men roused a mighty din, shouting clan war cries, firing muskets and, according to one source, playing the bagpipes.[25] The government soldiers thought they were surrounded by a great Jacobite force, and panic gripped them. Loudoun himself later described the incident (though he seems to have inflated the numbers that were firing against them):

> We marched prosperously to the Heght above the Watter ... [then] to my infinite mortification, I saw and heard, about a mile on my Left, a running Fire, from the whole Detachment. They saw, or imagined They saw, Four Men; on which They made this Fire. But the Consequence on the main Body was very bad, for it threw us into the greatest Confusion. I got my own Regiment, at the Head of which I was in the Front, saved from falling out of the road. All faced to where They saw the Fire, They were ten men deep, & all presented, and a good many droping Shots, one of which killed a Piper at my Foot, whilst I was forming Them. The rest fell all back out of the Road to the Right, a considerable way, in the utmost Confusion; and It was a great while before I could get them brought up and formed; and the Panick still so great, That It was with the

greatest Difficulty when the party came in, which They did in two & threes, That I could, standing before the muzzles of their pieces, prevent their Firing on Them. And when I came to count the Corps … I found I had lost the Five Companies in the Rear, of whom, after all the Search I could make, I could hear nothing.[26]

While this was a great boost for Jacobite morale—not least because Loudoun and his troops retreated out of Inverness as a result—it was a loss for Highland culture in another sense, for the piper who fell at Loudoun's feet was none other than Donald Bàn MacCrimmon; some say he was the single casualty of the entire episode. Legends quickly sprang up in response. One imbued Donald Bàn with second sight (i.e., prophetic vision) and had him composing, as he prepared to leave Skye the year before, a piobaireachd known as 'Cha Till MacCriumein'—'MacCrimmon Will Never Return'.[27] The other had him as a closet Jacobite, who, as he lay dying on the moor, gave his one and only performance of a composition, never to be played again, written in honour of the prince.[28] His death did, however, lead to the 'The Lament for Donald Bàn MacCrimmon', attributed to his brother Malcolm. The great twentieth-century piper and composer, Captain John MacLellan, has called it 'one of the longest and most beautiful works ever composed for the bagpipe'.[29]

The Rout of Moy encapsulates the apparent contradictions of the time, as a great bearer of Highland tradition, Donald Bàn, falls serving the Hanoverian king. Not only that, he both serves alongside fellow Highlanders and dies at the hands of a Highlander. It's even possible—it was almost certainly the case at Culloden two months later—that the sound of the bagpipes accompanied both sides as the rout unfolded.[30] Their stirring blast was not, in these cases, the sound of unity.

* * *

It's not our fault, however, if we think in less blurry ways than this. In many respects, the media of the time is partly to blame for making the picture far neater than it was. Already, in the first decade of the eighteenth century, we find at least two Grub Street satirists linking, in the most unflattering fashion, Scotland with Jacobitism and Catholicism. One places a well-known musician in hell and has him composing 'Scotch tunes for Lucifer's Bag-piper'[31] and, else-where, rails at the idea that 'a Man could Toot himself to Heaven upon the Whore of Babylon's Bagpipes' (the Whore of Babylon meaning the Roman Catholic Church).[32] The other satirist decries the prospect of attending church at St Paul's, London, which 'Jacobites and Papists use', and where 'Popish Bagpipes make a hideous Noise.'[33] No wonder that Williams can write:

> The bagpipe's sound provides the background music for all things unlawful, corrupt and unacceptable. Its connection with Scotland, in the eyes of many an English satirist, is so strong that its mere presence in literature or prints is enough to convey a plethora of signifiers which speak of Jacobitism, devotion to the Stuart dynasty and a Catholic monarchy, and the disruptive effects this would have on the English Establishment.[34]

The remarkable Woodhouselee manuscript, which captures first-hand accounts from eyewitnesses and participants of the Jacobite occupation of Edinburgh in the autumn of 1745, shows how much the bagpipes were viewed as *the* sound of the Jacobites, even though the Scottish regiments of the government forces had pipers too. At Edinburgh Cross, 'the pipes plaid pibrowghs when they were making ther circle'.[35] After victory at Prestonpans, '[t]he Prince ... came to the Palice on Sabath evening with bagpips playing'.[36] There is also this rather wonderful sentence: 'A popish Italian prince with the oddest crue [crew] Britain cowld produce came all with plaids, bagpips and bairbuttocks, from the Prince to the baggage man.'[37] No wonder Sir Walter Scott would one day say—well, he's said to have said—'twelve Highlanders and a bagpipe make a rebellion'.[38]

The Jacobites themselves were also responsible for simplifying the picture. Their literature was not averse to conflating the government forces with the English. Aonghas Mac Dhomhnuill's 1745 song 'Oran Brosnachaidh do na Gàidheil'—'An Incitement for the Gaels'—is a case in point. Here, Aonghas encourages the Highlander to 'Show the English / In the rout you're not gentle.'[39] Jacobite literature also reinforced the idea that the bagpipes were a distinguishing identifier of their cause. A poem by Sìleas Nighean Mhic Raghnaill (or Sileas MacDonald, c. 1660–1729) addresses the Jacobite officer Alexander Robertson of Struan in terms that can be translated: 'Laird of Struan from the mountainous Giùthsach / you have spent some time waiting in France. / Raise your pipe and your flag—/ now is the time to be active—/ and send the Campbells home in full flight.'[40] Note that final line, too. The enemy in this case is no English interloper: it's that most powerful of Scottish clans, the Campbells.

One of the MacDonalds of Clanranald, the remarkable Alasdair Mac Mhaighstir Alasdair (or Alexander MacDonald, c. 1698—1770), produced some other telling lines in his 'Tearlach Mac Sheaumais'—'Charles Son of James'. Alasdair is said to have sung these lines when the prince raised his standard at Glenfinnan: 'Between earth and heaven in the air I am sailing, / On the wings of exultance, battle-drunken, enraptured, / While the notes of the Great Pipes shrilly sound out their tune.'[41]

There can be no doubt that the pipes referred to in these poems were Highland Great Pipes—though we now know it's hard to be precise about exactly what that means. One thing's for sure: they were mouth-blown pipes. What's so fascinating (and this takes us full circle back to the start of the chapter) is that visual representations of Highlanders and Jacobites in the press of the second half of the eighteenth century—that is, subsequent to Culloden—usually depict the instrument as being bellows-blown. As we'll see in the next chapter, bellows-blown pipes took Britain by storm across the middle of the eighteenth century. They thus became the 'go-to' image for the bagpipe in the mind of the urbanised popular press, most of whose contributors would not have made the arduous journey to the Highlands themselves to see the Highlanders' native pipes in all their larger glory. The Highland Great Pipes were simply not in the imagination of the wider public.

How things have changed! To understand why things have shifted so dramatically, to know why cheek-puffing and three drones on the shoulder are prerequisites for almost all contemporary depictions of the bagpiper, we have to look at what unfolded once the Jacobites were quashed for good. The Highlands, having been a byword for suspicion and treason, could now be clouded with the romance and nostalgia for which their mist covered mountains seemed to have been made. But the pursuit of the authentic Highland image would lead, in some ways, to the death of Highland authenticity itself.

5

PIPES, POWER AND PATRONAGE

THE ENLIGHTENED REIMAGINING OF THE HIGHLANDS:
1746–1830s

He seemed then to be convulsed; his pantomimical gestures resembled those
of a man engaged in combat; his arms, his hands, his head, his legs, were
all in motion; the sounds of his instrument were all called forth and con-
founded together at the same moment. This fine disorder seemed keenly to
interest every one. The piper then passed, without transition, to a kind of
andante; his convulsions suddenly ceased: he became sad and overwhelmed
with sorrow; the sounds of his instrument were plaintive, languishing, as if
lamenting the slain who were being carried off from the field of battle. This
was the part which drew tears from the eyes of the beautiful Scotch ladies.[1]

So wrote the French geologist Barthélemy Faujas de Saint-Fond
after witnessing one of the very earliest solo competitions for the
Highland bagpipe in 1784. He was the guest in Edinburgh of none
other than Adam Smith, that towering figure of the Scottish
Enlightenment. Saint-Fond's bizarre description of the competing
piper mid-piobaireachd—as if John Cleese had been strapped with
a bagpipe before filming the Ministry of Silly Walks—is almost
impossible to believe were it not for the fact that Saint-Fond represented the epitome of the European 'disciplined and cultivated
mind';[2] he was not, in other words, inclined to the telling of tall
tales. It's tempting, however, to see more in this passage than just
a hugely entertaining description of eighteenth-century piobaireachd
performance (and one that seems to suggest that the art of piobaireachd has changed quite significantly over the centuries).[3] Taken

together with its context, the passage can act—though this was by no means Saint-Fond's intention—as a metaphor for the age itself.

Here we are in the city at the heart of the Scottish Enlightenment, where the rigours of human reason and the empirical approach ruled supreme. This was the Edinburgh of the great philosophical sceptic David Hume, who'd died just eight years earlier, and of Smith, the father of modern economics. The setting for the 1784 competition spoke of that movement. The pipers were performing in the hotelier John Dunn's new Assembly Rooms on West Register Street, made available for the first time that year for 'public entertainments'—events that would showcase the refinement and elegance with which the Enlightenment age is so commonly associated.[4] These annual piping competitions were organised through the Highland Societies of London, founded in 1778, and of Edinburgh, founded the year of Saint-Fond's visit. Again, these institutions were every inch the product of the age, modelled as they were on the Edinburgh Society for Encouraging the Arts, Sciences, Manufactures and Agriculture, which was itself an offshoot of the Select Society, a quintessentially Enlightenment body that boasted Hume and Smith as members.[5] The Highland Societies were largely composed of the landowning classes, and in their intentions to rejuvenate the Highland way of life that had been so affected after the Jacobites' defeat in 1746, 'the whole undertaking was underpinned by Adam Smith's declaration that the interests of the landlord and the general interest of society were one and the same'.[6] With such a basis, it's little wonder that it would be these societies that would first institute competition—that key driver within any model of capitalism—as a principal way through which rejuvenation, not least in the world of piping, could be achieved.

So, the entire set-up seems to speak of that age for which the Scots have become famous and that has led to one book being entitled *How the Scots Invented the Modern World: The True Story of How Western Europe's Poorest Nation Created Our World and Everything in It*.[7] And yet the image Saint-Fond presents of the piper is anything but an image of enlightened refinement. The convulsions, the violent emotions, the disorder and then the overwhelming sorrow that calls forth tears, all of this seems to speak of that other movement for which Scotland is famous: Romanticism. This Romantic element was not out of place. James Macpherson's *Fragments of Ancient Poetry*, which purported to be translations of ancient Gaelic poems on mythic figures in Scotland's past, was published in 1760. Together with his further collections of the 'Poems of Ossian', Macpherson's work proved to be one of the major catalysts for the wider international Romantic movement, with admirers ranging from Diderot to Thoreau, and of course Sir Walter Scott, 'the first to portray the Highlander as a "Noble Savage", all of whose sons were valiant and daughters virtuous'.[8] Together with Robert Burns (1759–96), whose *Poems, Chiefly in the Scottish Dialect* was published in 1786, these three men became the crowning trinity of Romantic Scottish figures.

The sense of overlap between the movements was more than just chronological. As Murray Pittock has so masterfully shown in his essay 'Enlightenment, Romanticism and the Scottish Canon', the two spheres of thought and feeling were continually bleeding into each other, feeding off each other, reacting to each other, to such an extent that 'the Enlightenment and Romanticism are inextricably intertwined in Scottish Romanticism'.[9] That is why Saint-Fond's depiction speaks so powerfully of the time. Not only do we have the Romantic figure of the Highland piper in the heart of Enlightenment Edinburgh, competing because of that Enlightenment, but the very words are indicative of the apparent contradictions of all this: 'The sounds of his instrument were all called forth and confounded together at the same moment.' 'Fine disorder' seems especially apt for capturing a mixture of the animating forces at the centre of the respective movements: Reason and Emotion.

* * *

The wider piping culture of the time was full of similar tensions. Just as the Romantic sphere was utterly enmeshed within the Enlightenment sphere (in Scotland at least), folk and classical—insofar as we can apply those terms to the eighteenth century—were similarly bound up with each other across this period. I mentioned in the previous chapter the boom in bellows-blown pastoral and union pipes that was now gripping Britain (I use the word 'Britain' deliberately; London was a hotspot for them), and a look at their backstory certainly disrupts the narrative that all bagpipes are essentially folk instruments.

These pipes and their music were developed and played in settings far removed from the rustic cottage or the inn. The baroque movement on the Continent, running across the seventeenth century and into the first half of the eighteenth, had produced new styles of music in the form of the opera and the cantata, and instruments were created or adapted to meet these fresh sounds. As the fashion for the 'pastorale'—music that deals with rural subjects—raged through Europe, France especially, it was inevitable that the archetypal shepherd's instrument, the bagpipe, would be caught up in this process. A raft of French composers across the seventeenth and eighteenth centuries wrote for versions of the French *musette*, and the instrument was refined in the process.[10] There were sonatas, concertos, cantatas and operas all composed to champion its sound.[11]

As the fashion spread across the channel, instrument makers in Great Britain pushed their creations into these new realms. The early forms of the Northumbrian smallpipes, given their small size and design, seem to draw on the *musette* fairly directly, but the pastoral pipes, a larger instrument, seemed to take things in a new direction while remaining true to the classical context.[12] Their volume range meant they were still suitable for playing alongside other classical instruments,[13] and like the Northumbrian pipes, the use of bellows meant the reeds weren't exposed to moisture, ensuring the instrument would stay in tune for longer. But crucially, they were designed so that the player could overblow on the new oboe-like chanter reed and thus range across the wide possibilities of an almost chromatic scale. There was now a set of twelve pitches available to the piper, far exceeding what was possible on previous incarnations of the bagpipe. It could thus match the baroque oboe in versatility, plus it had the advantage of the drone accompaniment.

Towards the end of the eighteenth century, an additional pipe, known as a regulator, was added to some of these bagpipes, with further regulators added in later decades. This came out of the bag from the same stock as the drones. It was 'stopped' at the end—that is, there was no hole at the end—and was fitted with four or five closed keys that a player could strike with his wrist while his fingers were occupied on the chanter. Once struck, another note was added to the drone chord, again heightening the sense of variation that was available. By the 1790s, the instrument had begun to morph into the union pipe—though pastoral pipes continued to be sold until 1842[14]—as the chanter underwent further modification. Having been shortened, this too could be 'stopped' by placing the end on the player's thigh, hence its clear links to what would become uilleann pipe-playing, which follows the same practice.[15] In this way, the player could jump an octave and also produce a staccato effect. The instrument's versatility was complete.[16]

I mentioned in the last chapter Geoghegan's 1743 book *The Compleat Tutor for the Pastoral or New Bagpipe*. A look at the cover image—with its evocation of 'an ideal landscape of classical antiquity'[17] and its 'Gentleman' of 'fine taste'[18] playing the instrument—shows how far we are from the rowdy world of the tavern. That these pipes were also expensive to make only added to the sense of social elevation. The maker would have to be skilled in woodwork, metalwork, leatherwork and capable of highly delicate reed making, plus he would have to source luxury materials from abroad, including boxwood, tropical hardwoods and ivory. There was no doubt this was an exclusive instrument, and there is a rich tradition, in Ireland especially, of 'gentlemen pipers', renowned for their skill upon it.[19]

That shouldn't make us assume that, correspondingly, the Highland pipes were the preserve of the poorer classes. Yes, there were many unlettered 'community pipers' who made no special claim to grandness,[20] but one glance at the ornate dress of the piper to the laird of Grant—that exquisite portrait of 1714, mentioned in Chapter 3—shows that piping and grandness could indeed combine.[21] In fact, hereditary pipers were very often tacksmen themselves, that is, they held leases of land from their chief, in exchange for their services, and then sublet the land to others. Of the MacCrimmons and the MacKays of Gairloch, Donaldson writes that they conformed to an expected picture for such established piping families, that is, 'the holding of lands rent-free by virtue of office, the social leadership entailed by the resulting tacksman status, the possession of servants, the easy familiarity with the lairdly family and neighbouring gentry, often permitting ... a degree of travel with consequent social polish and cosmopolitan outlook'.[22] (That said, we might note that certain MacCrimmons could only sign their names with an X on legal documents, so we might refrain from automatically adding literacy to the list).[23] Very often, close relatives of the chief were also tacksmen, and from these ranks came pipers too—they were patrons as well as performers, even composers in some instances. Indeed, Gaelic tradition of the eighteenth century makes much of such 'gentleman pipers' who starred on the Great Pipes.[24] The piping demographic of the late eighteenth-century Highlands was far from monochrome.[25]

We also ought to be wary of the idea that, just because the pastoral pipes brought new musical possibilities for the instrument and were at home in 'classical' settings, they somehow outshone, musically, the Great Pipes in sophistication. As Barnaby Brown, a musical historian, flautist and experimental piper, reminds us: 'Greek musicologists 2400 years ago praised tonal restraint and composers in recent centuries have repeatedly reacted against chromatic excess. Historically, delight in many pitches has predictably been followed by delight in fewer pitches, with indulgence and discipline ebbing and flowing.'[26] A tune such as 'The Royal Chance' in Geoghegan's *Compleat Tutor* has been called a 'glittering showpiece', and no doubt it is, but can it be said to match the finest piobaireachd?[27] Admittedly, not everyone would view the latter with such respect, Saint-Fond being one of the doubters. 'I confess that it was impossible for me to admire any of them', he wrote after watching the piobaireachd competitors of 1784. 'I thought them all of equal proficiency; that is to say the one was as bad as the other.'[28]

Yet even in the Highlands, bellows-blown pipes would have been played. A 1913 article from *The Oban Times* provides an eyewitness account of piper Sandy Bruce in the 1840s—'sturdy and well set, of a ruddy complexion, clean shaven ... [wearing] a tartan coat, with flaps embellished with silver-gilt bullet-shaped buttons, and trews'—and what music he played. Crucially, his instruments of choice are referenced too: 'Pibrochs were his forte, but he also played marches, salutes, and dance music when necessary. He would scorn to play the latter—the dance music on the *piob mhor*, or large pipe. He reserved it for the *piob shionnaich*, or bellows pipe, which he generally carried about with him.'[29] Further confirmation of this Highland diversity came when the National Museum of

Antiquities of Scotland was gifted a set of Lowland or Border pipes in 1983 by the descendants of Malcolm MacPherson (1833–98), to whom the pipes had once belonged (MacPherson was the father of Angus, mentioned in the Introduction, and will be the subject of further comment in the next chapter). Judging by the paintings of Egbert van Heemskerck, these bellows-blown instruments—before they were ever called Lowland or Border pipes—were being played in London and Oxford by the end of the seventeenth century.[30] Unlike the pastoral and union pipes, they sounded and tuned just like the Great Pipes, with the exception that they were quieter. According to MacPherson's family, it was typical for professional Highland pipers in MacPherson's era—the mid- to late 1800s that is—to have a set of both kinds of pipes, with the bellows pipes being used for accompanying dancing and indoor playing.[31] Given the words of John Ramsay of Ochtertyre, quoted in Chapter 3, that openness to variation was well established by the time Bruce and MacPherson were on the scene.

Just as the Lowland or Border pipes were originally free from the geographic ties suggested by their name, the pastoral and union pipes were in vogue *across* the British Isles. Judging by the material evidence available from about 1760 onwards, such pipes were being made in Dublin, Edinburgh, Aberdeen, Glasgow, London and Newcastle, and the north-east of Scotland in particular has been described as a 'special enclave' for them.[32] This may make us pause before any confident expressions about the uilleann pipes being an entirely indigenous Irish instrument. In fact, so rich is the material evidence for the bellows pipes, especially the pastoral or union pipes, across this period in Scotland and the wider United Kingdom one would be forgiven for thinking that *this* type of bagpipe was *the* national instrument of the time.[33] Until recently, however, there has been near silence about the instrument in the written histories of the bagpipes.[34]

The classical and the folk coalesced again in the repertoire of the pastoral pipe, as captured in Geoghegan's *Compleat Tutor*. This took well-known folk tunes and then spruced them up with a host of technical variations in a manner in keeping with baroque convention. In this respect, it followed a wider practice of the time, as is evident from the ornate variations provided in two early manuscripts of music for the Border pipes, one dating to 1717, the other to the 1730s.[35] It's an approach taken again in James Oswald's famous songbook, the *Caledonian Pocket Companion*, published in six volumes between 1745 and 1760, before Oswald, a London-based Scot, went on to become chamber composer to the king in 1761. Oswald's volumes covered a wide selection of Scottish material from both Lowlands and Highlands—yes, even Jacobite songs were popular across Britain while the remnants of Jacobitism were being brutally suppressed—as well as music for the London theatre and pleasure gardens. But the variations Oswald provided upon the tunes were new elements that were intended to make 'a product associated with the ideas of simplicity and tradition more palatable to an elite group of metropolitan customers'.[36] Geoghegan and his successors were similarly ambitious, with later Northumbrian pipe music dating to 1770 and 1800 following the same practice.[37]

The repertoire of the Highland bagpipe was not immune to this 'classical' context either. An article of 1972 said of Scottish fiddle music:

> Most people do not realise how far Scottish folk-fiddle music was influenced by classical music; it is usually thought of as an indigenous growth, untouched by civilisation, transmitted by illiterate farm workers and vagrant players. But in fact folk-fiddle playing, as it exists in Scotland today, was almost entirely an eighteenth-century creation; and it was developed by educated musicians, most of whom were at home in the classical music culture.[38]

Pipe music often fed off the fiddle repertoire. The earliest collections that we have of light music for the Highland bagpipe, starting with *A Collection of Quicksteps, Strathspeys, Reels, and Jigs Arranged for the Highland Bagpipe* by Donald MacDonald in 1828—though we know that dance-music in the Highlands stretched much further back than this—show this influence clearly, drawing notably on the hugely popular collections of fiddle music by Niel Gow and his sons, which first started to appear in 1784.[39] The contemporary repertoire still shows signs of these links: tunes such as 'Within a Mile of Edinburgh Toun' and 'The Piper's Maggot' could be seen as pure baroque. Incidentally, Highland versions of reel dances, accompanied by piper or fiddler, were often danced in Lowland Scotland, which means that any claims about hermetically sealed repertoires for the respective regions—one abounding in piobaireachd, the other delighting in 'lighter' forms of music—are hard to maintain.[40]

Likewise, it would be wrong to think that the worlds of the Highland Great Pipe and that of the pastoral and union pipes were in vacuums separate from each other. The spread of instruments being made by the illustrious Edinburgh bagpipe maker, Hugh Robertson (1730–1822), reflects this. Not only was he producing the 'Prize Pipe' for the winners of the Highland Societies' competitions for the Great Highland Bagpipe—and in doing so, standardising the instrument into roughly what we know it as today[41]—he was also creating large numbers of pastoral and union pipes for the gentry. But many within the Scottish gentry, especially those based in London (mainly as a result of the political union of Britain in 1707), remained intent on fostering the Great Pipe because it was considered the archetypal instrument of war[42]—and here again we run into a contradiction or tension.

* * *

The martial spirit that had once been associated with the so-called 'barbarism' of the Highlands was now transformed into an essential feature of Enlightenment progress. Thus could Henry Home, Lord Kames (1696–1782), a patron to Hume and Smith, write in *Sketches of the History of Man* (1774) that 'a military and an industrious spirit are of equal importance to Britain; and that if either of them be lost, we are undone'.[43] As Donaldson has pointed out: 'The [Highland] Societies' approach was entirely utilitarian: they considered that the pipe had a single purpose—to keep up the military spirit of the Gael and, by so doing, to sustain the gallantry of the Highland regiments. A steady flow of pipers into the army was the ultimate goal.'[44]

If you have read about the destruction of the 'Highland way of life' after Culloden through legal and military measures emanating from London, then this talk of the establishment rousing the 'spirit of the Gael' may come as a surprise.[45] It's true that the Act of Proscription 1746 made it illegal to wear 'Highland clothing' and any of its accoutrements (contrary to popular belief, the Act makes no mention of bagpipes or bagpipers and no-one was ever convicted of piping under its stipulations).[46] It's also true that the execution of the act—as expressed in the extreme punitive measures of the duke of Cumberland and his troops against anyone who could be said to have aided or abetted the Jacobite cause—was especially focused on Gaelic-speaking regions.[47] And yet, it's equally true that there was a speedy rise in recruitment among the Highlanders into the British Army, to the extent that, between 1740 and 1799, a total of fifty-nine Highland units were raised.[48] One reason that has been offered for this concerns the colonial and political ambitions of Great Britain across vast portions of the globe at the time. In the context of the Seven Years War (1756–63) and the War of American Independence (1775–83), not to mention the expansion of the British presence in India, it seems unsurprising that military leaders would look to the Highlands as an ample recruiting ground for cannon fodder. The prospect of a secure income in the harsh economic climate of the region would prove very alluring to its inhabitants, so the argument goes, and the War Office seemed to want to add to the allure by making 'a blatant appeal to the old loyalty to the clan and its leaders' through allowing the proscribed Highland wear (not repealed until 1782) in this military context.[49] Renowned military historian Hew Strachan, however, argues against this narrative:

> The recruiting of the Highland regiments was carried by the needs and ambitions of highland landowners and their kinsmen. Tenants traded military service for security of tenure ... Highlanders remained unhappy about serving away from home, particularly when such service—as it often did—contradicted their terms of enlistment. Mutiny could result. Others disliked having to wear the kilt: this was a matter of expense as well as comfort, since soldiers were docked money from their pay to cover the additional costs of Highland uniform. The higher standards of education prevailing in Scotland as opposed to England suggested that there were other routes by which an ambitious Highlander could promote his career without having to expose himself to the privations of military service.[50]

Either way, as Colonel David Murray writes,

> the piper was to be found in the ranks of the companies which formed the newly raised battalions, none considering itself complete until

each captain had his piper at his elbow. Records exist showing the inducements which were extended to persuade pipers to enlist, usually in the form of increased bounties, the money offered to each recruit on enlistment. Family influence was also invoked.[51]

Interestingly, it was not just Highland regiments that had 'Highland' pipers—though the term 'piper', with one exception, was unofficial in the military until 1854.[52] We know from a picture of 1769 that the 25th Regiment, later to become the King's Own Scottish Borderers, had a piper kitted out in Highland garb.[53] The 1st Battalion of the regiment that would become the Royal Scots, the oldest infantry regiment in the British Army, was authorised to have a piper— that is, the army itself would pay for him, not the officers, as was standard practice—throughout the eighteenth century, 'a unique privilege extended to no other regiment, Highland or Lowland'.[54] In a sense, this slight blurring of the boundaries reflected what was happening to the geography of piping in that century. The heartland of Highland piping, historically speaking, has sometimes been taken to be the Western Isles; it has been viewed, in other words, as a pursuit that flourished on the fringes. Yet, by the late eighteenth century, one of the most dominant counties for the Highland pipe was Perthshire, at the very centre of Scotland, through which the Highland Boundary Fault runs and thus where Highland and Lowland meet. The very first winner of the Highland Society of London's competition was Patrick MacGregor, a native of that county. (MacGregor was also admired for his capacity to play his pipe chanter with the usually superfluous pinkie finger of the left hand, having lost his ring-finger, a skill that earned him the nickname Patrick *na Corraig*, Patrick of the Finger.) Both first and second prizes of 1784 went to Perthshire men. But beyond geography, the fact that non-Highland regiments boasted their own pipers may tell us something of the development of the nation's self-understanding.

After the political Union of 1707, there was a growing sense of Scotland as a province of 'North Britain'.[55] Indicative of this were the very names that were given to the country's regiments in the first decades of the eighteenth century. The Royal Regiment of Scots Dragoons (later the Royal Scots Greys) became the Royal North British Dragoons in 1707; as for the Royal Scots Fusiliers (as they would become), they were named the Royal North British

Fusiliers in 1713. But as Scots regiments and Scots commanders, such as Sir Ralph Abercromby and Sir John Moore, began to win fame for themselves on the battlefield, a sense of Scottish identity could start to reassert itself against such Anglicising forces. That the bagpipes could sometimes feature in the fame only helped matters. In 1760, the pipers of the Fraser Highlanders were reported as representing the 'turning point' in a key battle during the capture of Montreal.[56] In 1781, during the Battle of Porto Novo, British troops, fighting on behalf of the British East India Company, were grossly outnumbered by the opposing soldiers of the Kingdom of Mysore. It's said that one piper belonging to the 71st Regiment (Highland Light Infantry) played near continuously for eight hours while the fighting went on. Remarkably, the battle went the way of the British forces. Apparently, the British commander Sir Eyre Coote rode up to the exhausted piper after the battle and extended his hand, saying, 'Well done, gallant fellow, you shall have a silver set of pipes for this!' Coote kept his promise, and the pipes became a treasured heirloom of the regiment.[57] Given the Anglicising forces that had previously been in play, events such as these, which highlighted something specifically Scottish—whether Highland bagpipe or kilt or tartan—became prized for their capacity to distinguish the country from its southern neighbour. Thus, features specific to the Highlands became critically important across Scotland for their capacity to speak for the nation's individuality.

It's perhaps for this reason that, although most of the Scottish soldiers who fought against Napoleon at the beginning of the nineteenth century were Lowlanders, their image was Highland.[58] That the British Army was now disproportionately made up of Scots— 17 per cent compared to 10 per cent by UK population—only added to the sense of pride. The Highland Society of London made much of the military exploits of the Scots, and in the process converted 'the highlanders' image from one of primitivism to one of Scottish national valour'.[59] It's in this context that we have to understand the growing exhibitionism of Scottish displays of nationhood after the decisive victory at Waterloo in 1815, which reached their apogee in the royal visit of George IV to Edinburgh in 1822, where Sir Walter Scott and other leading figures sought 'to transfer the charisma of the Stuarts to a Hanoverian chief of chiefs' through 'political theatre'.[60] Playing their part in the theatre were of course the bagpipes, and three pipers were there at Leith Pier to welcome the king, before piping him up to the King's Park (now known as Holyrood Park) and onwards to Holyrood Palace in a 'grand procession'.[61] What they wore is not recorded, but the Celtic Society had a detachment of Highlanders, acting as His Majesty's bodyguard, dressed in a manner that might give us some clue. Each one wore a belted plaid, a tartan jacket (at a time when the idea of a 'clan tartan' was only just starting to emerge),[62] a scarlet vest, a cocked bonnet with a clan badge and cockade, a pair of hose, brogues with clasps, a gun, a broadsword with shoulder belt, a shield known as a targe, two pistols with a belt, a knife (dirk) and belt, a shoe knife called a sgian, a powder horn with chain and cord and, last but not least, a pouch for ammunition with a belt across the shoulder.[63] It leaves the costume department of *Braveheart* in the shade.

* * *

The Highland Societies followed the trend, and their competitions of the early 1820s featured 'troops of garishly accoutred dancers, cute little boy pipers ... grizzled war veterans with chestfuls of medals, all in spectacular "Highland Dress"'.[64] Not only this, but the organisers arranged for a depiction of romantic Highland scenery to act as the backdrop for the performances. By 1838, there were prizes for the 'best dressed' performer.[65] Referring to these competitions, Donaldson writes: '[P]iping was seen first and foremost as spectacle, with music coming a distant second to theatrical razzmatazz.'[66]

The societies contributed to these new ideas about the Highlanders in other ways. It had become the societies' habit, as they set about publishing works of Highland music, to attach essays to them, written not by the compiler of the music but some other 'expert'. The problem was, these experts were not necessarily fully aware of the reality of, and history behind, Highland cultural life. An essay entitled 'Of the Influence of Poetry and Music upon the Highlanders' was added to Patrick MacDonald's *A Collection of Highland Vocal Airs* of 1784, but the evidence suggests it was written by John Ramsay of Ochtertyre, though everyone took the author to be MacDonald himself. With claims about the 'very high antiquity' of the bagpipes, the probable Norse origin of piobaireachd and the rapid decline of this noble art, Ramsay's essay has been described as 'pretentious, ill-informed and taking the fashionably gloomy view of Highland culture'.[67] I would be reluctant to speak so strongly about a man whom Burns and Scott regarded highly and whose views are not actually that far from Patrick's brother, the knowledgeable Joseph MacDonald, when he wrote to his father (the italics are mine):

> O! that I had been at more pains, to gather those admirable remains of our *ancient* Highland music, before I left my native country ... in order that those sweet, noble, and expressive sentiments of nature, *may not be allowed to sink and die away*, and to shew, that our poor remote corner, even *without the advantages of learning and cultivation*, abounded in works of taste and genius.[68]

These words were quoted by Patrick in his preface to the book and stand alongside Ramsay's essay. But the picture Ramsay's words present, and to some extent Joseph MacDonald's too, was indeed rather 'gloomy' and probably unjustifiably so. Research has shown that Highland piping after Culloden was in fact surprisingly robust and rich.[69]

Echoes of Ramsay's views were proffered to the public once again in 1803 when an introductory essay was attached to Joseph MacDonald's *Compleat Theory*, finally published more than forty years after its compilation. This essay has been described as 'even more militaristic and jingo-patriotic' than Ramsay's, with the bagpipes presented as 'the badge of a modern xenophobic nationalism, and as a metaphor for a vanishing world of antique heroism'.[70] This is largely true, though I struggle to see the xenophobic element. What's important to grasp here is the overall image of Highland Scotland that's building up in such essays: the sense of a country that is backwards looking, hankering after a lost past and oriented towards the importance of prowess in battle.

For a nation that just a few decades previously could boast of being in the very vanguard of forward-thinking cosmopolitanism— Smith had published the *Wealth of Nations* in 1776—this sort of narrative seemed to be taking Scottish identity in a different direction. Yet this kind of narrative would be both the making and breaking of

Scotland in the nineteenth century and beyond: making, because the mythologisation of the Highlands has come to underpin the nation's worldwide fame; breaking, because, paradoxically, it allowed for a radical detachment from the reality of Highland life for a large majority of its inhabitants, a reality of extreme economic hardship, famine and ultimately of mass emigration.

Before I say more on that, it's important to qualify the mythologising narrative somewhat. Some authors appear to suggest that this nineteenth-century perspective on the Highlands was almost pure invention, and that from it spring those things that have lazily been taken as quintessential aspects of the Highlands from time immemorial, whether that be the kilt or clan tartan. Even at the time, Alasdair MacDonell of Glengarry, fifteenth chief of his clan, said of the Celtic Society that 'their general appearance is assumed and fictitious ... they have no right to burlesque the national character or dress of the Highlands'.[71] Yet it's probably better to see these developments more as an exaggeration of, or expansion upon, an authentic existing tradition. One document of 1704 records what the men of Badenoch and Strathspey ought to wear when called for their laird's 'hosting or hunteing', and the costume is perhaps only a lighter cousin of what the Celtic Society Highlanders of 1822 wore: 'Heighland coates, trewes, amd short hoes of tartane of red and greine sett broad springed and also with gun, sword, pistol and durk.'[72] The laird in question was the chieftain of clan Grant. He clearly had a penchant for a good show. When he formally handed over his estate to his eldest son, he 'made all the gentlemen and commons of his name wear whiskers, and make [sic] all their plaids and tartan of red and green, and commanded them all to appear before him at Ballintome, the ordinary place of rendezvous, in that uniform, in kilt and under arms'.[73] The beginnings of the 'clan tartan' idea can be seen here; not an 'ancient' reference perhaps, but certainly long before George IV graced the streets of Edinburgh.

The famous portrait of Grant's personal piper is once again a useful reference point on this issue. There, the piper's clothing is about as ornate as you can get: he wears tartan, he wears a kilt—though not one that simply ties around the waist like modern kilts—his drones flutter with the bratach or heraldic banner of the family. Castle Grant and its surrounding mountains nobly provide the

Highland backdrop. And this is dated to 1714. Or look at Giuseppe Chiesa's 'Lady Louisa Lennox with Her Husband's Regiment, 25th Regiment of Foot', dated circa 1769–71. The piper in that painting is every bit as finely turned out, with his belted plaid of government tartan. His yellow coat with red facings is very handsome indeed. The decorative element had thus long been important. The developments of the nineteenth century simply took this further and put a focus on the visual element that seemed to outweigh the music.

Nonetheless, precisely at the time that Highland Scotland was being hailed as the stomping ground of Britain's most elite group of warriors; precisely at the time that the wealthy officers of the Highland regiments bedecked, at their own expense, their pipers in ever more extravagant Highland dress;[74] precisely at the time that Scott was penning the novels that would make Scotland the seedbed of Romantic nationalism across Europe, the novels that would tempt hordes of foreign visitors to the west coast in search of 'a people that were "unchanged", appeared unworldly and offered a looking glass into an earlier time';[75] precisely as these things were going on, many inhabitants of this apparently wondrous land were being rounded up and evicted from their inland crofts to allow the more profitable sheep to graze freely across heather and hill. It was, in other words, the time of the infamous Highland Clearances. The people were sent first to the coasts of Scotland, where it was hoped they could make their living through fishing and kelping (kelp is a substance made from seaweed and was used in the soap and glass-making industries). As this proved untenable for many, and with the demand for kelp declining after the Napoleonic Wars, the only hopeful choice for thousands of Scots—and this included Lowlanders too—was to emigrate, usually to Canada (the cheapest and quickest option), but also to Australia and New Zealand. The music and culture they took with them will be revealed in later chapters. It's not that most were actually forced to leave the country by their landlords, embarking the ships wrapped in their plaids with laments and tears (the classic, misconceived view, so potently depicted in Thomas Faed's painting 'The Last of the Clan' and John Watson Nicol's 'Lochaber No More'). In fact, most went out of circumstance and many went proudly, unwilling to succumb to the social deprivation they felt was being forced upon them.[76] And, as Professor Graeme Morton has

pointed out, the forces of the free market, in this new age of capitalism, were also significantly at play, and these 'inexorably, to contemporaries, pressed Scots to leave their homes for a livelihood elsewhere'.[77] According to Morton, the 'near constant movement in
search of work was the norm for most, and for many that journey
took them overseas'.[78] Nonetheless, the clearances and the capitalistic context within which they took place were signs that the popular
conception of the Highlands was largely a fantasy. Piping would feed
off the fantasy, as the cleared estates became the settings of 'stage-
managed Celticism on the grandest scale'.[79] But in some of its other
forms, piping would die because of that fantasy.

The various bellows-blown pipes did not conform to the image
of what the Scottish (in other words, Highland) piper should play
in all his martial glory. With town clocks introduced in the late
eighteenth century and urban populations ballooning in the
Lowlands with the onset of the industrial age, the need for, and
practicality of, town pipers disappeared. There was no nationalistic
incentive to keep them alive, as there was with the Great Pipe.
They did not speak of a people.[80] They survived longer in the
Highlands, where—as we've seen—they were used to accompany
dancing, but even there they died out eventually. The contrast with
the Irish bellows pipes shows how agendas around identity often
drove such matters, for it needed the creation of the Gaelic League
in Ireland in 1893 to stop the Irish pipes—not yet called uilleann—
from falling into oblivion.[81] The other bellows pipes native to the
British Isles, ones that again pull strongly on identity, are the
Northumbrian variant—distinguished by their four drones and a
chanter that is both keyed (in other words, you can flick metallic
bands that will allow you to extend the range of notes and add
sharps and flats) and closed (there's no hole at the bottom). But
pipe maker Robert Reid of North Shields (1784–1837) was only
just developing this instrument into what we know it as today at
the time that pipers in the Scottish Lowlands were laying their
instruments in their boxes for good. In time, the Northumbrian
pipes would also come to struggle for their existence. Their survival owes much to a handful of families who kept the art alive
and—patronage again—the duke of Northumberland, who, even
after the disbanding of the 'Northumbrian Small Pipes Society' in

73

1899, stubbornly kept on his family's tradition of having a personal piper within the duke's retinue.[82]

But just as the smallpipes were dying out in Lowland Scotland in the early part of the nineteenth century, the Highland pipes were crystalising into what we call the Great Highland Bagpipe today. In some sense, the tradition was reaching what seemed to be the height of its blossoming, and in other ways it was grinding to a halt. The tensions within the tradition thus continued. One man would play a key role in the creation of these new contradictions. This was the tragic-fated, sideburn-wearing Sovereign's Piper, Angus Mackay.

6

A TIME FOR GIANTS

DEVELOPING A TRADITION OF INNOVATION
(AND MADNESS): 1830s–1900s

The dancefloor at Scotland's Spa Hotel in Pitlochry, Perthshire, is heaving. It's the early 1980s. Kilts whirl through the smoke-filled air as the ceilidh band fiddles its heart out. Amid the noise and the shrieks, a slight, scholarly looking figure is quietly smiling by the dance floor, glass in hand, basking in the sense of a day well spent. This is Hugh Cheape, much quoted in previous chapters, and at the time a curator at the National Museum of Antiquities of Scotland. He had been on a special mission that day. The well-known *Times* columnist, Miles Kington, had been tasked with writing an article on the most prestigious of all solo competitions for the Great Highland Bagpipe, namely the Glenfiddich, held annually in the magnificent setting of the Victorian Ballroom at Blair Castle. On its stage, flanked by a vast array of walled antlers and armour, the ten best pipers of the year battled it out under the glare of antique portraits, three bonneted judges and a crowd of 300 spectators. The winner would be adjudged the finest bagpiper of the year. The trouble was, Kington had no real understanding of the bagpipes. How would he be able to tell the difference between the piper tuning his pipes and actually playing his piobaireachd? How would he know how one player's performance was any different from another? That's where Cheape came in.

Having built up a bit of a reputation as a knowledgeable commentator on all things bagpiping, Cheape had received a call from Kington a few weeks prior to the competition asking for his help.

Would he accompany him and whisper in his ear at moments of potential confusion? Cheape was more than delighted to accept. Now, having satisfactorily completed his task, here he was at the post-competition ceilidh, to which he had insisted that he and Kington proceed, knowing it was the perfect opportunity to capture the stories, told with as much enthusiasm as happy slurring, that would bring the article to life. Kington had been swallowed up in the crowd, leaving Cheape alone. But not for long. He sees approaching him a journalist acquaintance from Glasgow. The two start to blether loudly over the strains of the Gay Gordons. The pressing thing the journalist wishes to know is what Cheape thinks of a book that had been brought out a few years previously, which had—in a most unlikely fashion for a piping publication—captured the headlines and provoked the wrath of the piping establishment. This was Alistair Campsie's *The MacCrimmon Legend: The Madness of Angus Mackay*.

What had made this book so controversial? Three things really. One was the claims that Campsie had made within its pages. He argued that the MacCrimmons' piping college at Boreraig on Skye was a myth; that the much-vaulted MacCrimmon pipers themselves were an invention; that their famous compositions were not theirs; and that the ultimate responsibility for this myth lay partly at the door of James Logan, an expatriate Scot living in London, who apparently wrote the historical accounts that accompany Mackay's 1838 *A Collection of Ancient Piobaireachd and Highland Pipe Music*, and partly at the door of Mackay himself, piper to Queen Victoria between 1843 and 1854. Not only was Mackay's piping pedigree questionable, according to Campsie, but his presentation of 'authentic' piobaireachd and his claims about the origins of individual pieces, especially their connections to the MacCrimmons, were less based on genuine knowledge of the tradition than the shattering effects of cerebral syphilis—in other words, they were the results of insanity.

Almost every piper knew the magical but tragic tale of Angus Mackay: how he had been born to a famous piping father in 1813; how he had won, aged only twelve, the Highland Societies' competition for setting pipe tunes in the new staff notation; how he'd then won the Societies' Prize Pipe itself, for the finest piper of the year, aged just twenty-one; how he became the most influential collector and editor of pipe music, especially piobaireachd, in the nineteenth century; how he had pioneered the 'competition' march; and how he had his appointment to Queen Victoria terminated because of acute mental instability. (He had, apparently, claimed he was married to Her Majesty, that her offspring were his and that Prince Albert was denying him his marital rights! Campsie, anticipating his readers' shock, took evident delight in quoting a man he calls 'the leading psychiatrist of his day', who described Mackay as 'the most violent patient in England'; Campsie also noted Mackay's 'predilection for enticing people to approach him, then punching or kicking them in the testicles').[1]

Most pipers also knew that Mackay had been confined to hospital, first at the notorious 'Bedlam' (Bethlem Royal Hospital) in London, then at the progressive Crichton Royal Hospital in Dumfries, and that at age forty-five he had drowned in the River Nith trying to escape the hospital attendants (though some have interpreted his plunge into the water as suicide). All this was known, but the consensus was that this terrible period came well after Mackay's great contribution to the study of pipe music. Now Campsie was claiming that modern medical perspectives on his condition would have Mackay insane from as early as the age of twenty, colouring all his major work. Since everything that came subsequent to Mackay was built on his edifice, the whole tradition behind the classical music of the Highland bagpipe came tumbling down if Campsie's claims were true.

But the claims were only one element of the controversy. The second element was the personal invective that stained Campsie's pages. His scorn for the piping establishment was palpable in every chapter. The third element was how he reacted to his critics. The widely admired Captain John MacLellan, one time head of army bagpiping at Edinburgh Castle, had published a review in his self-founded journal *The International Piper* and made his disapproval of Campsie's book more than clear. Campsie was having none of it, and MacLellan's wife Christine ('Bunty' to her friends) reported in the pages of *The International Piper* that he was harassing them at home with repeated abusive phone calls. But by putting this claim, which they could not prove, about Campsie's behaviour into print, the MacLellans had exposed themselves as liable for defamation. Campsie swiftly threatened legal action. It was not long before *The International Piper* ceased to appear, and Campsie is said to have gloated that he'd brought the publication to its inglorious end. In truth, the MacLellans were only too happy to have an excuse to wrap things up, having got into an endeavour that, with their advancing ages and health problems, had become a sizable burden. While most in the piping world didn't know this, they most certainly did know that voicing strong opinions on Campsie was a dangerous pursuit.

Back to Scotland's Spa Hotel. Cheape, knowing something of the above story, is trying to answer the journalist's question about the merits of Campsie's book in such a way that he'll keep out of trouble. He does not divulge his own doubts over the quality of Campsie's scholarship, though he does acknowledge that the orthodoxies of the piping world needed a shake up, and in this respect *The MacCrimmon Legend* had undoubtedly fulfilled a function. The journalist smiles. 'Well, you'll never know your luck.' He points over to the bar. 'Alistair Campsie's here!' And sure enough, propped up at the bar, a few whiskies in, is the lone figure of Alistair Campsie, looking thoroughly unimpressed by the festivities. 'I'll introduce you!'

The first thing Cheape notices as they approach the bar is the size difference between Campsie and himself, the former towering over the diminutive Cheape. The journalist, after the briefest of introductions, disappears, leaving the two men alone. Campsie looks at Cheape with what can only be described as contempt. Staring down at him, he asks, 'Who are you?' The tone is confrontational from the off. Cheape explains his background and tells of his interest in the history of piping. 'What would you know about it?' comes the response. Despite this discouraging start, Cheape doggedly continues, 'I must tell you, I was really interested in your book.' Again, the hostile response comes, 'What would you know about it?' Cheape forges on nonetheless, 'Well, I must ask, why did you say what you did about the MacCrimmon college at Boreraig?' This is too much for Campsie. His long arms shoot out towards Cheape's lapels; it's time for a fight. Cheape steps back in alarm with a flurry of placatory words. Campsie leans towards him and jeers, 'You're all the same! Ignorant, ignorant, ignorant!' There's nothing left for Cheape but to make a quick exit.

Outside, he meets his journalist acquaintance again. The Glaswegian can't stop laughing, having known full well what would happen. Cheape, feeling like the sacrificial lamb, is the opposite of impressed.

The Campsie saga would only get more bizarre. In 1995, *The Herald* published an article entitled 'Writer Tries to End MacCrimmon Recriminations', in which Campsie argued that, shortly before his book was published, someone tampered with his manuscript with the object of bringing the work into disrepute.[2] These alterations apparently accounted, in a major way, for people's strong misgivings about the book. The article explained that Campsie had made it his mission to have an erratum slip inserted into every copy of his book that he could find, and readers were told that the copy in the National Library of Scotland certainly had one. Reading this years later, in 2024, I quickly made arrangements to visit the library and ascertain what scandalous changes had been made to poor Mr Campsie's book against his will. Eagerly, I opened the front cover. This is what I found on the erratum slip:

> pp 155 & 156: 1799 should read 1797
> p 163: 'infectious' should read 'non-infectious'
> Author of Piobaireachd should read Seumas MacNeill

On the one hand, it was laughable. Did Campsie really think *these* slips were responsible for bringing his book into disrepute? On the other hand, it was also sadly ironic. *The MacCrimmon Legend* was an extended essay on the demeaning and damaging effects of mental instability, and yet here was what looked to be pretty stark evidence of the author's own paranoia. It was hard not to feel sorry for the man.

* * *

Why do I tell these stories? Well, it's because we have to understand what Angus Mackay and his legacy means to people in the piping world. In 2009, Mackay was hailed by the current president of the Piobaireachd Society Robert Wallace as 'a genius in the history of world piping', whose 'contribution to piobaireachd playing can never be over estimated'.[3] Indeed, with very few exceptions, every competitor at that 1980s Glenfiddich, and all Glenfiddichs before and after, would have been playing a piobaireachd based on the version of the tune as it was presented by Mackay.[4] As the most influential editor of Mackay's work, Archibald Campbell of Kilberry, once said of Mackay's 1834 collection:

> The book was accepted immediately by all pipers as their Scriptures, and their sedulous fidelity to it, in my youthful days, was sometimes grotesque. The prestige of Angus Mackay's book still stands higher than that of any other book of pipe music, and probably, among those who are able to estimate its worth, as high as any other book on any branch of Celtic art.[5]

Part of the reason for this was Mackay's claim that he was closely following the tradition that had been handed down to him by his father, the renowned John Mackay of Raasay, of whom the secretary of the Celtic Society wrote in 1821: 'The fame of this man is too well known to require any praise from me.'[6] Conventional wisdom conforms to what is written on the plaque affixed to John's burial stone, which describes him as '[t]he last great piper to have had lessons from the MacCrimmons. He was the best player, composer and teacher of his day, and through his expert pupils … the playing of the great music was carried forward faithfully to all the top pipers of the present time.'[7] He is considered, in other words, the key link point within the tradition back to the illustrious MacCrimmons. It's little wonder, then, that his son Angus's book was prized above all others; it had captured the MacCrimmon tradition for ever more. I use the word 'captured' on purpose.

This is not the place to get sucked into the details of the debate around John's connection to the famous Skye dynasty or his son Angus's faithfulness or lack thereof to what his father handed down, but before we move forward, we do need to put to bed any lingering suspicions that Campsie's book may have lodged in our minds about the very existence of the MacCrimmons themselves. A very thorough examination of the historical records has led the most knowledgeable of the MacCrimmon scholars, Ruari Halford-MacLeod, to assert:

> All these facts [in the historical records] take the legend out of the legendary MacCrummens, so that, by 1838, when Angus MacKay's

book 'A Collection of Ancient Piobaireachd and Highland Pipe Music' gave an account of the MacCrimmons,[8] this was not the beginning of the invented history but the end of at least 150 years of records and recollections.[9]

The quality of Campsie's research into the Boreraig site can be glimpsed by another Halford-MacLeod observation. Campsie makes much of an account written by one John Dalziel in the 1830s, in which Dalziel says he went to visit the site and found no trace of a MacCrimmon history there, not even the locals knowing anything of them. Of this, Halford-MacLeod says:

> I was sitting with Euan MacCrimmon last evening [this was 2001] ... Now Euan assures me that his father still has a tack [holds a lease] at Boreraig and his family has been living there all along. My only conclusion is that Dalziel went to the wrong Boreraig—there is another Boreraig near Torrin in Skye. The census returns in the 1840s and '50s show that there were still MacCrimmons at Boreraig and Euan was quite insulted to know that such had been written.[10]

The idea that insanity coloured all Mackay's major work also needs to be settled. Donaldson, a noted authority on such matters, puts the case succinctly when he describes the manuscript scores that Mackay assembled during the 1830s and '40s as 'a model of clarity and order'.[11] There is simply no explicable way in which a deranged man could have produced them. But Donaldson is also aware that the intentions and consequences of Mackay's work were not, and have not been, entirely positive in every respect. He identifies three aims behind Mackay's collection: '(i) to stabilise the repertoire for the purposes of competition and instruction; (ii) to replace the rich diversity of oral versions with a standard fixed score; and (iii) to substitute for the traditional varied palette of ornament a uniform simplified style'.[12] This may be making slightly too much out of the evidence, but certainly, in the words of Mackay's own Preface, he wished to 'preserve, in its native simplicity, the ancient music of Caledonia'.[13] The legacy of the collection has thus been viewed two ways, either—and this is the historically dominant interpretation—as the preservation of a unique tradition and the creation of a level playing field that would allow the proficiency of all pipers to be assessed evenly from then onwards, or—and this is the more recent but growing interpretation—as the coagulation of a once diverse tradition, stemming the long flow of creativity and musicality that had preceded it.

There is a third interpretation, however. Why not view it as a combination of all these things? The problem lies less in Mackay than in the psychology of the bagpiper, which is perhaps only a reflection of a psychological instinct native to all human beings. In other words, the instinct to take sides, to see matters in black and white, to shun ambiguity and nuance. We, the present author included, have to fight this urge and try to see the good and not so good at the same time. Even if we do, the fact remains: Mackay is a giant of the tradition from whatever angle you look at it.

* * *

It was a time for giants. The nineteenth century produced an extraordinary array of talent and personality. One who stands alongside Mackay is his father's old pupil, John Bàn Mackenzie. Famously handsome, he had eloped with the daughter of a landed gentleman and married her in Crieff against her father's will. Famously talented, he came third in the Highland Societies' Prize Pipe competition in Edinburgh in 1821, second in 1822 and first in 1823, before going on to win, in its first year, the Special Gold Medal for former winners in 1835. When Queen Victoria visited Lord Breadalbane, whom Mackenzie served as personal piper, at Taymouth Castle in 1842, it is said that she was 'much taken by Breadalbane's handsome piper'.[14] Apparently, she asked the noble lord where she could find a piper like Mackenzie. Breadalbane went to consult Mackenzie himself. For Mackenzie, it was a hopeless case: as he told his master, the queen would never find a piper as handsome or as proficient as he. The job, as we know, eventually went to Angus Mackay. If Mackenzie had pride and a sense of humour, he had deep feelings too. 'His Father's Lament for Donald MacKenzie', which he composed after his beloved son (himself a winner of the Prize Pipe) died of smallpox, is testimony to that. His talent stretched to pipe-making too, and he was therefore described as 'the last of the old school' and 'the complete piper', as he 'could kill the sheep, make the bag, turn the pipes, cut the reeds, compose the tune and play'.[15] Unsurprisingly, then, Mackenzie is often referred to by the title that was formally offered with his 1835 victory: 'King of Pipers'. A look at the portraits we have of him suggests that Mackenzie knew himself to be piping royalty.

How many other substantial figures could be named, whether that be Donald MacDonald (c. 1767–1840), the originator of written pipe music as we know it and in whose famous book *A Collection of the Ancient Martial Music of Caledonia called Piobaireachd* of circa 1819 we first encounter the claim—though probably made by a Preface writer who was not MacDonald himself—that the bagpipe is Scotland's 'national instrument';[16] or Donald Cameron (c. 1810–68), pupil of John Bàn Mackenzie and master player, collector and editor, honoured by many as the originator of 'the Cameron school' of piobaireachd playing; or Lt John MacLennan (1843–1923), a colossus as a writer and editor of pipe music and the father of two magnificently gifted players, George Stewart and Donald Ross (always known by their initials), who would come to dominate the next generation; or William (Uilleam) Ross (1823–91), a later piper to Queen Victoria, who has been acknowledged as one of the principal founders of the modern light music tradition. As their accolades suggest, these men—and yes, the main influencers were all men, though as we'll see in Chapter 7, women could play important roles too—were innovators, pushing the art of piping forward. With such names enshrined in piping history, it's easy to lose sight of the fact that, in their own time, they were not simply representatives of the 'old school' or just talented interpreters of what came before.

One of the main shifts across the timeframe of these 'giants' was the move to a greater focus on the written score and a standardising of technique in line with that score. Evidence from what could be found, until relatively recently, in the Scottish communities that had settled in eastern Canada, especially Nova Scotia, during this period shows that learning by ear had been the established way of learning for many pipers prior to, and during, the generation of those mentioned above. Indeed, diversity of technique was a given between players, rather than—as it is now—something to be frowned upon.[17] All of which is to say, in their efforts to produce and/or edit written pipe music for their contemporaries and posterity, the giants of 'the tradition' across the Victorian era were, in many cases, as much tradition breakers as they were tradition bearers.

One man who well exemplifies the tension between old and new is someone I've mentioned before: Malcolm MacPherson, known as 'Calum Pìobaire' ('Malcolm the Piper' in Gaelic). We already know something of MacPherson's piping pedigree from the words of his son Angus, quoted in the Introduction. Like John Mackay of Raasay—who taught MacPherson's father—MacPherson was viewed as a conduit of the MacCrimmon tradition and, like Mackay, his fame rests largely on the impressive collection of pupils he taught—though MacPherson was himself a great winner of medals. In fact, he was competing just at the time that the Highland Games circuit was coming into being, the first being held in 1837. As English or English-aping landowners turned their estates into ever more extravagant Highland playgrounds, the west and north of Scotland became go-to social destinations during particular seasons of the year. You could get a steamer from Glasgow, Leith and London just to see the Highland Games. The sporting aspect was secondary to the social, but the events themselves were extensive. Spectacles included boat and bicycle races, pigeon shooting, hot air ballooning and parachuting.[18] There was, in most cases, nothing particularly 'Highland' about the activities pursued.[19]

Piping was one of the exceptions, yet the act of making it competitive immediately dissociated it from its classic role within the community, which was to provide music for communal dancing.[20] It was in the context of the games that the craze for competition among pipers emerged—a craze that's still with us—and it's because of competitions that the written score became such an important factor over these years, providing an equal platform from which to judge a range of players. With the Highland Societies' Edinburgh competitions ending in 1844, the ultimate accolade became the competitions at the Northern Meeting in Inverness—where MacPherson won the Prize Pipe in 1866 and Gold Medal in 1871—and, of equal importance later within the century, the Argyllshire Gathering in Oban (where MacPherson took the top prize in 1876). A piper could earn good money from these games, especially if he had the talent to compete in some of the other events, as did the multitalented John MacColl in the generation that followed MacPherson's, who could earn £40 in an afternoon, more than £4,000 in today's money. For MacPherson, the allure of prize money must have been great, for he was willing to travel far and wide, even winning at the Portree Games in Skye. His success was based not just on exceptional technique and a wonderful bagpipe. MacPherson's sense of musicality is said to have been unsurpassed.

But he was keen to pass his mastery on. Through his pupil John MacDonald of Inverness, we have one of the earliest depictions of how instruction once took place:

> Each morning, he used to play Jigs on the chanter while breakfast was being got ready—he would sit on a stool near the peat fire as he played … I can see him know, with his old jacket and his leather sporran, sitting on a stool while the porridge was being brought to the boil. After breakfast he would take his barrow to the peat moss, cut a turf, and build up the fire with wet peat for the next day. He would then sit down beside me, take away all books and pipe music, then sing in his own canntaireachd the ground and different variations of the particular piobaireachd he wished me to learn. It was from these early associations of Malcolm MacPherson that I realized that piobaireachd must be transmitted by song from one piper to another in order to get the soul of it; the lights and shades.[21]

Prior to this, MacPherson had been the personal piper to Cluny MacPherson, chief of the clan. But the role of the piper within such a household was changing. Having once been a position of eminence, granting almost 'gentleman' status (according to one clan chief's piper in the eighteenth century, it was a poor estate that could not keep its laird and its piper without working),[22] the evermore money-conscious landed classes were now looking for 'added value'.[23] The personal piper was expected to take on additional tasks, whether as forester or chauffeur or similar, and to this time period—the mid-nineteenth century—we can trace the first stirrings of what would become quite pronounced in the twentieth century: the sense that piping was, with a few notable exceptions, essentially a blue-collar pursuit. As George Bernard Shaw (1856–1950) is said to have quipped: the definition of a gentleman is a man who can play the bagpipes but doesn't.[24] It was a sign of the times when, in 1881, the Scottish Pipers' Society—later the Royal

Scottish Pipers' Society—was founded in order to encourage '[b]ag-pipe playing amongst gentlemen'.[25] This was very much a rear-guard action.

It's hard to know whether these changes in social status had anything to do with MacPherson's retirement from his chief's service in 1877,[26] but what's fascinating to note is the self-created image of the old-world bagpiper that MacPherson took on. In the best-known photograph of him, MacPherson's immense beard seems to perfectly imitate his sporran, and the great spiralled walking stick he grasps in his hand makes you wonder if he's just wrestled an antler out of the head of a gargantuan stag. But, contrary to what the image might make you think, his past was not all Highland porridge and peat.

He'd worked as a teenager in the port town of Greenock, west of Glasgow, as a labourer and ship's carpenter, as well as a piper on a government boat enforcing revenue laws. He also joined one of the very earliest pipe bands, known as 'The Greenock Highlanders', led by another piper with illustrious forebears, Sandy Cameron. It's easy to skip over this communal playing without much comment—it's so much part of piping culture now—but we must remember how radically *untraditional* this activity was for the time. Prior to the nineteenth century, piping was fundamentally a solo pursuit. When pipe bands began to emerge, some purists even called them a 'modern excrescence'.[27]

It's hard to untangle the origins of pipe bands—by which I mean pipers playing ensemble with an integrated drum corps—but there is a reference in the *Edinburgh Courant* of 3 November 1803 to a military review in Hyde Park during which a regiment with the official title of the Highland Armed Association of London, but commonly known as the Loyal North Britons, entered Oxford Street Gate with 'their Kettle-drums and bagpipes playing the old tune of "Over the hills and far away."'[28] There is no evidence to suggest there was anything 'official' about this arrangement, and it may be that the Greenock Highlanders, to which MacPherson belonged and who were all volunteer soldiers within the Renfrewshire Rifle Volunteers, provide the earliest example of organized pipe band playing. There is also evidence that civilian pipers on the great estates were playing in large groups, perhaps even more than two dozen, before piping soldiers got round to it.[29] But the bands within the regular army certainly did come to dominate, towards the end of the century, the perception of what a pipe band was—despite the fact that by the 1870s civilian pipe bands were springing up in a formal manner too, with the town of Brechin potentially holding the title of oldest civilian pipe band in the world.[30] With the founding of the Boys' Brigade in 1883—around the time police bands were appearing—it wasn't long before a healthy seed ground for the rising adult bands was laid among their ranks. Boys' Brigade pipe bands were up and running by 1887.[31]

Before I say more on army pipers, a final word on Malcolm MacPherson. The part MacPherson played in the Greenock Highlanders certainly puts this great tradition bearer in a new light. He was, in a sense, at the cutting edge of piping endeavours in his youth. But in later years MacPherson seemed to distance himself from such a past. As John MacDonald wrote of his teacher: 'He hardly ever played March, Strathspey and Reel; only piobaireachd and Jigs.'[32] Taken together with the way he presented himself visually, we might start to question whether or not the bogeymen in the story of the Highlander's 'inauthenticity' is always the outsider—the Anglicised aristocrat, the Scott-reading foreigner. Indeed, the existing paintings or photographs of any of those 'giants' of the tradition mentioned in the last few pages would suggest that they themselves were more than willing to 'create' an image for themselves. And their images conformed to expectations.

This observation should make us cautious about the very language of authenticity, especially in this period. It might—*might*—once have been possible to talk of a dichotomy between *real* Highlanders over there in an actual physical space and *imagined* Highlanders over there in the minds of wishful-thinkers. But as the nineteenth century drew on, the lines became ever more blurred. Some Highlanders had clearly got caught up in their own romance. That's not to say, of course, that they were failing to be themselves.[33]

* * *

Mention of army pipe bands takes us to a crucial point in the history of the instrument, as it was these bands, travelling far and wide across the British colonies and on foreign campaigns, who would make the Highland bagpipe a global phenomenon. Their emergence within the army has been traced to the development of macadam roads after 1815 and the end of the Napoleonic Wars. Developed by Scottish engineer John Loudon McAdam, these were roads constructed by laying a firm base of large stones beneath another layer of crushed stone bound with gravel and doing so in such a way as to create a convex camber that would allow water to drain off the surface. These roads were hailed as the most significant development in roadmaking since Roman times, and they provide the origins for what we now call 'tarmac', short for Tar Macadam, which is simply a macadam surface that's been bound by tar. There had been small groups of pipers playing together for some time previously to the macadam road but nothing formal and lasting had ever been organised, nor had drums been included in the equation. The old style of road tended to be narrow and rough, making it pointless to attempt the act of marching in unison for long distances. That all changed with McAdam's invention.

But if pipers were to play at the head of the column on these marches, it did not necessarily guarantee a clear beat that the soldiers could follow. That's where the drums, especially the bass drum, became important. Drums had long been part of the military tradition, and their role was often to accompany the playing of the fife. As indicated earlier, it's hard to know precisely when pipers and the drummers started to play together, but the piper and historian of Scotland's regimental music Colonel David Murray has found at least one instance of them playing together in a military context in 1848—on the forecastle of a ship during thick fog, where they were told to warn other vessels of their ship's presence 'by their discord'![34] That same year, we find three marching tunes composed by three different pipers, from two different regiments, which are written in 2/4 time. As Murray explains:

> These three marches are, from their form and structure, intended to be played by the marching pipe band. None is difficult in the technical sense and all will stand repetition without becoming tedious. It is from this seminal era that we can trace the evolution of the bagpipe march as a musical form in its own right.[35]

The lack of difficulty may also tell us something about the quality of the average army bagpiper. Virtuoso pipers clearly existed, as we know from the prizes they won, but early books of army pipe music suggest that a very low level of technical proficiency was required by pipers in the band. One military man, born in 1877, recalled that '[t]he general level of individual performance was deplorably low'.[36] The reason for this was that bands required a certain minimum number to function, and it was often difficult to achieve the base number, so men within ranks, with no piping experience whatsoever, were plucked out and given hurried tuition. The benefit of having fairly easy tunes to play was most notable when certain gruelling ordeals had to be faced. There are stories—though the source of these stories is not always reliable[37]—of pipers playing for hours on end in the most uncomfortable of conditions, such as the time two pipers of the Seaforth Highlanders played alternately for thirteen hours straight on a 42-mile march during the Indian Rebellion of 1857.[38] In August 1880, during the Second Afghan War, Lieutenant-General Sir Frederick Roberts led British and Indian troops on a 320-mile march from Kabul to Kandahar to relieve a British force that was being besieged by Afghan forces. Only two pipers survived the gruelling ordeal; the rest were said to have 'played themselves to death'.[39]

For as long as pipers had been in the army, it had been a tradition that they, with very few exceptions, were to be kept 'against the establishment'—in other words, they were not on the army books and had to be paid for by the officers. Indeed, there are numerous examples of 'officialdom' taking a rather dim view of the value of pipers. When, for instance, in 1769 the marquess of Lorne, later 5th duke of Argyll, as colonel of the Royal Scots protested to an English inspecting officer about a threatened loss of their pipe and drum majors, he was met with the response: '[N]o person whom I have consulted is of opinion that a drum-major or piper can add to, or take from, the honour of that most respectable corps.'[40] Not all non-Scots saw things this way. In 1852, it came to the attention of the duke of Wellington (of Anglo-Irish descent) that Major General J. E. Napier planned to have all pipers removed from the 92nd Regiment (the Gordon Highlanders) as contrary to regulations. Wellington protested to the general: 'I am surprised that an officer who has seen, as you must have seen, the many gallant deeds of Highland regiments, in which their pipers have played so important a part, should make such a report.'[41]

Two years later, though the 'Iron Duke' did not live to see it, a more promising development for army piping took place. As war with Russia looked increasingly imminent, every battalion was ordered to raise their numbers to 1,000, and a footnote within the order authorised for each of the Highland regiments to have one pipe major, with the rank of sergeant, as well as five more pipers. These six pipers were ordered to join those companies within the battalion who were to serve abroad. Gradually, and in a rather piecemeal manner, the numbers grew, and bands became more formally recognised and better provided for; but, really, this didn't settle into anything like a norm until quite late in the nineteenth century.[42] If that's surprising, so too will be the fact that of the eight Highland regiments who were to have their six pipers in 1854, three of those regiments were non-kilted. The pipe bands of the 71st Highland Light Infantry, the 72nd Duke of Albany's Own and the 74th Highlanders (and from 1864, the 91st Argyllshire Regiment) all marched proudly in trews (from *triubhas*), in other words in tartan trousers.

In noting that the pipers of the Highland regiments were to serve abroad, we're reminded of why the Highland bagpipe came to be considered *the* bagpipe in the minds of so many across the world. Tales are legion of how they've enthralled and terrified in equal measure. A classic occurred at the Siege of Pondicherry in 1793. There, a young British lieutenant recorded in his journal the moment when the officer in charge of the British trenches, Colonel Campbell, requested that the piper of the Grenadiers play a piobaireachd, despite the severe French cannon fire that was raining down on them. The reaction was unexpected. The cannon fire first slackened then ceased entirely. The lieutenant recalled in his journal that '[t]he French all got upon the works and seemed more astonished at hearing the bagpipe than we with Colonel Campbell's request'.[43]

It has been said by Strachan that 'Highlanders hogged the limelight in the great imperial sagas of the 1850s',[44] and certainly their part in what became known as the Siege of Lucknow, India, was headline news in 1857. The siege on Lucknow's British Residency was conducted by dissatisfied native Indians, while inside the barricaded Residency British troops and civilians (including hundreds of women and children) and Indians loyal to the British, 3,000 of them altogether, fearfully waited for relief. The troops that were sent to perform this task included the 78th Highlanders (later known as the Seaforth Highlanders), and the strains of their bag-pipes as they approached the Residency achieved widespread fame in the song known as 'Jessie's Dream'. As one survivor of the siege recounted: 'The shrill tones of the Highlanders' bagpipes now pierced our ears. Not the most beautiful music was ever more wel-come, more joy-bringing.'[45] What some of the Indians may have thought of these strange instruments can perhaps be sensed from a tale in which three soldiers of the 78th and a piper by the name of Gibson were caught isolated by six mounted Indians during the relief. Getting within 20 paces of the Highlanders, Gibson, lacking any weapon himself, turned his pipe drones towards the advancing cavalry and blew hard into his pipe bag. It's said the Indians stopped immediately, turned and 'flew like the wind, mistaking the bagpipe for some infernal machine'.[46]

But the bagpipes weren't always felt to be so foreign, and there are some stories that remind us that the Great Highland Bagpipe was anything but the only bagpipe out there. Shortly before the Battle of Salamanca in 1812, soldiers of the Black Watch were surprised to find a piper among the French they had taken captive. The Frenchman's instrument was, naturally, a *musette*.[47] Given the small-pipe tradition within Scotland, this discovery probably caused less surprise than did another experience, which, if we can be allowed to jump forward briefly into the time period of our next chapter, took place over 100 years later. During the First World War, the Macedonian Front provided many Scots with their first taste of Greek, Serbian and Bulgarian bagpipes. On one occasion, the offi-cers of the Royal Scots found themselves at a dinner with their opposite numbers among the Greeks, who were delighted to offer their guests a taste of their own musical heritage. There, round and round the table, marched ten Greek bagpipers playing a version of the instrument without any drones at all. Apparently, it was not an enjoyable experience for the Scottish officers.[48]

But, returning to the nineteenth century, when the Scots played their instruments it often left a lasting impression. When the young maharajah of Patiala, for instance, heard the pipers of the 93rd Regiment (the Argyll and Southerland Highlanders) playing strathspeys and reels, he is said to have exclaimed, 'Beautiful! *That* is the music for me. Can I get such a band? Can I buy it?'[49] Told that it might be possible to have one of the pipers discharged by purchase, the maharajah soon found a certain John Mackay at his command. Mackay was more than satisfied with his lot: a large salary, a good house, several cows, a horse-drawn carriage and abundant gifts. Before long, a pipe band of fourteen Indian pipers, clothed in the green cloth tunics and tartan trews of the 93rd, were merrily playing together. Mackay himself, interestingly, wished to assimilate, in dress at least. When the surgeon general of his old regiment received a visit from him some time later, he found Mackay in a glorious outfit consisting of a scarlet tunic covered with gold lace, blue-cloth trousers with lace down the seams, a blue and gold turban and a matching sash around his waist. For five years he stayed in this happy state, before returning to Scotland to start a business with the sizeable sum he'd saved.[50]

Though many Scots returned, the instruments remained, not least because an industry had sprung up among local tradesmen whom the British soldiers tasked with repairing their pipes. We know of a set of Highland pipes being made by an Indian as early as the 1830s, as this set was commissioned by Elizabeth Jane Ross, Lady D'Oyly—a key female figure in the history of piping, Raasay-born, and the originator of 'Lady D'Oyly's Manuscript', a wonderful 1812 collection of music, which includes five pieces of piobaireachd. Eliza, as she was known, was living with her husband in India when she had the pipes commissioned and sent them back to Scotland for inspection. The recipient was an old acquaintance from Raasay days: John Mackay, Angus Mackay's acclaimed father.[51] Evidently, the Indians showed an aptitude for the task, and soon companies were established for this purpose, such as Nadir Ali & Company in Meerut, 50 miles north-east of New Delhi, which started trading in 1885. The company still produces bagpipes for local pipers, though the owner admits they are 'a poor copy of what is made in Scotland'.[52] In the Pakistani city of Sialkot, there are at least ten companies making and selling bagpipes, according to Google, though there may be many more. In 1987,

Sialkot was said to be the home of the largest Highland bagpipe making industry in the world; its output was even said to surpass the combined output of all the bagpipe makers in Scotland and North America put together.[53] Yet, if the practices of Nadir Ali & Company in Meerut can be taken as indicative, the technology involved in the production appears to have changed little since the time of the British occupation.

The technology may have advanced in Scotland, but the instruments themselves have remained largely with the same design ever since the days of master pipe maker Hugh Robertson of Edinburgh, mentioned in Chapter 5. But as the army took their more or less standardised pipes abroad—most of which were essentially modelled on the Prize Pipe Robertson had created for the Edinburgh competitions in the late eighteenth century—they also took with them the message that *this* is what bagpipes should look like, and, in their dress, that *this* is what a bagpiper ought to look like. Hence the appearance of the pipe bands that sprang up among the many different peoples of the subcontinent, whether Sikhs, Gurkhas, Pashtuns or Dogras (by 1987, there were an estimated 300 pipe bands in India alone).[54] Fascinatingly, however, there are examples in both Pakistan and India of bagpipers playing Highland forms of the instrument who seem to know nothing of their Scottish origins.

In 2000, the Edinburgh-based academic Mark Trewin visited Pakistan for research purposes and discovered to his surprise that 'as far as the [Pakistani] Army pipers were concerned, most were unaware that the bagpipe was a Scottish instrument. Their perception of what they were doing was completely different.'[55] It's in this context, where a certain freedom from a binding tradition can be felt, that we might understand the rather outlandish (to Western eyes) practices that are to be discovered in some parts of Asia and the Middle East. In Pakistan and Oman, for instance, there are pipe bands that perform on camels (McCallum Bagpipes make 'camel-friendly blowpipes' for the players to avoid dental damage),[56] while in Ladakh, India, you can find a band that's decided it would be a good idea to combine bagpiping with ice-skating![57] Some bands attempt wildly choreographed performances, with split-second 360 degree spins, goose stepping, penguin-like waddles and something approaching the can-can.[58]

The sense of freedom behind such performances is not one that is universal across the subcontinent. A particularly revealing interview with a Rajasthani bagpiper, Shyopat Julia, for the programme *I Believe Art Matters*, portrays a man very much bound to a tradition.[59] Julia says he carries on precisely what was handed down to him from his father, who took his practices from his own father. Julia plays the Highland bagpipe but makes no mention whatsoever of its Scottish roots and names the instrument the *mashak*, a variation on the name given to indigenous, sometimes droneless, Indian pipes known variously as the *masaq*, *mashaq* or *bin baja*.[60] With the exception of the last name, these relate to the word that is commonly used for a water-carrying skin bag. Julia plays music that is recognisably Indian in character, and he is dressed in highly elaborate Indian clothing. All trace of Scottishness has disappeared, not only visually and aurally but psychologically too. The instrument now evidently feels entirely native to his people. But not only his. In the central Himalayan region of Garhwal, for example, the presence of *mashki*, as bagpipers are known, has been called 'an almost indispensable part of the rural wedding procession'.[61] And it goes beyond Rajasthan and Garhwal; they seem to be integral parts of communities right across South Asia.[62]

There are few pieces of evidence to tell us how such a tradition came into being, but we might see something of a *mashki*'s forebears in this 1896 account by Lady Wilson:

> While we were having a romp in the evening with Jack after his bath, we heard, to our amusement, the familiar sounds of the bagpipes proceed from the temple enclosure, the player, so Akbar informed us, an Indian soldier at home on leave. You can imagine how incongruous to the occasion the 'Pibroch of Donald Dhu' sounded, followed by 'Up wi' the bonnets o' Bonnie Dundee.'[63]

So, despite what we encounter now in the likes of Shyopat Julia, there was clearly a time when Indians were more than aware of the Scottishness of their instrument. Indeed, other research has shown that the colonial connections remain well known today to many in the subcontinent.[64] So why embrace the instrument so wholeheartedly? That there were indigenous forms of bagpipes already in existence may be part of it—in other words, the instrument wasn't so foreign after all. And even where the Great Highland Bagpipe differs from these, it retains that drone element that is essential to so much music in South Asia. The sense of cross-over is well expressed in the words of H. S. Bhatia in his *Military History of British India* of 1977 (though he is perhaps quoting an older source): 'All wild hill-men, you know, play the pipes, be they Pathans, Gurkhas, or Cameron lads, though their instruments vary from the Highland pipes of Scotland with a bass and two tenor drones, to similar pipes with only one bass drone down to the Eastern "sernai".'[65]

The Great Highland Bagpipe's survival might also have something to do with the far from unambiguous attitude to British rule in these lands. It's not a given that all things British are frowned upon; the Highland bagpipes are not a unique instance of the colonial legacy being proudly absorbed. The Indian and Pakistani armies are clearly part of the inheritance, and their pipe bands thus fit neatly within that context. Connected to this, ethnomusicologist Peter Cooke has identified the love of spectacle as a key feature of Indian culture, and there are few instruments more spectacular than the Highland bag-pipes, with their sheer loudness and the three drones allowing for all manner of ornamentation. Cooke recalls the 1986 Republic Day march-past in New Delhi, where many pipe bands, both regimental and school bands, were on parade. Yet their drones were mostly silent—'they served as spectacle only'.[66] (Cooke does add the prac-tical point that the climate makes it hard enough to get a good sounding chanter reed, let alone drone reeds.) The sense of spec-tacle is clearly a key part of the popularity of the non-military *mashki*, as the outfit and ornamented bagpipes of Shyopat Julia show. They rival any Highlander's paraphernalia in their splendour.

These elisions between the coloniser and the colonised may explain why the piping world in the West has failed to show any real wrestling with this colonial past. In fact, a number of tunes that were written to celebrate colonial victories or feats remain popular today: 'The Siege of Delhi' for instance or 'The 91st at Modder River'. The much-loved and highly atmospheric tune 'Hector the Hero' commemorates Major-General Sir Hector MacDonald, who achieved hero status at the Battle of Omdurman in 1898. That battle was part of the Anglo-Egyptian conquest of Sudan. Perhaps there's no reason to worry about any of this. Good music is good music, so we might say. Yet the fact that it doesn't even appear to arise as a question surely tells us something about the piping community. But what? A lack of interest in history or a simple acceptance that what has been has been? A concern solely for the music? A desire to rise above the so-called 'woke' agenda? There is no clear answer to this.

* * *

One tune that could be added to those above is 'The Heights of Dargai', a stronghold on the north-west frontier of India (now Pakistan), where, in October 1897, several thousand Afridi tribes-men, who had turned against the government of British India, were attempting to hold back attempts by the British Army to advance in what was known as the Tirah Campaign. Efforts had been made to storm the Heights but to no avail, and now three battalions were stuck beneath the stronghold, pinned down by enemy fire. That's when the order went out to the 1st Battalion of the Gordon Highlanders to advance through open ground and take the Heights. Five men led the way: Pipers Findlater, Fraser, Wills and Kidd, with Lance-Corporal Piper Milne at the head. Before long, Milne was shot in the chest and fell (he survived). The others continued, but Piper George Findlater soon took a glancing blow to his left foot, only to be followed by another shot that utterly shattered his right ankle. Even his chanter was hit, though not to the point where it was unplayable. In fact, not one to let a little thing like a bullet wound put him off, Findlater hauled himself against a boulder and struck up his pipes once again, playing 'The Haughs O'Cromdale' as his comrades pressed on. Incredibly, the Gordons took the Heights and scattered the tribesmen. Of the five pipers, only Piper John Kidd reached the Heights.

Word soon spread of Findlater's exploits, and before long there were poems composed in his honour, and prints and paintings of the scene spread across the empire. An offer of marriage came his way, as did sets of bagpipes and subscriptions for monetary rewards. Invalided home to Britain, Queen Victoria made a personal visit to his bedside to decorate him with the Victoria Cross in May 1898. Numerous other medals followed, and Findlater would go on to make large sums of money—up to £100 a week or roughly £10,000 in today's money—performing at concerts and music halls, where crowds flocked to see the heroic piper. Although attempts were made to put a stop to these money-making endeavours, Findlater brushed them off and continued to feed off his celebrity status until, in 1899, he married and settled down on a farm in Aberdeenshire. But that was not the end of Findlater's exploits. Come the outbreak of war in 1914, he enlisted once again in the Gordon Highlanders and rose to the rank of Sergeant Piper. Once again, he was invalided on active duty and was decorated with four different medals for his service. He returned to his farm and became pipe major of the local band, eventually dying of a heart attack in 1942.[67]

What makes Findlater's case so interesting, apart from the sheer drama of his continued playing in the action of 1897, is the sense of a man who is consciously fulfilling a role, perhaps even an expectation. His choice of tune as he lay there injured was probably not accidental. 'The Haughs O'Cromdale' is a strathspey (commonly played today as a march), with an uncertain compositional history and, when sung, with highly inaccurate lyrics conflating two different battles separated by forty-five years, those of Auldearn and Cromdale. But importantly, the lyrics linked with the moment Findlater found himself in, as, in the words of the song, 'The Gordons boldly did advance ... Upon the Haughs O'Cromdale.' More importantly still, tradition has it that at the Battle of Cromdale itself (30 April–1 May 1690) a mortally wounded Jacobite piper continued to play his pipes to bolster his comrades in battle. The Piper's Stone, where this display of valour is said to have happened, can still be seen to this day.

An earlier part of this chapter showed that the great figures in the world of nineteenth-century piping were not immune to fulfilling an image or an expectation, and it would seem to be no different with George Findlater. Indeed, he may well have known not only of the Jacobite piper at Cromdale but also of Piper George Clark, who, at the Battle of Vimiero in August 1808, continued to play in spite of wounds and achieved significant accolades once home. Findlater was probably conscious of being part of a tradition, which he hoped to live up to. And like the major piping figures of his own century, with their rustic or elaborate outfits, grand beards and fine sticks, Findlater's public displays in the theatres and music halls show a man who was not immune to being a spectacle. These men were more than willing to be romantic figures. But opportunities to enter the hallowed halls of piping romance were only going to rise as the nineteenth century gave way to the twentieth.

If this book has highlighted many a tension within piping history, there would be no greater tension than what was experienced between 1914 and 1918. For these years represented, simultaneously, the near extinction of a whole generation of pipers *and* the setting for stories that, like no others, brought the instrument and its players stunningly alive. The desire to fulfil an image or an expectation had clearly passed down to the generation of pipers who left British shores for the bloody battlefields of the Western Front. These scenes of horror were no less stages for heroism. The intention to prove the true martial spirit of the Scot burnt brightly in these young men—they 'acted out of their warrior identity', as Strachan has put it.[68] The presence of the pipes seemed to compel both player and listener—those 'devils in skirts' and 'ladies from hell' as the Germans supposedly called the kilted regiments—to a kind of madness. And on that note, it would appear the chapter has come full circle.

7

EVERYTHING CHANGES

THE GREAT WAR, WOMEN AND THE STANDARDISATION OF TRADITION: 1903–39

Piper Daniel Laidlaw, 7th Battalion, The King's Own Scottish Borderers, For most conspicuous bravery prior to an assault on German trenches near Loos and Hill 70 on 25th September, 1915. During the worst of the bombardment, when the attack was about to commence, Piper Laidlaw, seeing that his company was somewhat shaken from the effects of gas, with absolute coolness and disregard of danger, mounted the parapet, marched up and down and played the company out of the trench. The effect of his splendid example was immediate, and the company dashed out to the assault. Piper Laidlaw continued playing his pipes till he was wounded.

Announcement of Victoria Cross recipients, *The London Gazette* (Supplement), 16 November 1915[1]

Undoubtedly courageous though he was, Daniel Laidlaw was the sufferer of a fairly new condition that was plaguing the pipers of the First World War. Colonel David Murray called it the 'Findlater/ Dargai syndrome'.[2] The sense that *this* was the thing to do—to lead your comrades 'over the top' to the blast of the pipes—was ingrained in so many minds that the loss of pipers reached staggering proportions. Of the 2,500 pipers who served during the conflict, 500 were killed and 600 wounded.[3] The proportions could be higher within individual battalions. Of the ten pipers who led the 2nd Battalion of the Scottish Rifles into France, four were killed within two months, and a fifth fell the following year.[4] The 2nd Battalion of the Seaforth Highlanders lost six pipers before the close of 1915, with five others wounded within that time.

Those who survived out of the 2,500 more than likely did so either because the pipers and drummers were detailed to act as message or ammunition carriers or as stretcher-bearers, as was the long-established practice in many regiments; or because, after 1915, with loss of life so prominent among the trench-based pipers, it became customary across all regiments to leave pipers and drummers out of the trenches altogether. But even then, it could be dangerous. In the Scots Guards, for instance, where the pipers left their instruments behind during the course of the conflict and instead bore ammunition and stretchers back and forth from the trenches, only two pipers out of the original eight in the 1st Battalion remained at the close of 1914. The exact same proportion was lost among the pipers, acting as runners, of the 1/4th Battalion (territorial) of the King's Own Scottish Borderers while serving in Gallipoli. To compound the tragedy, five of the six who had fallen were all young men from the same town of Kelso. At the Battle of Loos (September–October 1915), where the pipers of the 5th Battalion of the Queen's Own Cameron Highlanders fought as soldiers in the trenches, the entire pipe band was put out of action: three killed, three wounded, one gassed.

These horrifying statistics should qualify any tendency to idealise or overly romanticise the scene depicted in the *London Gazette* at the top of this chapter. And yet it's hard to deny the pull of such a response. Just look at the remarkable footage available on YouTube of Laidlaw in later life, in 1934, where he speaks of the moment he went over the top:

> With men falling all around us in the trenches at Loos on the 25th of September nineteen and fifteen, when Lieutenant Young yelled out to me, 'Laidla', for God's sake do something with your pipes', I played them over the top and went right on through the first round of German trenches, on to the second line, where I was bowled over.[5]

Laidlaw then plays for the cameras the very tune he played that day, his regimental march 'Blue Bonnets over the Border', on the very same pipes. Though you are likely to have heard the pipes being played more skilfully elsewhere, and, if you're a piper yourself, the fingering will come as a surprise, there's no doubt that most viewers would agree with the viewer who commented below the video: 'Makes the hair on the back of your neck stand up.' The comments, in general, are indicative of how tales such as Laidlaw's are received:

There are no superlatives available to describe this man's courage!

The Scots have always been fighters and the backbone of the British Army and long may it continue …

Blue Bonnets … grabs you by the guts …

They do not make men like him anymore. Hero.

Laidlaw's actions were by no means the most emotion-raising among the pipers of the Great War. Two men stand out. One has been as lauded as Laidlaw and like him received the Victoria Cross. This was James (Jimmy) Cleland Richardson, a Canadian emigrant from Scotland, who was not yet twenty at the time of his service with the 16th (Canadian Scottish) Battalion of the Canadian Expeditionary Force at the Battle of the Ancre Heights on 8 October 1916.[6] Nearing the German position that day, Richardson's company became stuck behind barbed wire, and the number of casualties was rising speedily as German bullets and bombs rained down on their position. Richardson, as much a sufferer of the Findlater/ Dargai syndrome as Laidlaw was, turned to his company sergeant major and said, 'Wull I gie them wund?' (Will I give them wind?). Receiving the response 'Aye mon, gie 'em wind', Richardson stood up, got his pipes going and played back and forth beyond the wire 'with the greatest coolness' for a full ten minutes. This act of courage/madness created an instantaneous reaction, with the company immediately leaping at the wire, cutting through it and storming on to take their objective.

But the story took a disastrous turn for Richardson later in the day. As he was helping move the wounded back to security, he realised that he had left his pipes behind on the battlefield. He was told on no account to return for them, but he ignored all orders from his superiors and went back to retrieve the precious instrument. Richardson was never seen again. Two years later, he was awarded, posthumously, the Victoria Cross. Mysteriously, the bagpipes he played on the day he died were recovered in unclear circumstances and ended up on display in a small prep school in

Scotland. In 2006, the British Columbia Legislature repatriated the pipes to Canada, where they are now on permanent display in the main foyer of the Legislative Assembly.

That Richardson was allowed to play in such circumstances that day in October 1916, well after piping in battle had become frowned upon by the authorities, had much to do with the culture that had been fostered within Richardson's regiment by its commander Lieutenant-Colonel Cyrus Peck, himself a later recipient of the VC. Peck's views on the military value of a piper are expressed well here:

> When I first proposed to take pipers into action I met with a great deal of criticism. I persisted, and as I have no Scottish blood in my veins, no one had reason to accuse me of acting from racial prejudices. I believe that the purpose of war is to win victories, and if one can do this better by encouraging certain sentiments and traditions, why shouldn't it be done? The heroic and dramatic effect of a piper stoically playing his way across the modern battlefield, altogether oblivious of danger, has an extraordinary effect on the spirit of his comrades.[7]

You might think that every instance of piping bravery would have been as keenly praised as were Laidlaw's and Richardson's, but that was not the fate for David Anderson. He was a twenty-six-year-old pipe sergeant of the 15th Battalion of the Royal Scots when he lined up with his comrades on the banks of the Somme on 1 July 1916. In his trembling hands, he bore the same pipes that had been played in 1904 by Gilbert Kerr in, of all unlikely places, the Antarctic—resulting in a marvellous photograph of Kerr piping away on the ice next to an emperor penguin, which showed only 'sleepy indifference'.[8] If the photo raised a smile, there was nothing humorous about where the pipes found themselves twelve years later. Like Laidlaw, Anderson played his regimental march, in this case 'Dumbarton's Drums', as the whistle went to signal the troops' entry into No Man's Land. Despite the hail of German bullets and the men falling all around him, on strode Anderson, until he reached an occupied German trench. He was utterly alone and without a weapon. Yet the Germans threw up their hands and offered their surrender.

When the other lucky Scots who'd survived their dash across the battlefield arrived, they, with Anderson, forged on further and eventually reached a third line of German trenches. There, Anderson took a hit to the right side of his body and fell to the ground. Perhaps with the historic exploits of Findlater in mind, he hauled himself into a seated position and struck up the mud-spattered pipes once more. For a few minutes, regimental tunes flooded the battlefield. Then he was struck again by a bullet, this time passing through his leg. Piping was no longer an option. Anderson knew that he was in need of urgent medical help. Incredibly, he managed to get on two feet, only to find that a German soldier was waiting to engage him in hand-to-hand combat. Anderson knocked the man unconscious with his bare fists. He grabbed the German's rifle and fought on. Eventually, the loss of blood was too great, and he passed out.

Somehow, Anderson survived, though no Victoria Cross ever made its way to his chest. He was at least promoted to pipe major. The French could do better, however, and awarded him the Croix de Guerre. At the end of the war, Anderson returned to his day job with the Edinburgh City Police. There were no theatre tours like Findlater, no television appearances like Laidlaw, but, for sheer guts and determination, his tale is hard to surpass.[9]

While we're on the Somme, it's worth mentioning one final story from this most horrific of battles, as it highlights one key function of the piper in combat: his ability to evoke instantaneously, through the playing of a single tune, an illustrious military past.

The classic piobaireachd 'War or Peace' (Cogadh no Sith) had long been associated with the Napoleonic Wars. There was, for instance, the remarkable story of a piper from the Gordon Highlanders playing the tune at the Battle of Saint Pierre (1813) and being killed as he played. When a second piper took up the tune, he too was killed. It took a third piper to strike up his pipes and complete it.[10] A piper of the Gordon's was to play the tune once again at the Battle of Waterloo (1815), though it was a piper of the 79th Camerons, Kenneth MacKay of Tongue, who lingered in the national consciousness for his rendition of the tune elsewhere on the battlefield, specifically in the immensely exposed position outside the defensive square formed by his fellow infantrymen, while the French cavalry advanced upon them. Subsequently, a stirring portrait of MacKay playing amid the battle by J. B. Anderson was endlessly reproduced and sold around the British Empire.

Remarkably, a great-grandson of the less famous Gordon Highlander who played 'War or Peace' at Waterloo was present at the Somme. When the regiment's chaplain discovered the soldier's connection to the celebrated 1815 victory and learned that he too could play the pipes, he said to him: '[T]his is the anniversary of Waterloo and you will lead the men out to that very tune which your great-grandfather played on that great day.' When the colonel heard of the plan, he responded, 'Ah! padre, we'll do better than that. You will tell the men about it, and I will call them to attention, and your piper will play his tune in memory of the men of Waterloo.' The chaplain later remembered the moment in vivid terms: 'And so it was done, and a thrilling incident it was as the men stood rigid and silent in full marching order, and the piper strode proudly along the ranks, sounding the wild, defiant challenge that stirred the regiment a hundred years before.'[11]

Making sense of our emotions over such stories is no easy task. And it's no good saying these emotions are tied to the Scots specifically. Too many examples to the contrary can be cited, but my favourite is the response described by the English journalist Robert Blatchford, who, on a visit to the front, felt depressed by all he saw around him. Everything changed when he and his fellow pressmen

> caught a whiff of sound that made us all start. 'The pipes! the pipes!' It was a company of Highlanders on the march, the pipers at their head. I—well, I took my hat off. It was the only thing to do, and my companions did the same, and in silence and with beating hearts we moved slowly past the line. Oh the good Scots faces, grim or gay, the wild elation of the pipers! I could have shouted, or danced, or cried, or—anything. But being British I did nothing. But it was some thrill.[12]

Of course, not everyone would feel like that. One comment beneath the 1934 Laidlaw video puts forward a different perspective: 'The Germans would never fire at a piper for fear of hitting the bag and making the noise even worse.'

The dry, academic response to all this is to dismiss the valorisation of the likes of Laidlaw, Richardson and Anderson, seeing them instead as rare examples of survival among what was overwhelmingly an achingly futile act of walking straight to one's death. But I think we need to be careful about outright dismissal. There is clearly a deep-seated human need to find glory in such moments of horror. It was precisely these kind of stories—of pipers, as symbols of a whole nation, stepping out courageously to face the enemy—that kept near-broken spirits afloat back home. At the front itself, to witness a piper do such a thing, so the testimonies tell us again and again, aroused in the near-broken men cowering behind their walls of clay and mud an otherwise unthinkable willingness to do what their commanders asked of them, and rise over the top. 'The effect of his splendid example was immediate', says *The London Gazette* of Laidlaw; of Richardson, 'The effect was instantaneous.' Veteran William Charles, interviewed for a film on instruments of war, remembers of the pipes: 'They put everything out of my mind but action. I wouldn't be afraid of anything. In fact, the bagpipes when they bled I felt like I could go through hell, anywhere.'[13] Obviously, in an ideal world none of these young men should have been going over the top at all. But that was deemed to be the right thing then, and from that perspective we can say: thank goodness for the likes of Laidlaw, Richardson and Anderson providing a moment of hope amid the despair. And when, at the Armistice, despair gave way to relief, the pipes were there to register that too. A grand sight it was to see the pipe major of the King's Own Scottish Borderers marching up and down a French high street with his pipes on the evening of 10 November 1918, wearing nothing but a shirt and pair of boots.[14]

As with so much else in British culture, the First World War was a watershed moment for bagpiping, and nothing in that world has been quite the same since. Sir Bruce Seton's words in *The Pipes of War* (1920) tell a story: 'Scotland—and the world—must face the fact that a large proportion of the men who played the instrument and kept alive the old traditions have completed their self-imposed task ... something must be done to raise a new generation of players.' Seton then adds, 'it is a matter of national importance that this should be taken in hand at once, and that the sons of those who have gone should follow in the footsteps of their fathers'.[15]

While preservation was felt to be all important, the war also opened up the possibility to think afresh about piping. This dual aspect would explain much of what would follow in the twentieth century.

* * *

It wasn't all disruption. A number of illustrious players and tradition bearers (they were innovators too)[16] had made it through the conflict. The names of Willie Ross (1878–1966), G. S. McLennan (1883–1929) and John MacDonald of Inverness (1865–1953) will be familiar to pipers the world over, having dominated the realms of army and competition piping for many years after the Armistice (and before). But their influence was tempered by influence from another corner, a corner that had a very particular definition of preservation at its heart.

This was the Piobaireachd Society, which had been established by a number of 'gentlemen' (and one woman!) in 1903 with a view to making the rich tradition of piobaireachd more accessible and to encourage a wider variety of tunes to be played.[17] Yet by 1919 it was stipulating to competitors at society-funded competitions that only a particular range of strict interpretations would be acceptable to the society's judges (who were not, for the most part, particularly accomplished pipers themselves), a narrowing that would only grow more pronounced over the coming years.[18] The society's intentions were noble, and many have argued that, without their intervention, piobaireachd would not have grown to the levels of popularity that it has since the days of the society's founding. Yet the level of musical insight the society's representatives have displayed across its lifetime has been significantly questioned by a number of voices, who argue that the society's governing ideology has often seemed to be one that was suspicious of melody and musicality, preferring instead, so the argument goes, something that spoke of the wildness and irregularity they believed was appropriate to the music's Highland origins. Despite these and other reservations, the society was—and still is—widely influential, not least because, drawing on a fairly grand social world, it held the purse strings across multiple arenas, from competitions to media awareness through piobaireachd publications and the payment of instructors. As one onlooker told a society representative in 1920: 'Your Society "pays the piper" & is therefore entitled to "call the tune".'[19]

In the world of light music, it was much clearer that the performer not the patron held the reins, leading to a flourishing of composition and a very evidently 'living tradition', which managed to survive despite the war's devastation.[20] A growing body of technically challenging, musically exciting repertoire had been building up since the 1860s and had been well exploited by players on the solo competition circuit. But it took until the post-war years for pipe bands really to get involved in the action. Pipe band competitions had been important before the war (having started in 1905), with the Cowal Highland Games considered the pinnacle of the season, hosting what is generally considered to be the very first World Pipe Band Championship in 1906. But with a few exceptions, the standard of bands in these years was fairly low. Across the 1920s and '30s, however, 'the competing pipe band came of age', as Donaldson has put it;[21] they were 'the exact equivalent in ensemble terms of the top flight solo performer, at its best a walking marvel of problem solving—operating in a dynamically expanding competitive environment'.[22]

Part of the problem solving was just getting the vagaries of individual instruments into some sort of harmony; with bags still made of animal skin and reeds made of cane, not to mention the lack of moisture protection, it was never going to be a straightforward job. It was a lengthy process to get a band in tune. A story told by a well-known Scots Guard pipe major of a later era, Angus MacDonald, sheds a kind of light on the different approaches that were taken to this challenge. On tour in a foreign climb, MacDonald was asked by a local pipe major how he tuned up his band. The former responded with solid common sense: the pipers blew individually for five minutes, then collectively for another five minutes. He would then make minor adjustments to drones and chanters, after which the band would play together again, before a final re-tune ahead of the performance. The local pipe major was having none of it. 'That sounds a complicated system of tuning to me ... We just congregate in the band hut and drink until it sounds good!'[23]

According to a 2019 survey assessing the rise of pipe bands over the previous 100 years, it was probably in the 1920s that the quality of civilian pipe bands began to surpass that of the military bands.[24] That said, the latter were also improving as a result of the systematic training offered to piping soldiers in what was called the Army Class, first established in 1910 and blossoming after the First World War under the patronage of the Piobaireachd Society and the expert instruction of the above-named Pipe Major Willie Ross, who held sway in his little room at the top of Edinburgh Castle from 1919 until 1958.[25] The Army Class is the direct ancestor of today's Army School of Bagpipe Music and Highland Drumming—a title that has amused some because there is nothing 'Highland' about pipe band drumming, with the earliest drummers drawing on the rhythms of the English army and, from the 1950s, under the influence of the legendary Alex Duthart, from the drumming of the Swiss![26]

While the developments of the 1920s and '30s were hugely enriching for piping, the rise of the civilian pipe band also marks the beginnings of a fissure within the piping community that is still with us, namely the preference of some excellent players for the band context over the solo scene. As different personalities took their pick—one prizing the lonely road of perfecting a piobaireachd, the other cherishing the social delights and technical challenges of communal playing—a distrust, sometimes even contempt, grew up between the two arenas that has not yet been altogether eradicated.

Given that many of these players, especially on the band side, came through the ranks of the Boys' Brigade pipe bands, it's worth pausing for a moment to quote the tutor book of 1909 through which they would have learnt the basics of their art: J. Percy Sturrock's *Piping for Boys*. It's a good reminder that, for all the over-competitiveness and unpleasantness that has sometimes blemished the piping world, humour has been central too. Sturrock advises his young readers:

> If he should occasionally run up against some poor Sassenach [English person] who cannot endure the sound of a Pibroch, he must treat him more in sorrow than in anger, and remember that there is no law, even in Scotland, to prohibit such people from being at large. At the same time it is well to impress upon the beginner that he should respect the feelings of his neighbours, if he has any, and retire to practise at some distance from the haunts of men. This is especially important in the early stages of the recruit's career, when he will probably produce a good deal of discord before much music is forthcoming.[27]

This early training in determination was often put to good use by those lucky enough to make it through the war. To make a civilian band function was no easy matter. It cost £400 (over £20,000 today) to clothe one of the top bands of the 1920s in appropriate uniform, and then came the cost of rehearsal space.[28] The bands that were springing up within the mining communities could cost around £250 a year to run—£13,000 today—but were warmly communally spirited. Just as workers could pay a voluntary tax to support their local band, the band itself gave back through fund-raising beyond the point of covering its own needs. Thus the Michael Colliery Prize Pipe Band became known as 'The Charity Band', raising money, for instance, for the local soup kitchen by a march to St Andrews during the General Strike of 1926.[29] With free tuition also offered, such outward-looking community bands, playing at local gala days and festivals, have been called the 'unsung heroes' of Scottish culture by the former presenter of BBC Radio Scotland's *Pipeline* programme, Gary West, who himself was taught free of charge through his local band.[30] But, as we'll see, it's not a given that these heroes of the Scottish social tradition are prized for what they are.

With pipe bands appearing at an unprecedented rate, each operating as a law unto themselves, it became clear by 1930 that some sort of regulatory body was needed to bring order to the competition process. What arose was the Scottish Pipe Band Association— or SPBA—which became the Royal Scottish Pipe Band Association—the RSPBA—in 1980 (Australia could boast of such a body since 1924 in the form of the Victorian Highland Pipe Band Association). Though the SPBA's focus was principally on competitions, the second item on its four-point 'Aims and Objectives' list is especially worthy of note: 'To create and maintain a bond of fellowship with all Pipe Band personnel throughout the world without discrimination as to colour, race, nationality, ethnic or national origins.'[31] This was a very positive sign, a definite move away from the hints of xenophobia that have sometimes been detected among certain quarters during the previous century (see Chapter 5). Yet one word is conspicuously absent from that enlightened list: sex. Thinking on that front would soon have to shift because in the very same year in which the association was founded, so too was another exciting venture: The Dagenham Girl Pipers pipe band.

* * *

Women had played an important, if relatively silent, part in piping for generations. If folklore is to be believed, there were fine female pipers among the MacCrimmons, notably Bess and Euphemia. The former, we're told, married a famous piper on the island of Coll, piper to the local laird, and when she played out of sight one night in her husband's absence, the laird's guests could not distinguish any difference.[32] I mentioned the Raasay-born Elizabeth Jane Ross, Lady D'Oyly, in the last chapter, but she was not the only woman with a keen ear for piobaireachd on the island. John MacKay's sister would 'dictate the words of Canntaireachd' and sing them as her brother played with his back to his pupils.[33] Indeed, it was not unknown in the nineteenth century to hear old women singing canntaireachd out in the fields as they went about their work.[34] And it wasn't all about imitation of what the men were producing: tunes such as 'The Caledonian Society of London', 'Jeanie's March' and 'The Scottish Horse' were all composed or part-composed by women.[35] One of those women, Helen ('Nelly') MacDonald—sister of John MacDonald of Inverness—was wonderfully forthright on some of the major light music composers of the day. For Nelly, the tunes of John MacColl and William Laurie simply had 'nae bite'.[36] Though the judgement of women was not commonly sought on such matters, it's at least something that at the Lorn Ossianic Society Games in Oban of 1875, a Miss MacGregor of Oban was named among the piping judges.[37]

The men who otherwise dominated the scene could be important conduits for female talent. Malcolm MacPherson's daughter had six highly proficient piping brothers, but one of them, the Angus of our Introduction, is on record saying, 'My sister Sarah could play as well as any of us.'[38] Willie Ross was not only taught by his mother, Mary Collie, but in 1924 his daughter Cecily won at the Mòd for playing marches, strathspeys and reels on the piano. The Mòd festival had been founded in 1892 to celebrate the linguistic and cultural heritage of Gaelic, having been modelled on the Welsh Eisteddfod, and continues to flourish as The Royal National Mòd. This mention of Gaelic culture brings to mind another key female voice of an earlier generation: Marianne Clephane (née MacLean, d. 1843), who hailed from Torloisk in Mull. Though not a piper herself, she was an accomplished harpist and keyboard player whose great authority on Highland music is no better demonstrated than in the story that is told of her visit to Abbotsford in 1819, where Sir Walter Scott proudly showed off his handsome personal piper. 'Is he not an elegant man?', asked Scott, fishing for compliments from the great lady. Her response was not encouraging. 'He is a pretty man; but he understands little of his pipe ... His drones are not in tune with his chanter. He wants the Highland style altogether.' To add to Scott's humiliation, his uncle then chirped up: 'His ear is false and he will never play well.'[39]

But male agreement with female opinions was not always so forthcoming. Lizzie Higgins (1929–93) was the daughter of the celebrated Scottish folk singer Jeannie Robertson and was brought up around male pipers. Desperate to learn herself, she sought instruction from her uncles, which went well until her father Donald ('Donty') Higgins found out. Roaring that 'he would have no *she-pipers* in his house', he threw her chanter in the fire. Perhaps out of guilt, he then spent many hours painstakingly taking her through the traditional song repertoire, in a style that was heavily influenced by his piping background, laying the bedrock of a career that would eventually see Lizzie entering the Scottish Traditional Music Hall of Fame, posthumously, in 2019.[40]

With Lizzie being born in 1929, we can see the momentousness of what happened a year later when the Dagenham Girl Pipers pipe band was founded. It should be clarified that female pipe bands were not an utter novelty. As early as 1904, a local doctor in Broxburn, West Lothian, by the name of Dr Kelso, offered piping lessons to the girls who accompanied the town's male pipers with Highland dancing and soon formed the 'Lothian Lasses' pipe band—probably the first all-girl pipe band in the world, with five of its members notably showcasing their skills and using their pipes as a protest instrument at the Edinburgh suffrage demonstration in October 1909, which the magazine *Votes for Women* described as 'the most gorgeous political pageant that Edinburgh has ever seen'.[41] Playing alongside the West Lothian girls was a nine-year-old girl from the capital, Elizabeth 'Bessie' Watson, known as 'the Suffragette Piper Girl', who lived an incredible life: at fifteen years old, during the Great War, she became the official piper for the 'Edinburgh Recruiting Car'; shortly after this, Watson became one of the first women to join a male pipe band;[42] in 1938, she became the official piper for the Auxiliary Territorial Service and the first woman to pipe in a regimental dinner for officers in the British Army; and after the war, she became the founder of the first state school pipe band in Scotland at Broughton High School—all described with great flair in Watson's autobiography *Lone Piper*.[43] But not every woman had to be a lone piper, especially if she lived in Australia, where the first all-woman adult pipe bands appeared. The South and Port Ladies Band was founded in January 1918, and the Australian Ladies Pipe Band (whose members had to have Scottish-born grandparents) was established two years later, swiftly becoming a touring sensation;[44] they even won the Murray Cup for band discipline ahead of forty male bands at the 1924 Cowal Gathering and shortly after performed for the king and queen at Braemar.[45] But it was the Dagenham Girl Pipers who became the byword for this new phenomenon in the piping world.[46]

Their story is an intriguing one, not least because Dagenham is a suburb of East London! It's founder, the Reverend J. W. Graves, was an eyebrow-raising character. In his youth, he'd been buried alive, had survived being knifed in a New York doss-house and had lived through a plane crash. Though a congregationalist minister with a degree from Yale, in a former life he had been a 'jewelry store detective, a bronco-buster in Saskatchewan and a medium for a professional hypnotist'.[47] But Graves had a passion for the pipes—and, one suspects, an eye for money-making schemes—and so, in his fiftieth year, while still a pastor, he recruited twelve girls from the Sunday school and, for instruction, a pipe major from the King's Own Scottish Borderers. Meanwhile, Mrs Graves got to work on the uniforms, which meant the full 'Scottish' shebang: kilts, velvet jackets, tartan socks and tam-o-shanters. Within eighteen months, the girls were ready for their first performance before a swarm of local journalists.

Their presence seemed to be a sign of the times. As one newspaper put it after seeing them perform at the 1932 Lord Mayor of

London Show: 'Girl Pipers of Dagenham, we salute you. Marching through the sanded streets of an historical city you succeeded more forcibly than any other feature in portraying the spirit of the age. You were like a fresh breeze from the mountains.'[48] So successful were they that Graves resigned from his position within the church and became the manager of a full-time professional outfit. Any girl who had reached school leaving age became a paid employee on £5 a week, and by 1936 the band was performing at some 400 functions a year.

Their example was clearly inspiring. In 1934, the Braemar Girls' Pipe Band was formed, and within a year they were competing at the juvenile competition at the Cowal Gathering. When the *Queen Elizabeth* was launched by the Queen herself in 1938, it was the girls from Braemar who did the piping honours. Though some established bands did admit women—Bessie Watson was in the East Edinburgh Pipers in 1916, and there was at least one woman in the Craigend Pipe Band in Falkirk in 1938—further girls' and ladies' bands appeared across the decade, with Canada proving a particular hotspot.[49] These all-female bands could compete against male bands, but in 1938 the very first Ladies' World Championship took place, held in the Western Park, Renfrew, with Scottish Ladies (Coatbridge and District) taking first prize.

As for female competitors in solo piping, it was Australia once again, with its strong Scottish immigrant community, that led the way. As early as 1900, there were female prize-winners at the Lismore NSW Caledonian Society Highland Gathering. It did not go undisputed, however. 'In this event a protest has been entered against the winner', so the papers recorded.[50] In Scotland, Christina Mowat of Fife was competing by 1907, taking a second prize in the march competition at the Culross Games and would go on to take many more prizes thereafter, becoming, in the words of one of her main competitors, 'The champion lady piper of Scotland.' Other highly regarded players followed who would be equally worthy of the title, Helen Wilson and Edith MacPherson especially. One prominent male pipe major of later years remembered going for tuition to his uncle, who happened to be Edith's instructor too, but his uncle only said: 'If I were you I'd put my pipes in the box. I've a girl coming who will put you to shame.'[51]

Some women, however, didn't do the cause of their sex any favours. The British variety entertainer, Rena Hall, was asked in 1934 about women and piping, and her answer will puzzle contemporary players:

> The crux of the whole question is physique. For a woman I am exceptionally well endowed physically, but I feel it would be preposterous on my part to contend for honours with male performers. The truth of the matter is that few women are strong enough to become proficient bagpipe players, and even the strongest of us must be at a great disadvantage in a piping contest with men. Bagpipe playing demands a standard of physique which few women possess, and that is why—I admit it readily—my services have been in demand.[52]

Men could of course say yet more damaging things. A not atypical comment came from a male member of the Canadian Parliament in 1938: 'Although women may become efficient mistresses of the bagpipes, in so doing they are losing their natural feminine charm. Most women pipers looked knocked out of shape, their bodies acquiring an unnatural twist from strenuous blowing.'[53]

Yet even with this kind of discouragement, overall the scene since the end of the Great War had been brightening. The rise of the civilian pipe band and the new visibility for women players suggested things were on the up. The war had not, after all, been as destructive for piping as many had feared. The old art of piobaireachd—for all the squabbles about the beneficial impact or otherwise of the Piobaireachd Society—remained a cherished part of the culture, while light music composition and performance went from strength to strength. Optimism, however, was about to become harder to sustain.

In August 1937, the Dagenham Girl Pipers pipe band travelled to Berlin, where they played in front of Adolf Hitler. Much taken by what he saw, Hitler announced that the Fatherland ought to have a band just like them. The Dagenham girls returned to Germany two years later and toured the Black Forest. A fortnight later, war broke out across Europe.

When the Roman Emperor Nero was described playing a pipe 'with a bag tucked under his armpit' he became the first named bagpiper in history. There are few other references to the instrument in the ancient world.

2. After a long hiatus during the 'Dark Ages', the bagpipes re-emerged in multiple sacre
settings across Europe, though not always in the most flattering light. This carvi
adjacent to the Percy tomb at Beverley Minster, Yorkshire, shows that, for some, t
instrument's sound was a little too reminiscent of a squealing pig. The sow was alsc
symbol for lust. The carving's early date (c.1340) provides evidence to suggest that t
bagpipes were in England before they reached Scotland.

This exquisite early fifteenth-century nativity scene from the *Belles Heures of Jean de France, duc de Berry*, by the Limbourg Brothers, reinforces the long connection between the instrument and shepherds. Notice Joseph's apparently pained expression—did the wailing pipes have anything to do with it?

4. In this marginal doodle from a 1487 manuscript titled *De Caelo, De anima*, a pig plays pig's bladder as a bagpipe. A jester dances behind the pig, mimicking the animal as h pushes one hand to his chest—housing his own air—while the other hand grasps his ow penis and testicles. It has been suggested that depictions of animals playing animal ba; pipes are reminders of human masturbation.

Albrecht Dürer's engraving of a peasant piper (1514) is one of the earliest representations of the bagpipes in a secular context.

6. Many versions of the 'Danse Macabre', or Dance of Death, appeared in the wake of th
Black Death to remind viewers of the shortness of life and the nearness of death. Often
the bagpipes feature with clear phallic overtones, as in this depiction of the Fool in Han
Holbein the Younger's *The Dance of Death* (1523–5).

7. Pieter Bruegel the Elder's *The Peasant Dance* of 1567 confirms the long and intimate connection between piping and dancing. That connection has often been overlooked when it comes to the history of Scottish piping; the extended, stately tunes known as piobaireachd have sometimes dominated thinking about the past. In fact, dancing to the pipe was an essential part of Scottish culture until the nineteenth century, as it was elsewhere.

8. Bellows-blown pipes did not appear until the sixteenth century, but they took hold in Scotland in a major way and were of equal cultural significance to the developing Highland Great Pipe. Pictured is a mid-eighteenth century engraving of the Haddington town piper James Livingstoun and drummer Andrew Simpson, accompanied by 'fool' Harry Barrie. Livingstoun plays the bellows-blown Lowland pipes, which were common across Scotland until the early nineteenth century. They were revived with zeal in the 1980s.

9. Richard Waitt's 1714 painting of William Cumming, piper to the laird of Grant, is the first uncontested painting of a bagpipe with three drones in Scotland. It is our best visual insight into pre-Culloden Highland piping, and shows the high status of the hereditary pipers. The more common 'community pipers' would not have been turned out so splendidly, however, and not every set of bagpipes would have looked like this. In fact, it was common in the west of Scotland to have only two tenor drones and no bass drone at all. Diversity of form was taken for granted until the nineteenth century.

THE
Compleat Tutor
for the
PASTORAL or NEW-BAGPIPE
Containing

All the necessary Instructions for such as are
desirous to play that Instrument and attain
the true knowledge of all the Principles thereof;
never before Published merely by Mr. Geoghegan.
To which is Added
A Collection of some familiar Airs, light Jigs, &c.
Curiously Adapted to that Instrument.

Printed for & Sold by John Simpson
at the Bass Viol & Flute in Sweetings Alley
opposite ye East Door of the Royal Exchange

London (1740)

Where may be had Bagpipes, & Books of instructions
for any Single Instrument

10. The first printed music for the bagpipes in the British Isles, published in 1743, was not for the Highland pipes at all, but for an instrument known as the pastoral pipes, inspired by baroque developments on the continent and the precursor of today's uilleann pipes, which were made not only in Ireland, but in Scotland and England as well. The instrument can be seen in the frontispiece of the volume (pictured)

1. Iain MacGillivray piping on Culloden Moor during the filming of *Outlander*. The series is to be commended for its attempts to remain visually true to the mid-eighteenth century (notwithstanding the T-shaped zip handle which hangs from the base of MacGillivray's bag and some other more modern elements), but no series could ever capture the complexity of the culture at the time. Highland pipes came in many shapes and sizes, and pipers were just as prevalent amongst the government forces as they were amongst the Jacobites.

12. The nineteenth century produced a high proportion of larger than life piping personalities. Portraits and photographs, such as this one of Malcolm MacPherson, probabl
taken in the 1880s, suggest they were more than aware of the romance of their char
acters and did little to live it down; if anything, they did quite the opposite.

13. Much of the Great Highland Bagpipe's global popularity today goes back to the army's colonial activities. George Findlater (pictured) was just one of many pipers engaged in those activities, but he became a household name for his heroic playing, even whilst seriously injured, at the Battle of Dargai (in modern-day Pakistan) in 1897. Many an army piper would subsequently seek to follow his example, often with disastrous results.

14. The Rajasthani bagpiper Shyopat Julia provides a fascinating example of the absorption of the pipes into Indian culture after the British left. Other than the design of the instrument, no trace of its Scottish origins can now be found, neither in Julia's dress nor in the terms in which he speaks of the instrument.

5. In some quarters, it has been tempting to think that by the late 19th or early twentieth century the bagpipes were synonymous with the Great Highland Bagpipe, but as this image of a Belarusian bagpiper reminds us, the instrument still retained its regional variants in many areas across the globe.

16. Elizabeth 'Bessie' Watson, known as 'the Suffragette Piper Girl', pictured here aged eleven (centre with sash) at the 1911 Women's Suffrage March. Watson was a pioneer in more ways than one. She eventually established the first ever state school pipe band in Scotland, ... High School in 1947

O'TOOLE PIPERS, DUBLIN

17. The pipes have often served as instruments of protest. Pictured is Dublin's St Laurence O'Toole Pipe Band in 1912; they were formed in 1910 in the context of Irish struggles for independence from Britain. It has been said that the pipes, 'quite literally, mobilised national identity', in Ireland.

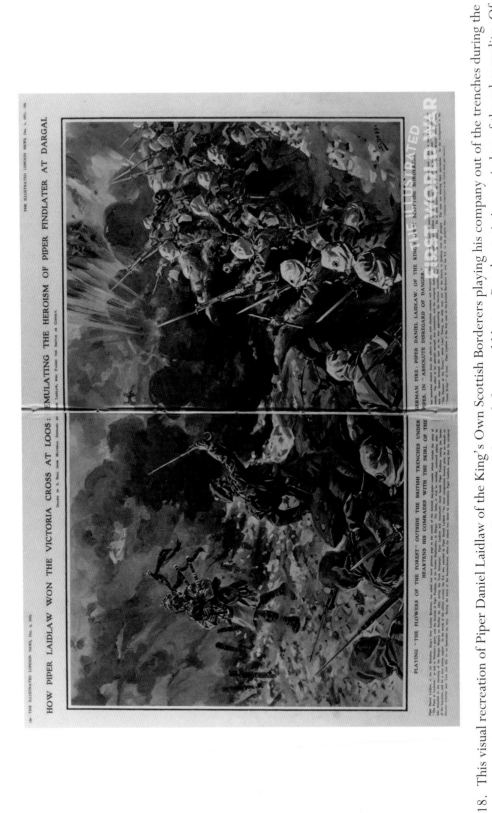

18. This visual recreation of Piper Daniel Laidlaw of the King's Own Scottish Borderers playing his company out of the trenches during the Battle of Loos in September 1915 shows the 'hero status' that such feats could bring. But the statistics remind us of the sober reality. Of

19. The Dagenham Girl Pipers pipe band was founded in 1930 and was one of the first all-female bands to be established in the British Isles. Their success, at home and abroad, meant they quickly became a byword for the rise of women pipers, though Australia was the real trend-setter, with the South and Port Ladies Band founded in 1918. The male world was not always appreciative, with one member of the Canadian Parliament commenting, 'Although women may become efficient mistresses of the bagpipes, in so doing they are losing their natural feminine charm.'

20. Piping heroics did not end with the First World War. Perhaps the best-known piper
of the Second World War was Bill Millin (standing), personal piper to Simon Fraser
Lord Lovat, who led the 1st Special Service Brigade into France during the D-Day
landings in Normandy in June 1944. It's said that when they got off the boat under
heavy German fire, Millin proposed that he walk up and down the beach as he played
'The Road to the Isles'. Lovat responded, 'Oh yes, that would be lovely.'

1. Seumas MacNeill, pictured here with Catriona Campbell (now Garbutt), at a competition in the early 1950s. MacNeill was a great supporter of women pipers, and became the most prominent figure in Scottish piping across the second half of the twentieth century, not least as co-founder and principal of Glasgow's College of Piping. But his conservative approach to the instrument and his acerbic wit meant he made many enemies. Pipers used to say you were a nobody in the piping world if you hadn't been savaged by Seumas.

22. Nova Scotia, especially Cape Breton, has a long-established tradition of piping which is characterised by a fast, rounded and dance-focused style. It has been suggested that this is a remnant of the style prevalent in Scotland up until the time of the Highland Clearances, and that its disappearance was largely due to the rise of written music and piping competitions, which led to a standardisation of playing and technique, removed from the context of dance. Alex Currie (pictured), who died in 1997, was probably the last of the traditional Gaelic-speaking, ear-learned Cape Breton pipers; but his style has managed to cling on and is even experiencing a renaissance.

3 The Czech ethnographer Josef Režný, pictured here in 2007, was a key figure in the reawakening of interest in indigenous piping traditions across the globe. In 1955, Režný founded the precursor to what is now the hugely popular International Bagpipe Festival in Strakonice, Czech Republic.

24. Pipes known as *gaitas*, as seen in this traditional Galician bagpipe and drum group, have
been central to Galician life for centuries. The instrument struggled to thrive, however, under Franco's push to produce a unified Castilian Spanish culture. After Franco's
downfall, one of his former ministers drove a revival that has led the region's most
famous piper, Carlos Núñez, to say, 'We have more pipers than policemen, or priests,
or pharmacists … it's great!'

25. Canada's 78th Fraser Highlanders celebrate on the bus after their historic win at the 1987 World Pipe Band Championship in Glasgow—the first non-Scottish band to take the title. From left to right: Tom Bowen, Bruce Gandy, Michael Grey (with bottle), Beverley Gandy, Scott Brown, J. Reid Maxwell, Gordon MacRae, Julie Wilson.

26. The Bagad de Lann-Bihoué is the French Navy's Breton *bagad*, the name for the music ensembles that emerged after the Second World War in Brittany, but which were inspired by Scottish pipe bands. The bands incorporate Brittany's native *bombard*, a reeded but bagless pipe, and play the region's own distinctive repertoire. Their bagpipes are nearly identical to the Great Highland Bagpipe but are known as *biniou bras* ('big bagpipe') and are widely considered to be a development, rather than a rupture, of the region's longstanding piping tradi-

27. These Northumbrian smallpipe players at the 2007 Alwinton Show, Northumberland, continue a long tradition of English regional bagpiping. The Northumbrian smallpipes would have probably died out at the end of the nineteenth century had it not been for a handful of faithful families and the Duke of Northumberland, who insisted on retaining a piper within his retinue.

28. Gordon Duncan (pictured) has been called the 'Jimi Hendrix of the pipes' for his innovative playing. His epochal 1994 album *Just for Seumas* was named after that great resistant force to innovation, Seumas MacNeill, who, at a competition the year before, had described Gordon's playing as 'garbage'. The excitement and experimentation in today's piping scene is hard to imagine without Gordon's influence.

29. Paddy Keenan, the legendary uilleann piper from Ireland and co-founder of The Bothy Band, pictured here playing at the Katharine Cornell Theater at the University of Buffalo in the late 1990s/early 2000s. Keenan's playing had an enormous influence on Gordon Duncan, as did The Bothy Band's playing on the Scottish folk and piping scene in general. It's a reminder of how important Ireland has been in the story of the pipes, with the country even acknowledged as the 'wellspring' of the culture out of which emerged the earliest piping in Gaelic Scotland.

30. Martyn Bennett (pictured with fiddle) and his band Cuillin perform at the Buddha Bar, Paris, before the opening match of the 1998 World Cup between Scotland and Brazil. As this picture proves, Sean Connery and Ewan MacGregor were amongst the famous audience members who unexpectedly took to the floor. Though a classically trained violinist and pianist, Martyn was also known as 'the techno piper' for his approach to the instrument, blending it effortlessly with the 'sound and scale, tension and release' of '90s electro-dance music.

31. The Canadian piper Jack Lee competing at the 2017 Glenfiddich Piping Championship, the most prestigious solo competition in the world for the Highland bagpipes. Held in the grand ballroom of Blair Castle, Perthshire, with its antlers, armour and banners, it is a magnificent spectacle, but also an interesting example of the Scots living up to, or even exceeding, the stereotypes of Scottish piping in its most romantic form. The cameras beam the event around the world.

32. The most famous contemporary bagpiper worldwide is no Scotsman, but an American woman, Allyson Crowley-Duncan, known to her millions of fans as 'Ally the Piper'. Ally has brilliantly exploited the marketing possibilities of social media to create formidable following. Though her inventive repertoire and style are unlikely to b adopted by the piping community at large, Ally is undoubtedly achieving her aim of breaking down stereotypes about the bagpipes and introducing new audiences to the instrument.

8

PIPING CHARACTERS OF THE OLD WORLD ON THE CUSP OF THE NEW

ROUSING THE ROMANCE FROM WITHIN: 1939–1970s

Had the 'Findlater/Dargai syndrome' died a death along with the many other millions of deaths in the First World War? Not quite. While the hostilities commencing in September 1939 did not invite the kinds of piping heroics that the earlier conflict did, and piping casualties were probably far lower than in the First World War (there are no precise statistics), the Second World War could not utterly remove the opportunities for repeating history.[1] The North African Campaign (June 1940–May 1943) was one of the few arenas where pipers did, on occasion, lead troops into battle. But that was all to come to a halt after the Second Battle of El Alamein in northern Egypt.

This was really a series of battles between the Axis army of Italy and Germany on the one hand and the British Eighth Army on the other, lasting from 23 October until 11 November 1942. Victory for the Axis would mean the ability to link up with the Germans advancing in the Caucasus and thus the potential to overrun the whole Middle East. Victory for the Allies would mean the very first victory by the British Army upon the Axis powers, with all the implications for morale that that would bring. In Churchill's inimitable rhetoric, it would be 'the end of the beginning' of the war.[2]

But the conditions were challenging to say the least. The Axis troops were shielded by some half a million mines, most of them anti-tank mines, in an area known as the Devil's Gardens. The British commander of the Eighth Army, General Bernard Montgomery, having taken time to build up a stronger force than his opponents, decided to release an almighty artillery bombardment on the Axis position immediately prior to sending the infantry through the mine-field by night, as the men would be too light to set off the anti-tank mines. The foot soldiers would then be followed by engineers who would clear paths for the Allied tanks coming up behind. It was a plan that incurred many setbacks but eventually succeeded.

With darkness, smoke and sand to contend with, the advancing infantry, which included the 51st (Highland) Division, had a hard time of it. They were to progress in lines about a mile and a half wide, with 5 metres between each soldier. To stay in formation, each company was assigned a piper. The memories of Lieutenant Colonel C. A. Cameron MC of the Cameron Highlanders attest to the usefulness of this addition, and the weight of piping history upon the regiment:

> Having captured our objective [named] 'Inverness', we dug in, and we heard the Black Watch coming up behind with bloodthirsty cries and clearly bent on destroying everything in front of them. Knowing that clear orders do not always get down to each private soldier, I feared that they would mistake us for the enemy and fighting would ensue between us. I therefore told our company piper, Donald Macpherson, to get hold of his pipes again and play the Pibroch of Donuil Dubh so that the Black Watch could not possibly mistake who was in front of them. Unfortunately, after the Black Watch had passed through safely, Piper Macpherson was killed by a direct hit … This is possibly the last time the pipes were played in the middle of a battle, certainly in the Camerons. It carried on the tradition set by Piper Mackay at Waterloo.[3]

Black Watch pipers could make similarly important interventions during the battle. When companies of the Gordon Highlanders and the 5th Battalion Black Watch came under fire from a German sniper, members of the Gordons went out to find the sniper and eradicate the menace. This they did successfully, but they couldn't find their way back in the darkness. Not, that is, until they heard the Black Watch piper playing the B company march 'Monymusk'. Only then could they make their way safely back to their position.

But it was the exploits of another Black Watch piper, Duncan MacIntyre, that showed more clearly than anything else that the

Findlater tradition still burnt brightly. MacIntyre had had a successful piping career before the war, even winning the Strathspey and
Reel competition at the Northern Meeting in 1938. He was playing
the regimental march 'Highland Laddie' as his company unknowingly made its way into the fire of a German machine gun. Wounded,
MacIntyre continued to play until he was shot again, this time
fatally. But on he played until no more breath was in him. When his
body was discovered the next morning, his pipes were still under
his arm, his hands cold upon the chanter. He was twenty-eight years
old. That he was recommended for the Victoria Cross but not
awarded one suggests that the mindset of officialdom had changed
somewhat since the previous war.

* * *

The mindset of the Germans also seems to have changed, because
bagpipes became one of the few items they allowed into their prisoner of war camps. According to *The Oban Times*, in camp Stalag 383
there were no fewer than thirteen pipe majors in 1944. Thanks to
piping societies back home and the Red Cross's ability to facilitate
transport, ten sets of pipes found their way into the camp, and a
Piping Academy was established, as well as a pipe band with drums
supplied by the camp orchestra. Others were keen to get involved,
and so practice chanters were also sent out from Scotland. A learn-
ers' class of thirty members was the result. Not all the German
guards were appreciative. In the camp known as Oflag VII.B, where
another band was established, one prisoner was careful to stand as
near to the guards as he could when he practised, simply for the
enjoyment of watching them wince.[4] In other camps, it was suspicion that the sound of the pipes was keeping out the noise of tunnel
diggers that put the guards on edge.[5] Still, this willingness to have
the pipes in camps stands in contrast to what apparently happened
in Poland. It's said that the Nazis made a point of banning the Polish
bagpipe throughout the war years as it was believed to rouse up
Polish national identity with too great a force.[6]

Amazingly, a certain type of bagpiping was also repressed in
Scotland. Given the profusion of buskers in Scotland's capital today,
it's startling to discover that in 1942 it could get you arrested—

well, if you played badly enough it could—as the *Evening Times* reported in August of that year. Veteran William Sinclair Rosie, who'd served for three years with the Seaforth Highlanders in the previous war, was arrested while playing the pipes in the street. A total of £3 in small change was found in his pocket. The charge? Begging and breach of the peace. The police report stated: 'His efforts were not in keeping with the traditions of the national Instrument.' Upon questioning in court, Rosie blamed a wartime shortage of reeds for his poor playing. Showing his pipes to the judge, the latter responded: 'You deserve to be sentenced for playing those pipes.' And sentenced he was, on both counts. Rosie was jailed for twenty days.[7]

One man who certainly had 'the traditions of the national Instrument' in mind during these years was the legendary 'Mad Jack' Churchill. This was the soldier who once said, 'Any officer who goes into action without his sword is improperly dressed.'[8] A bow and arrow, as well as the bagpipes, were additional parts of his gentlemanly armoury. When serving in the commandos in 1941, he was second in command of two companies that were ordered to raid a German garrison at Vågsøy in Norway. With incomparable dash (he had acted in films before the war), Churchill stood upon the lead landing craft, pipes blaring, playing 'The March of the Cameron Men', before leaping off and hurling the first grenade. Charging onwards 'into the thick smoke, uttering warlike cries', he wielded a basket-hilted sword or claybeg in his hand—a weapon that has been called 'a beacon of Scottish identity'[9]—as if to make sure his enemies were in absolutely no doubt of his origins. And yet, there seems to have been barely a drop of Scottish blood in Churchill's body.

This might all sound slightly ridiculous, but it was undoubtedly effective. Having shot with the bow at the World Championships in Oslo in 1938, it was deadly in his hands. With the claybeg alone, he once captured, during the Salerno landings of 1943, forty-two German soldiers in a night. He would later say: 'I maintain that, as long as you tell a German loudly and clearly what to do, if you are senior to him he will cry *Jawohl* and get on with it enthusiastically and efficiently whatever the … situation. That's why they make such marvelous soldiers.' As for his pipes, they could be both boon and bane. In battle, they stirred in the classic manner (one German, on the receiving end of Churchill's onrushing pipes, described 'the doleful sound of an unknown instrument'), but in camp Churchill was none too admired for his habit of striking up his pipes just as his comrades were settling down to a good night's sleep. Still, it didn't stop him earning *two* Military Crosses.

It was only when mavericks such as Churchill came along that the pipes found a place in the European battlefields of the Second World War. Hence what happened when another maverick, Simon Fraser, Lord Lovat, twenty-fourth chief of his clan, led the 1st Special Service Brigade into France during the D-Day landings in Normandy of 6 June 1944.[10] At his request, he had with him his personal piper, Bill Millin, whose exploits that day have been immortalised in the film *The Longest Day*. The story goes that Millin protested at Lovat's request for the pipes to be played, citing War Office regulations that forbade it. 'Ah, but that's the *English* War Office', came the response, 'You and I are both Scottish, and that doesn't apply.'[11] To reassure any doubters, Millin was the only man during the landing who wore a kilt, the same kilt his father had worn in the First World War. The sole weapon on him was his *sgian-dubh*, or 'black knife', tucked inside his kilt sock.

Despite this apparent vulnerability, Millin was desperate to get off the boat, having suffered from terrible seasickness during the crossing. As they waded through the waves of Sword Beach, Lovat called over 'Give us a tune, piper.'[12] The strains of 'Highland Laddie' now filled the air between shell blasts, winning a smile from Lovat. Reaching dry land, piper and commander stood side by side wondering what to do next. Lovat thought it would be a good idea if the twenty-one-year-old Glaswegian played 'The Road to the Isles'. Millin asked if he should walk to and fro along the shore in classic piping fashion. Lovat was delighted. 'Oh, yes. That would be lovely.'[13]

But it wasn't too lovely for Millin, who felt the sand shaking beneath his feet as the mortar fire rained down. Every now and then, the dead body of a comrade brushed against his legs as it rolled in the surf. Thankfully, the surviving troops were eventually able to make it off the beach, and the march to Pegasus Bridge—then named Bénouville Bridge—began. They were due there by noon, where they planned to relieve the 2nd Battalion of the Ox and Bucks Light Infantry. Millin played throughout the 6-mile march, at one point learning, upon swinging around, that he was the only man standing, the rest of the troops having dived into cover at the presence of a German sniper. Arriving at Bénouville, the spirt of Daniel Laidlaw was evoked as Millin broke into 'Blue Bonnets over the Border'. The famous 'coolness' of past battle pipers was native to Millin too. Marching down the main street, the commander of 6 Commando called out for the men to run the length of the road. But that was not becoming of a piper. Millin walked. And, having reached the Ox and Bucks and having received his orders from Lovat, on he strode further, pipes still going, right on over the bridge amid the bullets that killed twelve of his compatriots, most of them shot through their berets. 'It seemed like a very long bridge', recalled Millin.[14]

True to form, Millin later downplayed the heroics of all this. Asked in a 1994 interview if he didn't feel terrified and vulnerable, he responded: 'Well, not really because I was concentrating on the bagpipes. And Lovat is a bit of a critic of the bagpipes so I had to watch what I was playing. So I had no time to think about anything else. It kept me going actually.'[15] In a sense, the pipes really did save his life. When one of the captured German snipers was later asked why they hadn't shot at the bagpiper, he replied that they thought he must have been a 'Dummkopf', which could be translated in this context as a fool or a simpleton. In other words, they took pity on him for his apparent madness. Yet, there was method in his madness. As Millin's son John would later observe: 'The pipes were motivating [his comrades], snapping them out of their fear.'[16] Lovat said in his old age: 'I think [the presence of the bagpipes] rises people to the occasion; it certainly did that day.' It is telling that the only statue of a soldier to stand on the Normandy beaches is a statue of this so-called Dummkopf. At the statue's unveiling in 2013, three years after Millin's death, his son John, who had learnt the instrument specially for the occasion, played one of his father's old favourites, 'Amazing Grace', accompanied by 500 pipers and drummers from all across the world.

As such numbers suggest, it's almost impossible to resist the romance of the heroic Scottish piper in this context. But I think it would be slightly off-piste if we thought this was a romance conjured from afar by adoring, rose-tinted foreign eyes, unacquainted with the brutal realities of war. Just as we saw the 'giants' of the tradition in the Victorian era gladly living up to expectations of the Highland bagpiper, it's possible to detect a sense that for the likes of MacIntyre, Churchill and Lovat (Millin, too perhaps), there was a willingness—keenness even—to cultivate or promote a particular image of the Scots military piper, predetermined by the precedent of history. The Scots—and let's include the Englishman Churchill with them—were rousing the romance from within.

* * *

Some things, of course, don't need any extra push from humankind to capture the imagination; they inescapably send shivers down the spine. These stories do not even require the workings of myth-building time to conjure such responses. The story behind the great modern piobaireachd 'The Phantom Piper of Corrieyairack' is one. After the war, in the days of National Service, a group of eighty servicemen was being led by Colonel David Murray—the man who first gave a name to the 'Findlater/Dargai syndrome'—over the Corrieyairack Pass, from Fort Augustus to Garvamore, in their final training exercise in February 1958.[17] Leading the way were three pipers (not including Murray, who was a fine piper himself). Halfway up the hill, the wind got up, and the snow that had been lying quietly was now being driven off the drifts. Visibility became very poor. To keep together, Murray ordered each man to hold the end of the rifle of the man in front of him. As they trudged on through the blizzard, Murray was reminded of something that had been said to him in the days previously by a famous figure in piping, Sheriff G. P. Grant of Rothiemurchus. Hearing that Murray planned to walk the Corrieyairack Pass, Rothiemurchus (as he was always known) said: 'I wonder if you'll see the ghost army.' This was an old belief that the forces led by the marquess of Montrose, who had taken that route to reach the Battle of Inverlochy in 1645, still haunted the pass. Rothiemurchus continued, 'If anyone sees them, David, it will be you, a Highland soldier.' Such was the thought that was in Murray's mind as they made their way onwards, with one of the pipers, a shepherd in civilian life, finding a track forward by following a pair of ptarmigans, who waddled on ahead.

Only when they reached the top of the pass did the birds fly off. The troops had 9 miles still to go before they reached Garvamore, where the colour sergeant-major was waiting for them with a hot meal and tea. When they eventually arrived, Murray was surprised to see everything set up for them, with the food still hot, as if they'd got there just on time when in fact the march had taken the group much longer than they'd anticipated. 'Well done', said Murray to the colour sergeant-major. 'Och, we knew you were on your way because we heard the pipes coming down the glen, Sir.' Shaken, Murray said, 'But no-one was playing the pipes. The pipes were soaked through.' But the colour sergeant-major, who was also a piper, was insistent, as were the cooks. It was definitely the pipes they'd heard. With the wind still whistling round about them, and the darkness coming on, Murray felt there was only one appropriate response: 'Let's get the hell out of here.'

The story made its way into the newspapers, and one of the people to read about it was Captain John MacLellan, director of the Army School of Bagpiping after the long reign of Willie Ross. A prolific composer, MacLellan named perhaps his finest composition after the incident. 'The Phantom Piper of Corrieyairack' is now an established piece on the piobaireachd repertoire.

Though others had written fine piobaireachd over the previous century, the Phantom Piper was one of the very few 'modern' compositions to make it on to the set tune lists for competitions.[18]

There seems to have been a widespread assumption that only pieces of significant age were 'real' piobaireachd. The communal acceptance of MacLellan's piece was a relatively rare example of open-mindedness about pipe music itself in the post-war setting. In fact, conservative forces—which, in some cases, were propagating fairly new outlooks, assumed to be 'traditional'[19]—had been in the ascendant since at least the foundation of the College of Piping in Glasgow in 1944 and the appearance of its linked monthly publication the *Piping Times* in 1948. Seumas MacNeill (1917–96) is the name most associated with these endeavours (though the co-founder of the college, Tommy Pearston, should not be forgotten), and it was a name to be reckoned with.[20]

* * *

Much that MacNeill did was profoundly positive. Unlike 1918, the end of the Second World War brought no fears for the survival of piping. Quite the opposite. First, most of the vaunted tradition bearers had made it through, having served as pipe majors of their respective battalions—the piobaireachd-saturated 'Bobs of Balmoral' (Robert Brown and Robert Nicol, who both worked at the royal estate on Deeside) and 'Wee Donald' MacLeod, for instance, all of whom had learnt at the knee of the great figures of the previous generation. The presence of such men ensured a sense of continuity, but there was also—perhaps as a result of the recent military ferment—a mass of young people longing to learn, with one Glasgow pipe maker toiling through a waiting list for practice chanters that reached the astonishing number of 900.[21] The intention behind the College of Piping was partly to ensure that the instruction of these newbies was systematised and of a high standard. Wee Donald MacLeod and a host of other luminaries were thus employed as instructors.

This longing for quality was surely laudable, as were other aims, notably 'to provide facilities for all boys, especially those of limited means, to learn the Art of Piping'.[22] Despite the gendered language, girls were soon admitted for instruction, and two of them, sisters Rosemary and Hazel Currie, would go on to serve on the editorial board of the journal. MacNeill's staunch support of women pipers was by no means universally felt. When, in 1957, a photograph was printed in British newspapers of a young woman tuning up at a band contest, a raft of derogatory comments came flooding back. One Englishman expressed his views thus:

> Arms too short to go round the bag, head cocked on one side, left shoulder at 45°, and the blowpipe rammed into the throat. No wonder the result is an ear splitting din so unique as to be indescribable. No wonder the simple Englishman looks on with bewilderment and awe and grudges not one penny of the amount he has paid to see this parody of a pipe band. Many a phoney has got away with gulling an easily gullible public, but the girls' pipe band has no superior in this so-called form of entertainment.[23]

MacNeill's contrary view was summed up later that year when he wrote a piece in the *Piping Times* on the female pipe major of the

Nova Scotia Gaelic College Pipe Band. It was entitled 'Heather Mackenzie, or a Defence of Lady Pipers'. His second sentence said it all: 'Even to mention lady pipers in the "Piping Times" seems to be a sure way to stir up a load of trouble these days, but this time let the die-hards snort their disapproval, for Heather is probably a better piper than nine out of ten of them.'[24]

This mention of Nova Scotia points to another forward-thinking aspect of MacNeill's approach, for it was thanks to him that the college organised summer schools across North America, and later in Germany too. Much of today's global interest in the Highland bagpipe can be traced to these schools. MacNeill's presence in Canada, however, was not without its issues. In Cape Breton at that time it was still possible to find players who preserved a form of bagpiping that probably came across from Scotland with the settlers of the eighteenth and nineteenth centuries. The style was intimately connected to dancing and was not confined to one 'correct' method of performance. This stood in contrast to the mindset that had developed in Scotland subsequent to the clearances, where the focus on competitions had wrenched piping out of its dance context and had standardised the technique that was expected of players. MacNeill, steeped in this later culture, was therefore unable to recognise what he was hearing for what it really was. Notable piping figure Hamish Moore has put it this way: 'He [MacNeill] had witnessed a true jewel in the crown of Gaelic culture and because of his prejudice hadn't even been aware of it.' According to Moore, who's spent his life championing this emigrant Gaelic style, half of the Cape Breton pipers attending MacNeill's summer course at that time simply packed up their pipes at the end of their week together and never played them again, 'such was the shame they felt by being ridiculed about their style of playing'.[25]

There's an irony to this, because both MacNeill and his college co-founder Pearston were keen Scottish nationalists (tellingly, MacNeill's first name at birth was James, but he insisted on being called Seumas, the Gaelic form of the name, in the piping world), whom we might therefore have expected to be more inquisitive about the origins of these alternative styles. But it's hard to decipher what brand of Scottish nationalism they were promoting. The college was originally overseen by a nationalist youth organisation known as Fianna na h'Alba (Warriors of Scotland), founded in 1942, though its name would change shortly after the college's foundation to Comunn na h-Alba (The League of Young Scots). MacNeill and Pearston were both members of the organisation. In the face of what it saw as the Anglo-Americanisation of Scotland, its activities included 'the study of Scottish history, the Gaelic language and literature, Scottish crafts, Highland dancing and all outdoor pursuits',[26] ultimately with the aim of making 'young Scotland mentally and physically fit to play a useful part as future citizens in the reconstruction of Scottish national life'.[27] If this sounds rather well organised and focused, the reality—according to one of its founding members, Jimmy Jennett (1928–2018)—was that it represented 'a loose association of young people with a belief in Scotland and a desire for change in the current order'.[28] It was not, it should be said, a politically nationalist movement,[29] and merry cultural endeavours, such as the walking group known as the Inverscotia Nomads and the singing group known as the Inverscotia Singers, seemed to be among their most prominent activities.[30] If this all sounds fairly innocuous, it did, on at least two occasions, become much more sinister.

In an extraordinary scoop from my good friend, the teacher and historian Donald Mackintosh, to whom I'm immensely grateful for the following material, it can now be revealed—though the facts are there for all to see in a little-read article in the March 2018 edition of the *Piping Times* and in at least two other non-piping publications—that this organisation Fianna na h'Alba, so critical within the history of piping, was 'the first Scottish nationalist group to commit an act that would be considered terrorism'.[31] It turns out that six teenagers, aged between seventeen and nineteen, affiliated with Fianna na h-Alba, were imprisoned for eight or nine months for carrying out two separate attacks on the Imperial Chemicals Industries (ICI) building in Glasgow on Christmas Eve, 1943 and on 7 January 1944.[32] Having raided a Home Guard ammunition depot, the first was conducted with cordite, the second with hand grenades.

All of those convicted were connected in some way—sometimes very significant ways—to the College of Piping. Terence Macdonough became the first editor of the *Piping Times* and was a director of the college; John 'Iain' Thomson was the college's first ever pupil, one of its earliest treasurers and later became pipe major of the college's band; Robert 'Rab' Sharples regularly donated to the college; George Telfer, later known as Seoras MacDonald Telfer, was one of MacNeill's first piping pupils and the creator of the *Piping Times'* famous 'Donald Drone' cartoons; John Randolph Wilson Kennedy was the younger brother of MacGregor Kennedy, who was the first honorary secretary of the college, and later a director; and Ronald Robertson Kerr Taylor was described in Jennett's obituary as a founder member of the college, along with those above. Though at least four of these men retained lifelong links to MacNeill, MacNeill himself does not appear to have been involved in the bombings in any way (though he was not above joking about letter-bombs).[33] He was slightly older than these fellow members, and it would seem their actions on these two occasions were conducted more out of youthful naivety than out of hardened political motives. As one paper reported on the defence they gave in court: 'The lads were worried because Scottish industry was drifting south and they wished to draw the attention of authority to this fact.'[34] Jennett's obituary describes it as a protest against the ICI's drafting of Scottish girls to work in England.

The danger of their activities shouldn't be downplayed, however. They only narrowly missed killing four fire watchers who had only just left the board room into which the grenades were thrown.[35] It is perhaps because of the press these actions garnered that the organisation changed its name. It certainly can't have helped that Fianna na h-Alba clearly drew on the Irish youth organisation Na Fianna Éireann, founded in 1909, which took on a militarised, insurrectionist character and participated in the Easter Rising of 1916 and the Irish War of Independence (1919–21). The League of Young Scots may have unsettling overtones—early editions of the *Piping Times* referred to the College of Piping officially as the 'League of Young Scots College of Piping'—but it is surely less inflammatory than these connotations.

Scottish nationalism was by no means mainstream at this stage, though the secret removal of the Stone of Scone, also known as the Stone of Destiny, from Westminster Abbey in 1950 and its short-lived repatriation to Scotland showed how strong nationalist feelings were among a minority. At a less political level, however, the establishment of the School of Scottish Studies at Edinburgh University in 1951, which had the preservation of Scotland's cultural traditions at its heart, was a sign of a general growing awareness about the importance of the nation's identity and history. That the Edinburgh Tattoo (now the Royal Edinburgh Military Tattoo) also took off around this time, pulling in 100,000 audience members across twenty annual performances, served as a further indication that Scotland's heritage—in this case its musical heritage within the armed forces—was of major public interest. The founding of the College of Piping, then, was in keeping with the times, despite the clearly nationalist impulses behind it.

Its political dimension was expressed in more ways than just its affiliations. MacNeill and Pearston's famous 'Green Book' of 1953 (originally titled *The College of Piping Tutor for the Highland Bagpipe Part 1*), which was the first well-written book for self-taught learning, begins in a telling manner. The opening tune is 'Scots Wha Hae', that great unofficial nationalist anthem with a melody that is said to have been played by Robert the Bruce's army as they marched into battle at Bannockburn in 1314 and with lyrics by Burns commemorating those Scots who died fighting with Bruce and William Wallace for a 'free' Scotland. MacNeill and Pearston, in their comments upon the tune, leave their readers in no doubt about its intent. They even add this most revealing of asides: 'If you can't sing "Scots Wha Hae" you should not be learning the pipes.'[36] For MacNeill and Pearston, there seems to have been a clear link between Scottish nationalism and the national instrument. For an instrument that had long transcended political and geographical boundaries, this type of thinking was not exactly progressive.

Yet, so much was forward-looking. Apart from the elements already mentioned, there was also an impatience on MacNeill's part, shared with his friend and champion piper John MacFadyen, to exploit developments in broadcasting, and MacNeill would come to be the face and voice of the instrument for generations of people in Scotland. MacFadyen, a headteacher by day (MacNeill, fearsomely intelligent, was a classical physicist at Glasgow University), would go on to be the driving force behind bringing piping tuition into schools, eventually leading to the introduction of an O-Level in piping in 1976. But for all their progressive outreach work, neither man wished for innovation when it came to the art of piping itself. One of their central messages was that solo piping, piobaireachd especially, was what piping was *really* about. There was an austere, high seriousness about their mission—a counterpart, whether conscious or not, to two of the dominating faces of Scotland's culture at the time, namely the outlook of the 'Kailyard' school (a type of writing that critics, poet Hugh MacDiarmid chief among them, lambasted for its apparent sentimentality and an idealisation of rural life) and that of Tartantry (an over the top parody of kilted, Highland life).[37] The MacCrimmon hereditary piper of the past, pursuing his art with the utmost gravity, was the idol for men of MacNeill's and MacFadyen's ilk, so much so that 'pipe band' was almost a dirty term in their mouths. In an article of 1949, MacNeill's feelings are laid bare with a particular unpleasantness. Imagining a Jacobite piper hearing a contemporary pipe band, he writes: 'The sight of the traditional music of the Scottish Highlands being combined with the aboriginal noises of Darkest Africa would assuredly send him back to the security and peace of the grave.'[38]

What fundamentally mattered was preserving what had been handed down from the pipers of old. As MacNeill wrote in his 1968 book *Piobaireachd*:

A few individuals at odd times have played non-bagpipe music on the pipe, or have tried modification of fingering, or have added notes, but these experiments have always been firmly opposed by the great majority of pipers ... There have always been Highlanders who would rather go to the stake than allow their pipe to be changed in any radical way.[39]

This kind of conservatism was coupled with a narrow orthodoxy concerning the history of the instrument, which accounts for MacNeill's reaction to the alternative forms of piping he encountered in Cape Breton. His own view was summed up when he wrote that

the predominance of the Highland pipe is due in part to the work of the MacCrimmons. This almost legendary family was largely responsible for the development of piobaireachd, and was certainly responsible for the dissemination of it throughout the Highlands. Without piobaireachd there would have been little incentive for the maestros of piping to continue the playing of the instrument in face of government opposition and the conflicting appeal of other types of music.[40]

The message that the MacCrimmons were preeminent above all others and that piobaireachd is the life-force of piping was not one that sang of open-mindedness or an awareness of the nuances of history. Most of the serious historical work on piping history since these words were written has shown how much qualification, perhaps even rejection, such claims require.

Nonetheless, MacNeill saved the best of his famously caustic wit for those who strayed from his vision of good piping and correct history. To take one example from many, after the prize-winning Canadian piper Bill Livingstone had appeared before MacNeill at the Open Piobaireachd at the Argyllshire Gathering in 1973, where he played the classic tune the 'Big Nameless', MacNeill wrote up an account of the performance in the *Piping Times*. There he stated: 'The trouble with these big tunes is that although they enhance the piper's repertoire tremendously, they all require a great deal of study … They are music for the mature and the experienced, not to be confused with the pot boilers which normally win the average competitions.'[41] But, as pipers used to say, you were a nobody in the piping world if you hadn't been savaged by Seumas.[42]

MacNeill's veneration for the classic repertoire did not cloud his approach when it came to evangelising his vision of piping, where all avenues were open for exploration, however untraditional. There was innovation, in other words, but it was strongly circumscribed, reflecting, perhaps, his brand of nationalism: pioneering in its support of the college and the journal but backwards looking—think 'Scots Wha Hae'—when it came to the substance of what was at stake.

These different sides to MacNeill's character mean that two narratives have emerged about him. For some, he's a hero; for others, he was a devil. But the well-known folk piper Dougie Pincock is probably more accurate when he says that both narratives are true. As Pincock puts it: 'MacNeill *was* a hero and he *was* a devil.'[43] We could back up that perception with numerous quotations, but MacNeill's editorial from the January issue of the 1957 *Piping Times* captures it perfectly. In one paragraph, we find these delightfully warm-hearted words: '[W]e should try to encourage and be appreciative of the piper who has no pretensions to becoming an expert performer. Too often we listen for the mistakes and not for the beauty. "All piping is good piping," says one philosopher, and we would do well to cultivate this attitude.' Yet, two paragraphs later, the same man makes 'a special plea for no comic songs on the bagpipes'. MacNeill continues:

> Most pipers would be indignant if it were suggested that they prostituted the instrument in this way, and yet this is exactly what many do. It is not necessary to play 'Nellie Dean' on the pipes in order to be an offender, for any tune which is not in character with the great instrument is quite out of order. 'Mairi's Wedding', 'The Old Rustic Bridge' and many other fine pieces are comic songs when played on the pipes.[44]

There is something mean-spirited and doctrinaire about this. Just look at the overblown language: 'prostituted', 'offender', 'quite out of order'. It's this sense of a man who could wither as much as warm that pervades MacNeill's mammoth contribution to the piping scene in the second half of the twentieth century. To say that one side of him was a 'devil' is perhaps too much, but MacNeill himself certainly never held back strong words when it came to those who departed from his opinions—as the next chapter will emphasise even further.

* * *

That MacNeill was very definitely a 'character' is a reminder that this was an age teeming with such 'characters'. MacNeill's co-author on the 1987 book *Piobaireachd and Its Interpretation*, Major-General Frank Richardson, is one obvious example. A high-ranking doctor in the British Army, he was also that very rare breed (perhaps he and Jack Churchill were the only ones): the officer who piped in combat. At the Battle of Keren during the Eritrean campaign of 1941, Richardson was busy with his medical duties when he realised that the Scottish battalions were not going forward with the momentum that was expected of them. Grabbing his pipes—always near to hand—he went among the men and, seemingly oblivious to danger, played them forward. According to his obituary in *The Independent*: 'This brave and inspired action raised the spirit of the men and they overran the Italian positions.'[45] A DSO (Distinguished Service Order) was Richardson's reward.

For all his heroics and booming public school tones, Richardson seemed to know what it was that made a military man insecure. Among a range of 'interesting' books he authored, one of them was *Napoleon: Bisexual Emperor* (1972), which made a connection between the Frenchman's reputedly small penis size and his out-sized military ambitions. Nine years later, Richardson published the no less revealing *Mars with Venus: A Study of Some Homosexual Generals*. In the Introduction to that book, he writes: 'Some of my views may not conform to the gospel according to certain apostles of The Sexual Revolution, who will find them old-fashioned.'[46] He adds that, for those who are reading the book and are struggling with their sexuality, his narrative may provide 'some indication of how they may better adjust their lives to the accepted patterns of society'.[47] And on this note we're immediately led to another standout figure of the second half of the twentieth century, someone who bravely paid no heed to the 'accepted patterns of society'. This was Sue MacIntyre (1929–2010), or, as she was formerly known, Farquhar McIntosh.

Even without her pioneering decision to change gender and sex, MacIntyre would—as Farquhar McIntosh—have been a key name in the history of piping in Scotland. A one-time pipe major in the Scots Guards, McIntosh was appointed as schools piping instructor on Skye in 1969 and was, in fact, the first official instructor of piping in schools in Scotland. But as she told the *Daily Mirror* in 1976: 'All my life I have felt I was living in the wrong body.'[48] The medical view, after tests, was that there had been a release of female hormones before birth. The unsettling feeling built and built until eventually she became suicidal and had to stop teaching. After three years of uncertainty, she returned to Skye in 1978 with an entirely new outlook, as she said:

> I left Skye as Farquhar McIntosh and came back to the same village as Sue MacIntyre. It was a difficult time but I got on with my life. I felt happier and never had any problems from that day. The most remarkable thing was the way Elizabeth [Sue's wife since 1954 and

mother of their two daughters] stuck by me. If it weren't for her I wouldn't have been able to carry on teaching.[49]

The couple did divorce two years later but continued to live together—like 'sisters-in-law', as Elizabeth put it.[50] Inevitably for the times, there were mutterings from various corners, but Sue gave as good as she got. Sometime after their move to Ayrshire in 1980, a fellow piper made some unwelcome comments, to which Sue responded: 'I'm more of a man than you'll ever be and more of a woman than you'll ever get.'[51] Her strength of character was also felt when it came to her drive for access to piping lessons for Scotland's young people, a drive that led to a long period of strife with the local educational authorities in Ayrshire but eventually resulted in a full-time position for Sue, covering a multitude of schools. Returning to Inverness, the town of her birth, in 1998, she continued to teach, and her lifetime of effort resulted in an MBE for services to piping in 2001. Sue's pupils were legion and include Malcolm Jones of Runrig fame.

Fame, in Scotland's capital at least, came to another piping character, Dr Roddy Ross (1921–2016), but not always for reasons connected to the national instrument. Ross was well known as the man to see if you were a young woman with an unwanted pregnancy. Certainly, his approach to medicine was unconventional for the time. When an old friend from the Hebrides dropped into his surgery one day in the hope of some relief from a skin irritation, he found the waiting room full and turned to leave. Just then, Ross happened to open the door and, spotting his old chum, told him in Gaelic to enter. To placate the waiting patients, Ross said in English: 'This man is an urgent case.' Having handed over the necessary prescription—in the name of a patient who rarely used the doctor—a bottle of whisky was fetched from the cabinet and two glasses appeared. Out came the pipes as well. A couple of piobaireachd later, the friend enquired about the people still waiting outside. Ross's reply was simple. 'If they are really ill, they will stay; the malingerers will go.' When the time came for the Hebridean guest to leave, the waiting room was almost empty.[52]

But piobaireachd seemed to mean more to Ross than anything else. His love for the art form stemmed from his friendship with the son of Angus MacPherson, who was named after his illustrious grandfather, Malcolm. The younger Malcolm was hailed as one of the greatest interpreters of piobaireachd that ever lived—'genius' is not sparingly used about him—and it is said that even as a baby he refused to go to sleep until his father had sung him one of the great tunes.[53] It is thanks to Ross, however, that Malcolm's approach to piobaireachd lives on in the classic music book and record series *Binneas is Boreraig*, Gaelic for 'Melody and Boreraig'. And yet, for all the majesty of his playing and the prizes he won, Malcolm's life was scarred by tragedy. Alcoholism—a common curse among pipers, as we'll see—and failed relationships dogged his life, and, in 1966, he ended his days at his own hand with an overdose of barbiturates.

It was his friend Roddy Ross who organised the funeral. And what an extraordinary affair it was. Ross had wanted a squad of soldiers to send a volley of gunfire over the grave, but the soldiers refused, knowing that Malcolm had been dishonourably discharged during the war for his chronic alcoholism. Undeterred, Ross spoke to a former commando by the name of Captain MacArthur, who agreed to set off some highly explosive, not to mention illegal, gel-ignite from a nearby location. A witness recalled the bizarre, incongruous scene:

> The service was in the church in Laggan. After it finished, the mourners gathered around the open grave next to Malcolm's grandfather, the famous Calum Piobaire, and John MacLellan ... played 'Lament for the Only Son'. Malcolm's father, old Angus, watched impassively as the coffin was lowered, earth was shovelled in, and a small Rowan tree was inserted by an Edinburgh 'strong man', a theatrical touch arranged by the Doctor—who then disappeared behind the church with his camera. The plan was to use the flashbulb to signal to Captain MacArthur, lying on a crag across the glen to the south, with a car battery attached to the gelignite by a long wire. The next moment there was an ear-splitting explosion, like the Crack of Doom at The End of the World—totally out of proportion with the quiet solemnities being enacted. As the echoes rolled up and down the glen, a squall of rain swept in from the West, scattering the mourners, who fled to their cars and the nearest bar.[54]

133

If this all sounds rather far-fetched, all I can do is recommend searching YouTube for 'Roddy Ross at PS Conf 2009' and watching from at least seven minutes onwards. Having got some measure of the man from this, it's worth leaving you with one last vision of him. Bill Livingstone tells the story of the time he (Livingstone) was on stage tuning for the prestigious competition known as the Clasp at the Northern Meeting, held in Inverness's Eden Court theatre. Looking out into the crowd, Livingstone spotted Ross sitting in the middle-centre tier of seats. But it wasn't the doctor's bristling moustache that he noticed. No. Ross, legs indelicately splayed, was wearing a kilt. There was thus no escaping the sight of the good doctor's testicles hanging weightily to the floor. A serious effort was required on Livingstone's part to keep to the business at hand.[55]

* * *

The final 'character' to mention, belonging to this older world, though on the cusp of the new, is John D. Burgess (1934–2005). A child prodigy, the golden pupil of Willie Ross at Edinburgh Castle, Burgess became, at sixteen, the youngest ever winner of the Gold Medal at both the Argyllshire Gathering and Northern Meeting, winning them in the same year. Burgess was distinctive not just for his virtuosity and for his dandyish, immaculate Highland dress but also for having been privately educated at Edinburgh's most expensive day school and having a father who was professor of surgery at the Royal Dick Veterinary College. With such a background, it would have been more in keeping with the times for Burgess to go the 'gentlemanly' route of joining the Royal Scottish Pipers' Society, where the instrument could be played and enjoyed in an amateur setting, and remaining aloof from (unless judging) the competition circuit, which was traditionally dominated by players of working- or lower-middle-class origins. But Burgess broke the mould, especially in his decision to join the Cameron Highlanders as a regular soldier rather than an officer. Had he done the latter, of course, he would not have been allowed to play in the pipe band.

It was perhaps this background that allowed Burgess to relate to his 'superiors' in the army in an unconventional way. After his time with the Camerons, Burgess served as pipe major of a territorial unit, the Queen's Own Lowland Yeomanry. One evening, the pipers were playing for a function in the officers' mess, and Burgess was appalled to find the officers continuing their conversations over the sound of the pipes. A second set of tunes was planned for later in the evening, but when the mess steward alerted Burgess that the pipers were due on again, Burgess refused. This kind of mutiny was unheard of. The adjutant was summoned, and the pipe major made it very clear there would only be more music if the officers ceased from their chatter. The sheepish adjutant returned to the mess and begged silence. Order restored, the pipers returned for their second set.[56]

But, as a younger man, the power relations between the officers and men were harder to overturn, and in one crucial respect the results could be very damaging—they certainly were for Burgess. His friend Colonel David Murray referenced the issue in his moving eulogy for Burgess in 2005:

> Now 55 years ago, most pipers took a dram, and a good dram at that. Not all of them but the majority did, and there were always those punters on the fringe who were keen to be seen drinking with the star. It was a hard drinking Army too, and I include the Cameron Highlanders. At the Regiment guest nights, at the Officers Mess, after the pipers had played it was the done thing for the senior officers to have a word with the pipers and treat them to a large dram or two. Other officers did the same, the pipers were good company. It was 'good form' to give the pipers a dram or two, or three. Thus it was that all too many young pipers had too many drams forced on them at too early an age, in many cases with tragic results in later life. We can all name some of the casualties. And with the dram comes guilt, remorse, self-reproach, shame, repentance and stress and strain on the individual and those closest to him.[57]

It was only later in life, with the army behind him and with the firm support of his loving wife Sheila, that Burgess, after many difficult years, broke free from his addiction. Murray put it powerfully: 'Although John was rightly proud of his unrivalled piping record, his two Gold medals, his cups, shields, stars, banners, quaich or whatever, he was prouder by far by the victory he had won over himself.' Revealing a key part of the piping culture of the time more widely, Murray pointed out that the troubles Burgess had faced were ones that 'most pipers, at one time or another, have shared to some extent'. At least two of the 'characters' previously mentioned had their struggles in this direction, and, as we'll learn, such struggles would not disappear for later generations either.

The army culture evidently had something to do with this, but a full explanation for why so many talents fell prey to the bottle remains elusive. The drinking culture of the Highlands may play a part here. James Burnet, a prominent piping judge and school contemporary of Burgess, remembers travelling to the South Uist Games in the 1960s, where he and his fellow judge were met by an old Highlander in the main tent, who announced: 'Gentlemen, you're just in time', whereupon he pulled out a crate of whisky. It was just after breakfast. On day two, Burnet was escorted to his judging table by a local known as 'Watery Willie'. It was said that Willie only had to read the label on a bottle and he was pie-eyed.[58] When the Glasgow Police Pipe Band visited Barra to play at the funeral of the MacNeil chief in 1970, two band members—one of them being Allan Hamilton, the mastermind behind the *Pipers' Persuasion* series—used their downtime to explore the local hostelries, only to find the first one they entered open to the sky. It had lost its roof a fortnight previously in a fire, but that didn't stop it being open for business as usual![59]

Burgess's struggles, however, may have been tied to what Murray identified when he said: 'Although he was a man with literally hundreds of acquaintances, he seemed to have very few real friends. Hard though it may be to believe ... he was essentially a lonely man.' If talent and isolation are connected (it must be hard to relate to your peers when you seem to shine above them), then this may take us a step closer to understanding why the likes of Malcolm MacPherson (the younger), John D. Burgess and other luminaries suffered so severely in this way.

I hinted earlier that Burgess takes us to the cusp of the modern era. Why? His defying of class conventions is part of it perhaps, but one key part of Burgess's power to entertain was his willingness to showcase the 'tricks' that supple fingers can achieve on the pipe chanter. As with Roddy Ross, the best thing to do is visit YouTube and find 'John D. Burgess FINGER Tricks—incredible!!!' His opening words in the video show the contrast with the type of thinking exemplified by Seumas MacNeill's views on comic pieces on the pipes. Burgess says: 'I always think it's good fun to have a little laugh with an instrument. If you can't take a little bit of fun out of it, there's not much point.' He then plays on his practice chanter a strathspey in which he switches hands and runs his fingers across all the holes while remaining utterly true to the tune and goes on to give a demonstration of playing with the usually superfluous left-hand pinkie. Other highly unorthodox examples follow, as does a snippet from his own composition 'The Ballachulish Walkabout', where the F finger, in an entirely novel movement, flails over the hole to make an alarmingly comic sound. When, in another video, Burgess shows some of these tricks to MacNeill, the latter's response epitomises the conservative outlook I've tried to capture in this chapter: 'Well I don't know if you should have done that, there are going to be hundreds and thousands of young pipers out there doing this in the bands; there will be pipe bands playing in the World Championship and doing that.'[60]

I dated this chapter 1939–1970s, but this was MacNeill speaking in 1983 for a television series called 'The Piper's Tune'. Only by rewinding thirteen years, however, and beginning a new chapter there, can we begin to understand where MacNeill's anxiety came from. For the world of piping really was changing, and the (in)famous principal of the College of Piping was right to think that the new generation, who succeeded the old-world 'characters' outlined above, felt a kind of liberty to experiment that was alien to those who dominated the immediate post-war years. Thanks to them, the definition of a Scottish piper would be changed for good.

9

BREAKING FREE FROM THE SHACKLES OF CONVENTION

THE BAGPIPES REDEFINED: 1970s–1994

MacNeill's anxieties were not unfounded. The old order could no longer be relied upon. The ground had started to tremor in 1970 when the SPBA introduced Medley sets into their competitions, departing from the 'safe' confines of March, Strathspey and Reel. Now the subjectivity of the pipe major or musical director of the band could be felt, and a certain amount of experimentation was permitted. A further sign of change around this time was the appearance of women in Grade 1 bands (bands, that is, who perform in the highest tier of the competition circuit). When the first of them, the Canadian Gail Brown, initially sought to join the celebrated Shotts and Dykehead Caledonia Pipe Band in 1970, the pipe major tried to dissuade her as she was 'just a wee lassie';[1] three years later, when Brown was eventually included, the band won the World Championships. That didn't stop some other pipe majors muttering about the inappropriateness of Brown's presence.

Women became more noticeable on the solo circuit, too, though injustices remained. Had she been a man, Rona MacDonald's victory—she became Rona Lightfoot in 2010—at the senior piobaireachd at the South Uist Games would have automatically won her a place for the prestigious Bratach Gorm contest in London. It was only by vigorous advocacy that she eventually persuaded the organisers to allow her to perform. But when it came to the coveted Gold Medal competitions at Oban and Inverness, where *all* males were eligible, the authorities were unmoved. This resistance unleashed the very best of MacNeill, who wrote in 1971:

The mind boggles at the injustice here. Any man or youth, decrepit or immature, no matter how awful a piper, no matter how ghastly an instrument, be he Scot, Irish, Breton, Canadian, New Zealander, Bantu or Hottentot, may compete for the coveted gold medals. But a Highland lassie, a MacDonald of Clanranald, full of Gaelic language and Celtic culture, trained in the purest piping traditions, is not allowed to be heard. If this cannot be put right then we truly labour in vain.[2]

Put right it was, but more for legal reasons than for the humane outlook of the piping establishment. The Sex Discrimination Act of 1975 made it illegal to bar women from competing at the major solo events, and thus MacDonald's plight was never again repeated. The female stamp was now well and truly on the piping scene, and names such as Anne Spalding (née Stewart), Patricia Henderson (née Innes), Amy Garson (née Goble), Anne Johnston (née Sinclair) and of course Lightfoot's too have gone down as trailblazers in the annals of piping.[3]

But problems remained. One might be tempted to say, 'of course they did, misogyny was standard for the times', but there are some stories that suggest that the piping world may have been even more extreme in some respects than the world at large. Another Livingstone anecdote may make us think along these lines:

> I do remember at a particular Highland Games in the Seventies they gave the pipers a tent and it was pouring rain and almost zero degrees—typical Scottish lovely weather for a musical instrument. I said to my wife Lily, 'Come on in and get out of the rain.' She came in with me and all the pipers were there and each one of them had their little pipe case and their packet of sandwiches and maybe a couple of cans of Tennant's lager and had built little sort of shrines for each of their locations. Then when they saw Lily come in it was remarkable, they all began lifting their kilts and urinating against the tent walls, just like dogs marking their territory. It was astonishing. She never tried to do that again and I never encouraged it, but it was a cultural thing I think back in those days.[4]

This culture may have lasted longer than we'd like to think, for it was surely not a lack of skill that kept a woman from winning one of the major open competitions until 2003.[5] When we think of wider societal breakthroughs that were happening for women in the intervening years, it's tempting to think that the world of piping was lagging behind the general cultural trend.

* * *

Another change of the mid-'70s is linked to the explosion of interest in folk music that was occurring around this time. The influential Irish band Planxty, formed in 1972, were showing the world what was possible with uilleann pipes in a folk band context. The Bothy Band, also Irish, followed them in 1975. As various Scottish pipers started to explore the vibrant musical atmospheres of their own nation's folk pubs—chief among them the Scotia and Victoria bars in Glasgow and Sandy Bell's in Edinburgh—the question began to open up about whether or not the Highland pipes (we'll come to other pipes in a moment) could find a place in the world of folk.

This was controversial; MacNeill would call it a 'danger' in his 1983 conversation with Burgess. In the minds of the piping establishment, the Highland pipes were categorically not a folk instrument—it would be beneath such an instrument's dignity and gravity—and were to be kept a million miles from the totemic woolly jumpers of 'the Folkies'. Unsurprisingly, it was down to the 1970s 'bad boy' of Scottish piping to cross the Rubicon. This was Alan MacLeod, who even early in the decade, well before others, was bending notes—dragging his finger across the hole, sliding from one note to another—and playing the forbidden note of C-natural in his version of the Irish tune the 'Cook in the Kitchen'.[6] Joining the band Alba, MacLeod was unafraid to put the Highland pipes into action, generating a whole new tradition.[7] Alba was short-lived, and after breaking up, MacLeod and fellow bandmate Mike Ward joined The Tannahill Weavers, a major act that made the piper's presence not only acceptable but exciting.

Another well-known group, the Battlefield Band, picked this up, and by 1979 they had a young Duncan MacGillivray gracing the stage with them. MacGillivray was notable for being the son of a Gold Medal winner, Donald MacGillivray, and for being the man who played—perhaps ironically for a folk musician—the pipes that had once belonged to the poster boy of classical piobaireachd, John

MacDonald of Inverness (they came through Duncan's father, who'd been one of MacDonald's last pupils). Though MacNeill had told Burgess that 'it's a mistake for anyone who has ambitions to win the big prizes to go and play in folk',[8] the younger MacGillivray paid no heed to such sentiments and went on to win the Gold Medal at the Northern Meeting in 1997.

MacNeill was not around to see his winning performance, however, having died the previous year, though he did see the pioneering Rab Wallace win the Gold Medal at both Oban in 1985 and at Inverness ten years later—and this despite the fact that Wallace had been playing the bellows-blown Lowland pipes for The Whistlebinkies since 1974 (more anon). Wallace's and MacGillivray's competition success did not end the suspicion over pipers on the folk scene though, and it was not uncommon to hear competition players deriding the standards of the folk pipers. As piping polymath Iain MacInnes notes, there were fears that 'bagpipe-wielding charlatans with no real knowledge of the music would be mistaken for the genuine article'.[9] But it was the folk piper's playing style that was the main concern.

The question of playing style was a critical one for the piper who wished to cross the boundary to folk. The repertoire itself was still 'traditional', with folk bands content to play well-established pipe tunes, so much so that MacGillivray has said that the only difference between the competition and the folk scenes was that 'the tunes were given a different set of clothes'—that is, they had other instruments around them.[10] But he also had to increase the tempo of his playing to accord with the pulse-raising speed of folk, while simultaneously adjusting the 'phrasing' of the music. Because the bagpipes do not allow the player to emphasise elements of the music through playing louder or quieter, the only thing to draw upon, other than the finger embellishments, is the length of the notes. It had become standard practice among competing pipers, keen to show off their musicality, to 'point' certain notes—in other words, hold some long notes even longer, and to 'cut' some short notes even shorter, than the score indicated. But folk musicians play a more 'rounded' style, where long and short notes are held for the period indicated on the score. As a result, the contrast between the two is not particularly noticeable. For competing pipers, however, playing in a rounded as opposed to pointed style was a cardinal sin.

Dougie Pincock, one of MacGillivray's successors as piper for the Battlefield Band, remembers an incident from the 1979 Lorient Festival in Brittany that highlights this fact. Pincock was eighteen at the time and playing for the Glasgow-based band Kentigern, for whom he was more than happy to increase his tempo and play in a rounded fashion (Pincock, in keeping with many other Highland pipers who made the transition to folk from the solo and pipe band world, was struck by how much the non-competitive spirit made the music making that much more enjoyable). After their Lorient performance, the influential figure of Jimmy Anderson, who'd been watching the band in action, approached Pincock and took him aside. Anderson's was a voice to listen to, having not only won the World Pipe Band Championships three times in the late '60s with the all-conquering Muirhead and Sons but also, as part of The Clutha's line-up in the early '70s, for being the first person to play the bagpipe, in his case the mouth-blown 'miniature pipes', in a Scottish folk band (he would play Highland pipes too, but only in the intervals, so that MacLeod was the first to play that instrument *with* a folk band). Anderson had enjoyed a few drams by the time he'd taken Pincock aside so expressed his concerns to the youngster in an avuncular if colourful fashion: 'Now listen here, son. If you're going to play with these fucking Folkies, remember this. You're the fucking piper; you fucking tell them what to do.'[11]

Thankfully, this sense of division was alien to Pincock, as it was to most other Highland pipers in the folk scene. They had challenges enough. While the volume of their pipes could be kept on an even level with the other instruments thanks to sound-system developments, they still had the job of wrestling their instruments into the correct pitch for playing with their fellow band members. Interestingly, that challenge was actually easier then than it is today on a standard pipe chanter. According to Pincock, chanters in those days naturally pitched around B flat or 'concert pitch', which is what's necessary if the pipes are to play harmoniously with other instruments. With contemporary chanters now pitching somewhere between B flat and B natural, this only leads to cacophony when played with anything other than another set of pipes. As chanter pitch has risen over the intervening decades, a new market has opened up specifically for B flat chanters, sometimes called orchestral chanters, as well as for drone extenders that adjust that element accordingly. Back in the '70s and '80s, however, if a folk player's pipes were not conforming to the other instruments, the best he could do was apply tape to the holes and adjust the depth of the reed within the chanter. (As an aside, it's said that when Peter Maxwell Davies composed his now-classic *An Orkney Wedding, with Sunrise* in 1980 and sought to include a Highland piper in the finale, he opened an old Seaforth Highlanders book of pipe music and saw the tunes were written in the key of A. He composed his grand piece accordingly. Unfortunately, the pitch of the bagpipes had risen considerably since the book's publication, causing all sorts of headaches for the early pipers attempting the piece.)[12]

If these developments in folk were unsettling the conservatives, there was a new movement on the horizon that may have suggested—initially—that the old order, in its Gaelic 'purity' (whatever they thought that was), would be revived. This was the Fèis movement, which set up festivals (*fèis* means festival or feast) that allowed the young people of the Highlands to participate in Gaelic song, music making—bagpipes included—and dance, the first being held in Barra in 1981 (they are still going strong throughout the Highlands in forty-seven different locations). But because these festivals were purposefully non-competitive—unlike the only other comparable thing, the National Mòd—they were also non-restrictive and thus opened up a whole new generation to thinking about Gaelic music in an open and even experimental way.[13] One aspect of this was a willingness to see the shared history and affinities between what could be found in Scotland and what could be found in Ireland. In fact, echoing the ancient cultural exchanges explored in Chapter 2, developments in other lands would prove to be key in the next stage of moving the cultural dial in Scotland.

* * *

I mentioned Rab Wallace's playing of the Lowland bellows-blown pipes almost casually, but the revival of bellows pipes in Scotland was anything but incidental. Gary West (born 1966), who has spent his life surveying the highs and lows of piping culture, has called it the biggest change in the piping scene within his lifetime.[14]

Hamish Moore describes it as 'undoubtedly … one of the most influential and important revivals in Scotland's history'.[15] Although there were at least two players of the Lowland pipes still to be found in the post-war years, they had otherwise all but died out, and the vast majority of pipers were unaware that there was anyone in Scotland playing them.[16] The Highland pipes had come to be the definitive, seemingly the only, version of the instrument in Scotland. The idea of challenging this was made even harder in 1972 when the almost unthinkable happened and the Pipes and Drums of the Royal Scots Dragoon Guards, along with their Military Band, got to number 1 in the UK charts with 'Amazing Grace' and stayed there for five weeks, becoming the best-selling single of the year. *This* was the public face of piping. That sense was reinforced when Paul McCartney's band Wings released 'Mull of Kintyre' in 1977, which featured the Campbeltown Pipe Band, who in the music video march proudly down a Kintyre beach, kilts, bearskin hats and all. The song became that year's Christmas number 1, spending nine weeks at the top of the charts, and has gone on to become one of the best-selling singles of all time in the United Kingdom, with 2.09 million copies sold. In other words, in the '70s, to think beyond the paradigm of the kilted man with his Highland pipes took a mental leap indeed. And yet a few brave souls took it upon themselves—at first individually, then collectively—to question the prevailing assumptions.

Wallace, it seems, was the first to experiment. It just so happened that he was a member of Muirhead and Sons, that illustrious pipe band of which Jimmy Anderson was also a member (the band is sadly no more). When Wallace was then approached to join the folk group The Whistlebinkies in 1974, he drew on what he'd seen Anderson do for The Clutha and bought himself a set of mouth-blown miniature pipes.[17] But for Wallace, the instrument's inability to project its sound adequately left him wanting to find a more appropriate bagpipe for a folk setting. He began to research. First port of call was Francis Collinson's 1966 book *The Traditional and National Music of Scotland*, which opened his eyes to the existence of the Lowland bellows-blown pipes, which had once so dominated the piping scene, especially south of the Highland Boundary Fault. Wallace thought to himself: 'Christ, if only I could get hold of *them*!' Sometime after this, a Whistlebinkies gig brought him to Inverness, where he looked in on the local museum. There, he discovered a host of drawings of different forms of bagpipes, including the Lowland variant. Getting copies of the drawings from the curator, he returned to Glasgow and set himself the task of recreating the instrument.

First, he asked a friend's father, who was skilled in woodwork, to make a common drone stock for him according to the drawings. Miraculously, this stock perfectly fitted the three drones of a half-size set of Highland pipes that Wallace had sourced from elsewhere. Aware of the rich tradition of the Northumbrian smallpipes, he now simply took the bellows made for these instruments and attached them to his developing hybrid. As for the chanter, he found that the one that belonged to his half-size Highland pipes, with its conical bore (its tapered look tells you its conical), once again matched the dimensions of the Lowland chanter. Sticking in a large reed, the pitch was all wrong at first, and the sound was 'hellish'. But by taping the holes slightly and pushing the reed deeper into the chanter, he found he could get the instrument to pitch perfectly at B flat. Not only that—it also had the ideal level of volume projection for folk band playing.

Thus was born the distinctive sound of The Whistlebinkies. As their entry in the Scottish Traditional Music Hall of Fame records, the band 'pioneered' the use of the bellows, adding that they were 'the first group to bring the pipes, clarsach and fiddle into regular performance, a combination that seems commonplace now'.[18] Just as the Northumbrian tradition had played a crucial part in Wallace's project, the band's distinctive musical approach was a direct response to another outside influence: the Irish group The Chieftains, who seemed to be taking over the world at that time. The Whistlebinkies purposefully set out to do just what The Chieftains were doing, but to do it with Scottish music. Their subsequent success proved they were wise to do so.

* * *

That openness to Northumbrian and Irish influences would be critical to the other person who was questioning what bagpipes in a

Scottish setting had to mean at this time. This was Gordon Mooney, who recalls:

> As a student in Dundee in the early 1970's I remember hearing the wild and fluid playing of Northumbrian piper Billy Pigg on the BBC Radio 2—John Peel Show, and I recall buying a Finbar Furey album, curious about the Irish bagpipes. At that time, apart from photographs, I had never seen a bellows blown bagpipe.[19]

In 1976, Mooney—also, as it happens, a member of Muirhead and Sons—heard his bandmate Rab Wallace playing his Lowland pipes for The Whistlebinkies at the Linlithgow Folk Club. Inspired, he asked pipe maker after pipe maker if they'd make him a set. In stunning confirmation of the narrowness of Scottish piping in the '70s, all declined. Mooney's attempts to make his own drones at a night class ended in similar disappointment when the instructor banned him from using the engineering lathe. He then took it upon himself to make the drones out of aluminium. This worked, though they were noticeably heavier than wood.

All the while, Mooney was learning the Northumbrian smallpipes and was regularly driving down from Edinburgh to the Alnwick Pipers' Society. The musicians there 'had a very big influence on me … I loved the style and character of the Northumbrian music and the community musical values.' This last comment is telling, coming from a Muirhead man who had to contend with a pipe major who would drop a player if even a single grace note was missing from his playing.[20] Echoing what Pincock had found when he joined his first folk band, Mooney clearly felt the non-competitive spirit of these Northumbrian pipers to be not only deeply welcoming but also refreshingly distinctive from the culture out of which he came.

Thankfully, Mooney's abilities with the bellows outdid his skills with the lathe, and by 1978 he had them strapped to his aluminium Lowland pipes, producing an instrument of remarkable 'responsiveness and wild edgy quality'. Not content to stop there, in 1980 he bought a set of Northumbrian pipes that pitched at D and turned to another key figure in the story, the English pipe-maker Colin Ross, to provide a chanter in D from a 'new' instrument that Ross was adding to the bellows revival: the Scottish smallpipe. You read that sentence correctly: the Scottish smallpipe that we know today—

with its chanter reed based on the Northumbrian model, its cylindrical (straight) chanter and its quieter (than the Lowland pipes) sound—is largely the creation of an Englishman, though it has since been refined by Scotsman Hamish Moore.[21] Its design was based on an instrument that had once been part of the Scottish tradition but, like the Lowland pipes, had effectively disappeared.

Accompanying all this for Mooney was a historical awakening that put into question his own and his nation's relationship to the bagpipe and emboldened him to think afresh about where he sat within the musical tradition of Scotland and where he could authentically take it next:

> I discovered that Scotland once had *another* bagpipe culture—free of militarism of kilts and uniforms; a bagpipe that played for dancing at kirns and shearing the corn, accompanied songs, led wedding processions and played laments at lykewakes and funerals. It was the bagpipe of the Toun Pipers who woke the Burghs in the morning and sounded *Couvrir Feu* (Curfew) in the evening and who were the repositories of ancient ballads and wild otherworldly music ... Bellows bagpipes were therefore a valid, exciting and nuanced means of artistic expression in Scotland, free from the imperialistic, paternalistic, militaristic ethos that is often found in the marching pipe-band.

But Mooney's and Wallace's disparate attempts to reawaken a past of rich variety were yet to cohere into any kind of formal revival until the figure of Hugh Cheape (yes, he is rightly ubiquitous in this book) entered the story in 1979—an appropriate date given the widespread self-questioning of the nation at that time as a result of the referendum held that year for a devolved Scottish Assembly (a majority of 51.6 per cent voted for the new assembly, but a condition of the referendum was that 40 per cent of the total electorate had to vote in favour, otherwise the result would be repealed; the figure came back at 32.9 per cent). That spirit of self-questioning found expression in a talk Cheape delivered that year at the first ever Edinburgh Folk Festival entitled 'The Pipes and Folk Music'. He was determined to overcome the standard belief in Scotland that the pipes were not a folk instrument. Three years earlier, he and a colleague at the National Museum of Antiquities of Scotland had organised an exhibition called 'Pipes, Harps and Fiddles' (on a budget of £200, which tells you something about where the museum authorities ranked the importance of such matters in the '70s), and it was in the process of researching for this that Cheape's own assumptions about the nature of Scottish bagpipes began to be overturned. Examining an old set of pastoral pipes, which he expected to be of Irish provenance given their clear link to what we know today as uilleann pipes, he discovered to his amazement that the maker was one Naughton of Aberdeen.

The exhibition's success meant that he was further tasked to look into the small bagpipe collection held by the museum and to try to make some sense of it. Again, Cheape found his assumptions to be radically misplaced. Instead of finding evidence of a long, traceable history of Highland bagpipes, he found a hodgepodge assortment of widely varying pieces of instruments (there were very few complete sets), to which, in many cases, he could put no name. As he slowly tried to piece the jigsaw together, the overwhelming conclusion was that here was an instrument that had almost no fixity of form and no linear history until the nineteenth century, and that the bellows pipes had been integral to the story up until then. Moreover, the deeper Cheape went back in time, the more indistinct the line between 'folk' and 'classical' became, though clearly—in their multifarious uses within the communities in which they had arisen, not least as an accompaniment for dancing and festivities—many of the bagpipes in the collection could indeed be described as 'folk instruments'.

While Cheape made some of this clear to his audience at the Edinburgh Folk Festival in 1979, Gordon Mooney was in the audience and spoke to Cheape after the talk. After just a few minutes, it became obvious that their thinking—having developed independently of each other—was potently aligned. With their offices not far from each other (Mooney was a building conservation officer by day), the two began meeting regularly for lunch to discuss their shared obsession, and soon a third man, Mooney's friend Mike Rowan, was added to their controversial plot to widen the definition of Scottish bagpiping. Rowan was a larger than life character who worked as a performance artist known as 'Big Rory'. He also held an ambition to see the 'lost' bellows pipes restored to their rightful place within Scottish cultural life.

Rowan's presence was critical, for it was he who first suggested that a society ought to be established to revive the Lowland pipes. A meeting was therefore set up at the 1981 Edinburgh Folk Festival to discuss the prospect. With the support of Captain John MacLellan, who was at that first meeting and who subsequently published a notice in *International Piper* to alert the piping public to the plan, the Lowland and Border Pipers Society (LBPS) was officially founded in April 1983. By 1986, they had 100 members.[22] Since then, literally thousands of pipers, whether members or not, have picked up these bellows pipes and have not only played within this once-forgotten Scottish tradition, much old music having subsequently been found, but advanced it. Indeed, the first-rate young Highland pipers of today are more than likely to be first-rate bellows players too, and many of them cross easily between the competition and folk worlds without even registering the move. Instrumental diversity is part of the DNA of contemporary Scottish piping. That is a seismic shift since 1983.

* * *

In the same year the LBPS was founded, an album was released by Temple Records that started to shift perceptions around folk pipers. *A Controversy of Pipers*, with its aptly chosen collective noun, featured six of the leading figures from that scene, including MacGillivray, Wallace, Anderson and Pincock, playing the Highland pipes with all the prowess a Seumas MacNeill could hope for. The album also featured two men with the same name: Iain MacDonald. One of these Iains, piper for the band Ossian, was from a formidable trio of Gaelic-speaking piping brothers from Glenuig in Moidart and has gone on to play an important role in reintroducing a more 'Gaelic' style of playing (a style intimately connected to Gaelic song, as Iain's brother Allan has so cogently argued in print), not only as a piper but as a flautist and whistle player too. The other Iain was another multi-instrumentalist (as were MacGillivray, Anderson and Pincock) who could perform wizardry on Northumbrian pipes, Scottish smallpipes and uillean pipes, not to mention the Great Highland Bagpipe. As this spread of expertise suggests, this Iain was also a critical person in reconfiguring the focus of many a Scottish piper.

There could only have been one player on *A Controversy of Pipers* who put the album's selection of European dance tunes together.

Commonly known as Iain MacDonald of Neilston for his role as pipe major of Neilston and District Pipe Band, MacDonald was one of the preeminent collectors of bagpipes from around the world. Perhaps more importantly, he was one of the earliest pipe majors in Scotland purposefully to orientate his band members to piping cultures beyond their own country in the hope of finding inspiration and cultural exchange. One hitch was that the international festivals he wished the band to visit and participate in were often held at the same time of year as the big pipe band competitions in Scotland. Pinning his priorities to the mast, he chose the festivals. Neilston ceased to be a competing band.[23]

MacDonald would take them to places no other Scottish band would consider venturing: the Rothbury Traditional Music Festival in Northumberland for instance, and, even more exotically in 1978, for their very first foreign trip, they travelled to the International Bagpipe Festival in Strakonice, Czechoslovakia, founded by the great prophetic figure of Josef Režný in 1955 (see Chapter 2). That Neilston went at that time tells you something about their pipe major's adventurousness, because the country was still governed by a communist regime. In other respects, it was very good timing, not just because you could buy twelve pints of Budvar and get change back out of a pound, but mainly because this allowed the band to witness, and feed into, the early stages of multiple rediscoveries or developments in other lands regarding their bagpiping cultures.

Brittany and Galicia offer prime examples of the European piping renaissance that was occurring across these years.[24] I noted in Chapter 2 the striking similarities between the earliest depictions of the pipes in Scotland—those at Melrose, Rosslyn and Skirling—and the pipes played across the Iberian Peninsula known as *gaitas*, with their conical chanters, single drone and blowpipe suggesting a common ancestry. The Breton bagpipes, the *biniou* and the *veuze*, appear to be closely related to the *gaita*. It is partly to do with these similarities, perhaps even shared histories, that pipers within the Galician and Breton traditions were able to foster, especially with Irish and Scottish pipers (whom they considered fellow 'Celts'), the cross-pollination of ideas and practices that tends to characterise major revivals. But it's important to stress that the language of revival is slightly misleading in that it suggests the tradition before the period of revival was dead. This was not the case.

In both regions, bagpipe playing had been a continuous, if fluctuating, feature of communal life, not least for dances and public celebrations of one form or another. Nor should we think that, because they are commonly attributed to the 'folk' world, that the bagpipe in these places was simply a peasant's instrument, limited to a rural context. We've already seen how intimately connected the bagpipe was to the world of the church before the Reformation, but where Catholicism continued to hold sway, as it did in Spain and much of France, that relationship remained. From the sixteenth century onwards, there are numerous references to civil and religious institutions hiring a *gaiteiro* (*gaita* player) and *tamboril* (drummer) to play duets for various functions.[25] But, mirroring what we've seen repeatedly in the preceding pages, it was when the question of identity came sharply into focus that fresh attention fell on the importance of their indigenous instrument and the desire arose to give it greater prominence.

The language and literature of Galicia had been in what looked like terminal decline from the end of the fifteenth century, when a period known as the *séculos escuros* (dark centuries) commenced, lasting until roughly the end of the eighteenth century. Castilian Spanish had become the dominant language of the cities and professional life. But as Romanticism swept across Europe in the nineteenth century—with the Scotland of James Macpherson's *Ossian* and Walter Scott's *Waverley* partly responsible—a new sense of importance was given to the specific characteristics of individual regions. This found expression in Galicia in a movement known as O Rexurdimento ('The Resurgence' in Galician). One of the movement's central texts, and the first to be published (partially) in Galician, was a collection of poetry called *A gaita gallega* (The Galician pipes) in 1853. Here, the Galician pipes are symbolic of the language of Galicia itself, so that when, in one poem, the old *gaiteiro* says 'Please God these well-played Pipes / bring memories to the good Piper, / and may thousand more men, / where the first one played, / also come to play the beloved Pipes', he is also calling on the people to use their language and promote their culture with pride.[26] Ten years later, Rosalía de Castro published what would become Galicia's most famous book, *Cantares gallegos*, and again the pipes were a central feature.

With Romanticism came the Celtic Revival, and this too featured in the Rexurdimento agenda. That some of the other so-called Celtic nations or regions, especially Scotland, Ireland and Brittany, had strong bagpiping traditions only served to reinforce the sense of Galician difference from Castilian Spain.[27] In this context, the *gaita* flourished. But it was not to last. When Franco came to power in the 1930s, there was a drive to create a uniform Spanish culture— the Spain of the bullfighter and flamenco dancer. This did not altogether wipe out Galician piping, but only with Franco's death in 1975 and the advent of democracy could the spirit of the Rexurdimento be resurrected. Galicia's most celebrated contemporary *gaita* player, Carlos Núñez, paints a picture of the change:

> With the democracy, each small country in Spain started [to be] like: 'Oh the Catalans, we are Catalanish, we have our own music. Barcelona, Barcelona—listen world!' Same with the Galicians, same with the Basques, so in this moment there was a big revival of folk music. All the Celtic festivals in Galicia started in the seventies; the Galician people began to feel like a Celt, like a brother of the Irish and Scottish—and not the Spanish, Spanish is Moroccan, is South, but we come from the North.[28]

The pattern of suppression was repeated in Brittany during the Nazi occupation, where the bagpipe was once again seen by the authorities as too redolent of regional particularity. So effective was the suppression that by the end of the war the number of Breton pipers was below twenty.[29] But when their tradition could re-emerge, there was a debate to be had about what precise instrument ought to be promoted. For centuries, the principal bagpipe was the *biniwhere*, which looks like a small version of the *gaita*. It was played as an accompaniment to the more versatile bombard, a reeded but bagless pipe, especially for dancing. In the 1930s, however, a 'new' instrument entered the scene, the *biniwhere bras* (the big bagpipe), which appeared to be modelled on the Great Highland Bagpipe, though some argued it was a development—by adding two drones—of the ancient, though no longer played, *veuze* or *véze*, which belonged to the area of Nantes, in the south of Brittany, and was similar to the *gaita* in size and design.[30]

Though the debate has never clearly been settled, what emerged was a fusion that was in many ways even more exciting than what had come before. In the wake of the Second World War, the armed services sought to bring the bagpipe into their marching band units.[31] But as the *biniou* was too quiet to play with drums, the *biniou bras* was used instead. Crucially, the bombard was also incorporated, and the music that was played largely remained Breton music. As the bombard and the *biniou bras* have different but complementary scales, and the bombard can be overblown to enter a second octave, the musical effect of a bagad—as they call these bands—is quite extraordinary. That the bands are not welded to a long-standing tradition means there is a freedom in their performances that is alien to the Scottish pipe band model. That said, many of the top solo performers on the *biniou bras*, which to all intents and purposes is the Great Highland Bagpipe, have gravitated towards the latter's repertoire, piobaireachd especially. Thankfully, this has not meant the death of the traditional *biniou*, for that too, in its original role as accompaniment for the bombard, has regained its rightful place in Breton life.

Galicia has also taken to the band format. Surprisingly, it was one of Franco's ministers, the Galician-born Manuel Fraga Iribarne, who first took to the idea, having attended the Edinburgh Tattoo. As one of those who was able to straddle the end of the dictatorship and the transition to democracy, Fraga ultimately became president of the Xunta of Galicia in 1989, a post he held for fifteen years. Stunned by the power of the massed pipes and drums he'd witnessed in Edinburgh, Fraga tasked the man who would become the director of the Escola de Gaitas in Ourense, José Lois Foxo, to emulate what could be found in Scotland and in Brittany. This involved introducing a drum unit and increasing the numbers within the traditional ensemble, which had consisted of one or two *gaita* players, a drummer on the small tambor, a rattle accompaniment and sometimes an accordion or guitar player. By introducing *gaita* tuition within the province's schools, they were able to increase the number of *gaita* players to the point where marching bands, knowns as *banda de gaitas*, were possible.

The instrument itself was modified as well—though not without considerable complaint from those who wished to protect what they saw as the purity of their heritage.[32] But being in the key of C, the *gaita* was incompatible with pipe bands of the Scottish or Breton varieties who tended to play in B flat. This was excluding the Galician pipers from playing with pipers of other traditions when they came together at the major festivals. Chanters were adjusted accordingly, and one or two additional drones even entered the design, so that some modern forms of the instrument are, at first glance, indistinguishable from the Great Highland Bagpipe. In fact, differences remain: the two new drones are not two tenor drones but one baritone and one small treble. Importantly, as with Breton piping, the indigenous Galician music has continued to be central to their practice. That music, we might note, is interwoven with Latin American influences after the mass migration from Galicia to Central and South America at the end of the twentieth century, so that even the rhythms of the habanera and rumba feature on the bagpipe. The Galician willingness to hybridise was further reinforced when Os Resentidos—'The Resentful Ones'—became the first rock band to have a bagpiper in the early 1980s. Such developments were clearly popular, for by 1998 there were some 15,000 pipers in Galicia, which has an overall population of around 3 million, and an equal split between the sexes. As Núñez said in an interview that year, 'we have more pipers than policemen, or priests, or pharmacists ... it's great!'[33]

* * *

One culture that was struggling to retain a unique element across this period was the piping culture in Canada. The last generation of the traditional Gaelic-speaking ear-learned Cape Breton pipers was dying out (Alex Currie was probably the very last, dying in 1997), and it was becoming harder and harder to find their freewheeling, dance-based style among the piping community (thankfully, it does continue to survive, and is even coming back into prominence with the likes of fiddling and piping brothers Kenneth and Angus MacKenzie). The regimented competition, book-learnt, technique-focused culture, modelled on 'modern' Scottish conventions and long embraced by the inland provinces of Canada, was becoming a more obvious feature of the Nova Scotian scene.[34]

Before I say more on that culture, it's worth noting Michael Grey's compelling theory to account for the earlier embrace of the competition mentality in the more inland regions such as Ontario. He believes that the different kinds of emigration from Scotland that had taken place over the previous two centuries determined where one settled and the outlook one held. The wave of migrants who came with the early clearances were principally propelled by compulsion, so Grey argues, and thus settled in the regions that were immediately available to them directly on the eastern seaboard, where they hoped to recreate the Gaelic life they had known. They were followed by other waves of migrants later in the nineteenth century, carrying on well into the twentieth, who were more aspirational and less wedded to the life they had left behind. They pushed on inland looking for ever better growth and trading opportunities, and their capitalistic outlook may account for their quick uptake of the competition set-up, with all the focus on betterment and one-up-man-ship that it brings.

Whatever the reasons, after the Second World War it appeared that—in general—the Canadian scene was becoming more homogenised and more committed to emulating what was happening in Scotland. Indeed, when Colin MacLellan, the talented son of the famous Captain John MacLellan, moved to Ontario in the '70s and began to make a name for himself as a fine interpreter of pio-baireachd in his own right, he discovered that the people were almost more Scottish than the Scots themselves. 'People had their basements decked out in tartan,' recalls MacLellan, 'and made a great effort to be Scottish, which was great, but in a way that kind of thing felt sort of artificial.'[35] That said, the competition scene in Canada was at least willing to break ranks with the Scottish scene in one crucial respect. In Scotland, until recently, all junior players were dumped indiscriminately into the under-eighteen category. Canada, however, created a graded system to pit like for like, bringing opportunities for growth and confidence-building that were few and far between on the other side of the Atlantic.

But with air travel becoming more affordable across the '70s and '80s, it was inevitable that the great competitions in Scotland became the high points of the top Canadian piper's year, whether playing in a band or as a soloist. They came, at significant personal cost, even though they believed that the mentality among a number of the Scottish pipers and judges, at least in the '70s, was against them. It seemed that some Scots were convinced that when they met with Canadian piping prowess, it was not a result of talent or musicality but down to their well-known dedication and hard work. As one die-hard was overheard saying to another: 'These [Canadian] guys are all technique, and don't know how to produce any music at all ... I'd much rather hear a boy playing a good musical tune with a few technical blemishes, than one of these with nothing but technique alone.'[36] When Bill Livingstone was placed third in the Open Piobaireachd at the Cowal Games in 1973, it was a 'watershed moment', for as he says, 'it was rare to the point of nonexistence for a Canadian even to place in such a contest'.[37] As he used to say of those travelling over to Scotland and not getting any reward: 'It's a long way to come to piss in the pickles.'[38] Attitudes, thankfully, did soften, for in 1977 Livingstone was awarded the coveted Gold Medal at Inverness, followed by the Gold Medal at Oban two years later. Such success was partly a result of Livingstone's faithfulness to what he'd learnt at the knee of the master pipers of the previous generation. And yet, when it came to another arena of success—the pipe band—there was a clear sense that 'these Canadian guys' were far from willing to bow to Scottish convention.

In 1982, Livingstone became the founding pipe major of the Ontario-based 78th Fraser Highlanders, who were swiftly recognised as one of two Grade 1 bands willing to push the boundaries of what was 'acceptable' to the famously conservative pipe band judges. With an outrageously musical nucleus of players, prominently (in addition to Livingstone himself and some remarkable drummers) Gerry Quigg, John Walsh, Ian Anderson, Michael Grey and Bruce Gandy, the band was unusually open to the folk tradition and to developments in Ireland especially, and they had the capacity to translate what they heard into pipe arrangements of the most startling quality. For instance, their version of 'The Little Cascade'— in itself a brilliantly innovative piece by G. S. McLennan and rarely played by a pipe band at that time—was reworked in a bossa nova rhythm, with a playfulness to the timings that was unheard of. Daring, too, was their decision to play reels in a 'rounded' fashion—which, as we now know, was the height of audacity to the piping gods of the time—influenced, perhaps, by their willingness to mine the riches of the folk tradition and the music still to be found in Cape Breton. Newly composed pieces by members of the band were, if good enough, happily included in their repertoire (much of Grey's output is now a staple of pipe band repertoires across the globe) and orchestral-like pieces came within their ambit too. Their rendition of the jazz musician Don Thompson's 'Journey to Skye' utterly broke the mould for what pipe bands thought possible, laying down a bedrock for a whole new style of piping composition. Livingstone recalls:

> I always thought of it [the band] as a petri dish of musical invention and creativity, with ideas appearing from many corners. It is not disingenuous to say that it was all about the music, not the prize. I always felt, and said, that if we do what we want, and do it well, the prize will take care of itself. If was incredibly liberating, and created this rich atmosphere of music adventure and pushing the boundaries.[39]

The prizes did indeed take care of themselves. As a sign that the Scottish piping establishment wasn't quite as close-minded as some suspected, the 78th Frasers shot to meteoric success, going from fifth, to third, to fourth, to second at the World Championships between 1983 and 1986, before winning the ultimate prize—in the streaming rain of Glasgow's Bellahouston Park—in 1987: the first non-Scottish band to do so, and the single blip in the historic run of ten wins by the all-powerful Strathclyde Police Pipe Band.[40] To prove that it wasn't all about the competition arena, that year the 78th Frasers performed their now legendary 'Live in Ireland' concert in Ballymena, which became the largest-selling pipe band recording ever produced. They were heady times, as Grey recalls:

> You would step off the bus at the Worlds at Bellahouston Park or wherever and you'd get kids come running up with their programmes for you to autograph. I remember we did a concert in Leith Assembly Rooms [Edinburgh]. A few of us had gone out for something to eat and we came back to the hall in a taxi and the line went four deep right around the building and we felt like we were The Beatles; it was just an amazing thing. That really was a buzz.[41]

None of this stopped their endeavours from being highly precarious financially. At one point, the band manager, unknowingly to the band, had racked up a debt of around $70,000 on her personal credit cards just to keep them in existence.[42] Incidentally, that is roughly the figure that it takes to run a pipe band in Canada for a year if it also competes in Scotland.[43] Such expense doesn't seem to have put them off. With bands such as Simon Fraser University and the Toronto Police as well as the 78th, Canada has become one of the powerhouses of the pipe band world. The country's solo performers are equally impressive. In fact, so widespread is the instrument's popularity there, it is not ludicrous to say that the Great Highland Bagpipe is just as much the national instrument of Canada as it is of Scotland.

* * *

I said that the 78th Frasers were one of two bands that were pushing the boundaries in the 1980s. The other was a band from Pitlochry in Highland Perthshire, the Vale of Atholl Pipe Band. They, too, would know what meteoric success looked like, moving from Grade 4 to Grade 1 in the space of just seven years. But while the men from Ontario drew their musical boldness from a collective pool of strong characters, the Perthshire outfit, though pulsing with talent and creativity, has tended to hail one man beyond all others for theirs. If this chapter has depicted a piping scene breaking free from the shackles of convention, here was someone who personified piping freedom, and in so doing showed how flawed it was to reduce tradition to convention. His epochal album of 1994, *Just for Seumas*—teasingly named after the figure who had dominated Scottish piping for the past fifty years—was probably the start of an era that is still recognisably ours today. Though his life went the way of too many piping greats before him, he has changed how we think about the instrument forever. This was the Pitlochry bin man Gordon Duncan.

10

YESTERDAY, TODAY AND FOREVER

THE HEALTH, OR OTHERWISE, OF SCOTLAND'S
CONTEMPORARY PIPING CULTURE: 1994 ONWARDS

Gordon Duncan had just enjoyed an all-nighter with Shane MacGowan of the Pogues: not someone who was going to put him through his paces lightly. They were in Glasgow, where the annual Celtic Connections festival has been held every year since 1994. Next day, Gordon—calling him Duncan feels wrong—boarded the train to Perth, where he was to change trains for Pitlochry. He was looking forward to a wee nap. Unfortunately, having settled down in his seat, the nap took him all the way through Perth, and he awoke to find himself in Dundee. Alighting from the train, he thought he'd hang around the city for a couple of hours and just take the next train back to Perth. Fine. Back on the train, tiredness overtook him once more. When he woke, his bleary eyes peered through the train window to see where they were. The answer was Glasgow. He was back where he'd started.[1]

That is just one story about a man who has gathered a thousand stories around him. We could have easily begun the chapter with the escapade at the Lorient Festival when Gordon was spotted riding through town in the pillion passenger seat of a Harley Davidson, merrily playing his pipes; or the time he got his bandmates from The Tannahill Weavers to hold him by his feet so he could feel what it was like to play his instrument upside down. No wonder he won the Vale of Atholl's Esra prize (read the word backwards) six years running, awarded to the member of the band who'd done the stupidest thing that year. His bandmates have never forgotten the image of him atop the mast of the Rothesay ferry playing reels or, at JFK Airport, the sight of him going through the baggage security X-ray machine flat out on his back playing his chanter.[2]

In some respects, then, Gordon was a 'character' in keeping with the long line of characters the piping world has known and seems to attract. And, like them, he cared about his heritage. Being from Pitlochry, he was a proud son of Highland Perthshire, and his commitment to the Vale of Atholl, the local band, and to the Atholl Highlanders, the duke of Atholl's private army, was testament to that. He was also an accomplished player of the classic repertoire, knowing it inside-out and expressing it with 'a precise and fluent fingering style' that was 'the envy of the piping world'.[3] But if these things would have pleased a Seumas MacNeill, there were other aspects that were only going to ruffle the kilt pleats.

Gordon's love of AC/DC, his passion for Irish, Breton and Galician music, his penchant for personal experiment—all this took him and his pipes into unchartered territory. As Stuart Eaglesham of the band Wolfstone has said: 'Gordon was a kind of Jimmy Hendrix of the pipes in the way that both of them were doing things with the instrument that had never been done before.'[4] Along with Alan MacLeod, he was one of the earliest players to experiment with the C-natural, a note produced through a technique revealingly called 'false fingering'. Because of the popularity of his tune 'Andy Renwick's Ferret', it's through Gordon that many people have their first experience of hearing that alarming, vista-opening note on the bagpipes. The C-natural opened up the way for the F-natural too, thus creating an eleven-note scale, where for centuries there had been only nine—an abomination to MacNeill, who was on a mission 'to eliminate', as he put it in one letter, 'this false and foreign fingering'.[5] But Gordon wanted more than just an expanded scale. Listening to his hero Paddy Keenan, the influential Irish performer of the uilleann pipes and founding member of The Bothy Band, brought yet other dimensions, whether that be bending notes or playing in a rounded style. Apart from all this, there was the sheer pace of Gordon's playing and the frenetic, electric energy this brought to his performances.

But for all his individualistic virtuosity, Gordon had a creative pipe band brain too. His role as pipe sergeant and musical director of the Vale of Atholl (his brother Ian was pipe major) would come to mark them out as one of the leading innovators in that world and take them all the way to the heights of the Grade 1 tree. The soundtrack on the band bus was not the Great Pipe bands of yore or the Gold Medal winners but the defining folk bands of the time, both those from Scotland—notably The Tannahill Weavers (Gordon was their piper for a while) and Silly Wizard (co-founded, I'm proud to say, by my uncle)[6]—and importantly from Ireland too, whether that be Planxsty, The Bothy Band or Moving Hearts. Gordon would appear at band practice with copies of their tunes written especially for the bagpipes. As Gary West, another Vale player, has said, 'the judges didn't always like it, but we liked playing it. That's where Gordon first put his stamp on [things] ... arranging traditional tunes which weren't traditional for the Highland pipes.'[7] Given their rise through the grades, the judges must have liked it a fair bit of the time, as they did with the 78th Frasers' endeavours. But not everyone felt quite as open-minded.

In May 1993, the Scottish Pipers' Association held a knockout competition at Studio One of Broadcasting House in Glasglow. Gordon reached the finals, where he went head to head with another player of frightening ability and speed, Gordon Walker of the Royal Highland Fusiliers. The event was recorded by BBC Radio. The two men decided to let rip. At the end of the night, after the 260 audience members had cast their votes, it was announced that Walker would take the prize. The man who presented it was none other than Seumas MacNeill. His words are now part of piping lore:

> The piping tonight, I don't think there was a great deal of piping tonight ... I thought that some of it was very good, some of the march, strathspey and reel playing I enjoyed, but the rest of it ... was garbage. If this is what piping has come to, I'm going back to the fiddle.[8]

On the bus home to Pitlochry, Gordon sat at the back looking dejected, not because he hadn't won but because of what MacNeill had said. Sitting with him was Hamish Moore, that great advocate for the emigrant Gaelic styles of playing: fast, rounded and dance-worthy. Gordon pursued all three, and Moore—who'd walked out that night in protest after hearing MacNeill's damning verdict—was

163

intent to do all he could to make Gordon's artistry known to the world. As Moore recalls:

> I promised Gordie [as Gordon was known to his friends] that I would phone Ian Green of Greentrax Records and the next morning I suggested to Ian that he give Gordie a record contract. Immediately, he did. In his own beautiful way, Gordie had the perfect three-word response to Seumas MacNeill in naming his brilliant debut album, *Just for Seumas*.[9]

This record did not abandon the tradition, but it took it a quantum leap further.[10] You were simply not going to find another solo piping record at that time doing what it did. That was nowhere truer than in the title medley itself, with its multi-tracked bagpipes, its quartet of drummers, its indiscriminate array of other percussive instruments (bashed on by the producer) and its electric bass, playing a set that included the luminous piobaireachd 'Lament for Mary MacLeod' worked over Gordon's own composition 'Break Yer Bass Drone'. By unleashing such an album on the world, it's probably not an exaggeration to say that Gordon had also ushered in the modern era of piping. It was as if permission had finally been granted to play with freedom, to follow your interest and to experiment. No wonder *Just for Seumas*, together with Gordon's other two albums *The Circular Breath* (1997) and *Thunderstruck* (2003), would become Greentrax's biggest selling piping releases. His compositions were legion, becoming ubiquitous in the piping world, and some of them, such as 'Pressed for Time', 'The Belly Dancer' and the title track of his final album (his piping interpretation of the classic AC/DC tune) were quite simply genre-defying.

I said way back in the Introduction that the history of piping could boast of at least one figure that would not have looked out of place on a Rolling Stones album cover. That was Gordon: dishevelled hair, leather jacket, arm out the window, roaring down the road to band practice in his green Fiat Panda, rock music blaring, rolling a cigarette and steering with his knees. As Walter Drysdale, the highly respected piping judge, once said of him: '[H]e was the closest thing to a rock star the piping world has ever known.'[11] Ali Hutton, a leading multi-instrumental innovator today, recalls the first time he met Gordon and heard him play: 'I knew straight away that I wanted to play exactly like Gordon. Until then I'd never heard, or felt piping like his. Most youngsters want to be pilots, astronauts, or footballers. I wanted to be Gordon Duncan.'[12]

But for all his charisma and hijinks, Gordon was a gentle soul, with never a bad word to say about anyone. As pipe major of the Vale's Juvenile band, he dedicated much of his time to encouraging the young players to pursue their music with dedication and joy. The celebrated contemporary musician Ross Ainslie—often to be found playing with Ali Hutton, and whose whole style in appearance and playing reflects a close connection to Gordon—had his first band experience in this context. He remembers:

> [Gordon] was also in the Grade 1 band but we felt he was ours. He would travel home from competitions on our bus, not the Grade 1 band bus. His pipes would be brought out and passed around. He encouraged us all to play. I'll never forget these times and will always be thankful to Gordon for giving so much of his time and experience to us kids. All the time I was in the Vale it was one of the best parts of my life.[13]

And yet, as his escapades with Shane MacGowan suggest, Gordon knew what the inside of a bottle looked like. When out on his rounds as a bin man one day, he was approached by an American tourist who recognised the great piper. Shocked to see him in his overalls, the visitor asked him what he was doing in such a job. Gordon responded jovially: 'God, if I didn't do this I'd be steaming all the time!'[14] When alone, however, Gordon was not always so jovial. His gentleness bespoke a sensitivity of soul. Coupled with the drink, it would have tragic consequences.

* * *

The above may make it sound as if Gordon Duncan was the only pioneer of that era. He wasn't. The figures of Fred Morrison and Allan MacDonald could also be mentioned, but they belonged roughly to the same world as Gordon. Someone who put the pipes into a totally different space was Martyn Bennett. What made Martyn—Canadian-born but reared in Scotland from the age of six—such a unique figure was his spread of musical expertise and the palpable depth of his character, bordering, maybe even embodying, the spiritual. Though Martyn is usually remembered for his dreadlocks and topless performances, and is sometimes referred to as 'the techno piper', he was in fact classically trained at the Royal Scottish Academy of Music and Drama—now the Royal Conservatoire of Scotland—specialising in violin and piano, with the hope that he might eventually fulfil his dream of 'playing in a professional ensemble or Quartet'.[15]

That ambition was firmly re-oriented when he encountered electro-dance culture during what he called Edinburgh's 'Summer of Love', which he dated to 1994. He wrote:

> I think for a classically trained composer, the dance world is such an attractive place as it encapsulates the same musical ethos. It is principally about sound and scale, tension and release, power and detail—much like the orchestral canvas perhaps. It is no wonder that many of us end up composing using technology. Drums and beats became the focus of my days and I spent a lot of time with my Atari and Roland S760 sampling Bull-dog Breaks and incorporating my first tunes.[16]

Those tunes, and the impressive output that would follow, starting with his eponymous first album of 1995 and ending with his fifth and final record, *GRIT*, in 2003, would take the listener on a mind-expanding rollercoaster of sound and feel, one so clearly rooted in Scotland yet riding joyously through the many riches he discovered in the wider world. The power of his music was never so visible as the moment in Paris's Buddha Bar, when Martyn's band Cuillin—named after the Skye mountain range and including Martyn's wife Kirsten—played before an audience of celebrities and sportsmen gathered in the French capital for the opening match of the 1998 World Cup between Scotland and Brazil. Right in the middle of their set, who should leap upon the stage but Sean Connery, who began busting moves with abandon. Before they knew it, Cuillen and Connery were joined by a mass of famous names, including Ewan McGregor, Jackie Stewart and Alex Ferguson. As Martyn's website puts it: 'It was quite a sight to see James Bond getting it on with Renton from Trainspotting.'[17] Two years later, another of Martyn's bands, Hardland, ploughed a totally new folk furrow during their headline gig at the Cambridge Folk Festival. As *Mojo* magazine reported: 'Half the audience fled in fear of their lives ... Scots music has never sounded like this before. No music has ever sounded like this before.'[18]

But Martyn had his low points too. Back in 1993, just before his graduation, he was diagnosed with testicular cancer. Having successfully battled that, October 2000 brought yet more bad news with a diagnosis of Hodgkin's Lymphoma. It was during his eight months of chemo- and radiotherapy that he set up the studio to write *GRIT*, which, because of his weakness, had to be exclusively created out of archive material. Released under Peter Gabriel's Real World Records, *GRIT* is an extraordinary creative feat, where the evocative crackled sounds of Scotland's voices and song meet heavy drum beats and liquid guitar loops. It was Martyn's way of finding, as he said, 'a way into popular culture without diluting the origins of it'.[19] Or, as the singer Sheila Stewart expressed it about 'The Banks o' the Lee', a track they worked on together after the album was released: 'You have achieved what I hoped you were going to achieve, which was to bring the old to the new, and you've bloody done it!'[20]

But in its original release form, you would not necessarily know that a piper was behind *GRIT*, apart from what's suggested in the third track, 'Chanter'. In the 2014 reissue, however, two additional tracks were added, the last of which is 'Mackay's Memoirs', composed by Martyn in memory of his old piping instructor, Dr Kenneth Mackay of Badenoch. This spine-tingling interweaving of pipes, clarsach, strings and percussion has been described as the closest thing to an orchestral piece of piobaireachd that has ever been composed.[21] It was written to mark the centenary of Martyn's old high school in Edinburgh and was first performed at the opening of the new Scottish Parliament in 1999. When it was eventually recorded, it would be at an altogether less jubilant time.

Martyn may have produced what the folklorist Hamish Henderson described as 'brave new music', but it was anything but a flight into fancy. He conceived his final album in these remarkably clear-eyed terms:

In recent years so many representations of Scotland have been misty-lensed and fanciful to the point that the word 'Celtic' has

really become a cloudy pigeon hole. This album was a chance for
me to present a truthful picture, yet face my own reflection in the
great mirror of all cultures.[22]

It is this connection to the hard edge of music, to the grit of it, that
makes Bennett's output so compelling. It's why Finlay MacDonald,
director of the National Piping Centre in Glasgow and son of Iain
MacDonald of Neilston, compares the experience of watching and
hearing Martyn on stage in his prime with what it must have been
like to experience a piper playing reels in a Highland croft in the
1700s—the pure earthy energy of it and the connection to the
ground from which it sprang were surely just the same.[23] And since
this could probably be said of the music and playing of Gordon
Duncan, perhaps that's where we might glimpse something of
what's needed to secure for future generations the safekeeping of
the bagpipes. What the music of these two musicians tells us is this:
anything that is utterly divorced from the past is likely to vitiate and
ultimately die, but anything utterly stuck in the past will probably
cease to be art entirely. For the bagpipes to flourish, we need an
environment where those who play them, and those who hear them,
are open to the past, the present and the future in all their rich
abundance all at once.[24]

But neither Martyn nor Gordon remained with us long enough
to know if their lessons had taken root. On 30 January 2005, after
a long battle with cancer, Martyn died, aged thirty-three. A
recording of 'Mackay's Memoirs' by the pupils from Martyn's old
high school had been planned for the following morning. It was
decided that it would go ahead but that the news of Martyn's death
would be withheld from the performers until after the recording
was complete. For me at least, a piece that was already bitter-
sweet in its potent combination of the plaintive and the life-affirm-
ing becomes, in knowing this, that bit more bitter, that inexpress-
ibly bit sweeter.

When John D. Burgess died that June, his death may have come
more in the natural order of things, but the bagpiping world had
lost yet another great musical voice that spoke as much of the
future as it did of the past. Even then, 2005 was not done with its
ravaging work. It held a baleful bookend. On 14 December,

Gordon Duncan was found dead at home, having taken his own life. He was forty-one.[25]

* * *

Have their lessons taken root? Can we look to the future with confidence, knowing that this instrument, that is always so much more than an instrument, will flourish? Let's look at the Scottish context first, as that is undeniably the nation that is most closely associated with bagpiping in today's world—so much so that, in international sign language, a squeeze of the arm on an imaginary bagpipe is the established sign for 'Scotland'.[26] In the conclusion that follows, however, we can widen the lens once again and remind ourselves of just how global the instrument actually is.

Our take on the health or otherwise of the bagpipes in Scotland will depend on where we put our focus. If inclined towards pessimism, there's certainly enough to make you wonder if the language of 'national instrument' can really be sustained. The precarious nature of funding is perhaps the most obvious issue. There had been so much to give confidence in the years immediately after the establishment of the devolved Scottish Parliament in 1999, which set out bold plans for cultural renewal, resulting in initiatives such as the National Centre of Excellence in Traditional Music (including bagpiping) at Plockton High School in Wester Ross, one of six centres of excellence created around the turn of the century. While that funding is still ring-fenced, much else isn't, and a crisis in arts funding is taken as a given today. Even a charity such as the National Piping Centre (established 1996),[27] with the king as its patron, its three youth pipe bands, its exceptional outreach work and its joyously inclusive Piping Live! festival—even this organisation, regarded as 'the world's centre for excellence in bagpipes',[28] has had its funds from Creative Scotland, the Scottish government's arts funding body, at a standstill for twelve years.

Older generations might argue that for most of the bagpipes' history in Scotland there was no public funding whatsoever, so the overall progress is significant. Again, they might highlight that prior to 1969, there simply was no piping instruction in schools. Now, it is widespread and continues to be free—unlike most music tuition in England—but even here much frustration is felt. With Local Authorities deciding how their music budget is to be spent, certain regions feel left behind and note a continuing bias towards classical, orchestral instruments. Of the roughly 7,000 pupils who are learning the pipes and drums in school (I'm told that up to 20,000 would be learning if the resources were available),[29] a significant proportion of them are funded with the support of the Scottish Schools Pipes and Drums Trust, the charitable initiative of Edinburgh fund manager and philanthropist Angus Tulloch. Despite the noble efforts of the trust, the centre of gravity in the piping and drumming world has been increasingly moving towards the private schools—a stark contrast to fifty years ago, when the centre ground was very much held by the mining communities, the Boy Scouts and the Boys' Brigade, representing a very different demographic. But the private schools' capacity to pay full-time instructors and to offer one-on-one tuition is not only attracting some of the finest pipers to their staffs; it is also likely to create the next generation of standout performers.

In contrast to this, when the single instructor covering Dumfries and Galloway retired in 2012, the Local Authority chose not to replace him, and the vacuum has only subsequently been filled by the tireless work of the South West Scotland Piping and Drumming Academy, which was formed by local pipers in response to the crisis and is largely funded through a small band of wealthy benefactors. Once in the schools, conditions are not always ideal. Apart from the fact that group lessons are the norm, rather than the far more impactful one-on-one format, the physical spaces can be a challenge too. In one school in the region, the piping instructor was forced to teach in a janitor's cupboard and first aid room. And while the academy has formed a very successful schools' pipe band, it is one of only six pipe bands in a region that had once boasted around sixteen. Sheer expense is one of the principal causes of this decline.

The chance for bands to showcase their talents has also been hit badly by the financial uncertainties of the time. In 2023, one of the five major championships was unable to go ahead due to lack of funding from the Local Authority that was to host the event. For 2024, it looked likely that only two of the majors would be financially viable—though thankfully solutions were eventually found for all five. Sadly, a solution was not found in 2023 for BBC Radio Scotland's *Pipeline* programme, which had been running for decades. *Pipeline* held a special place in the nation's heart because it did not rely on the recordings of others or on old material but did its own original recordings from the studio or at the great competitions. Despite a worldwide petition gathering over 10,000 signatures, and a long Scottish Parliament hearing to defend the programme, *Pipeline* is no more. Again, funding seemed to be at the heart of the matter—the financial hole that needed to be covered just so happened to be about the same as the cost of producing the piping, Scottish classical and Scottish jazz programmes, all of which were axed. As the editor of *Piping Times* put it: 'Our national music has yet again become a victim of the bean counters.'[30] Though the programme has been replaced with *Piping Sounds*, which sits well alongside the established Gaelic-language piping programme *Crùnluath*, the loss of the original recordings has been sorely felt.

To stick with the pessimistic case for a moment, there's clearly much unhappiness among some sections of the piping community about the dominance of competition in the solo and pipe band worlds; a dominance nowhere better witnessed than in the three-part Sky Arts documentary of 2024, *Battle of the Bagpipes*, as it follows three Grade 1 pipe bands in their pursuit of the ultimate accolade, winning the World Championships. The drive and dedication of these bands matches any professional sports team. Some onlookers believe, however, that in recent years, musicality has been sacrificed at the altar of technical ability and unity of sound. In these latter respects, certainly, the top modern pipe bands are miracles of achievement—though the rise of synthetic bags and reeds since the 1990s, as well as electric tuners and devices to control moisture levels in the bag, has made the job of finding exact unity of sound much easier than it was in the past. But if we return to that key marker of flourishing as suggested by the lives of Gordon Duncan and Martyn Bennett, there are rumblings of discontent about the number of bands who are unwilling to experiment with the music, to take it to new places. Too often, it is claimed, there is a mind-numbing sameness to the sound year after year.

Not only this, but there are feelings of frustration at the format of the big competitions. The sets *must* begin in a prescribed manner;

the pipers *must not* cut out for any period of time to let the drummers take over; the band *must* form into a circle. And as that last criterion suggests, the audience experience does not seem to be taken very seriously; quite literally, the players turn their backs on you. Together with the background noise of the bands in other grades playing at the same time, it is not exactly easy listening. The final point, of course, is that these competitions are held outdoors, so that the competitors are at the mercy of the elements—and in Glasgow in August, when the Worlds are held, those elements can be rough indeed. True, the logistics, not to mention noise levels, of an indoor tournament would present major challenges, but there are plenty who want to see those challenges overcome. For the bands who spend hundreds of hours fine tuning their performances in indoor conditions, and even more so for those who travel hundreds, sometimes thousands of miles at their own vast expense to compete—in 2023, there were bands from Australia, Canada, the United States, Malaysia, Zimbabwe and Israel competing at the Worlds—it's a bitter pill to swallow when you find your instruments and performances ruined by a rainstorm.

While bands flood into Scotland from around the globe, the Scottish bands are often reluctant to travel even the short distance to the Northern Ireland competitions, citing the expense of it. There are those who read this, however, more as a silent arrogance: 'You can come to us, but we're not coming to you.' Yet the days when the Scots could be arrogant about their piping prowess are long gone. The most successful pipe band of modern times, the Field Marshal Montgomery Pipe Band, with a record breaking thirteen world titles at Grade 1, comes not from Lothian but Lisburn, Northern Ireland. In the solo world, meanwhile, most of the very top female competitors for the last ten or fifteen years have come from outside of Scotland: Jenny Hazzard and Andrea Boyd from Canada, Fiona Manson from New Zealand, Margaret Dunn from Ireland—these have been some of the most recurring names on the prize lists.

That said, the pessimist has yet more ammunition in this regard, for there are currently fewer women at the top solo level than there were in the 1980s. In the traditional music world—some people still use the F word, i.e., folk—the number of women performing is low, despite a star such as Brìghde Chaimbeul leaving most other Scottish smallpipe players in the shade. In the pipe band world, no noticeable increase in female pipers over the past few decades can be detected, and a photo from 2024 that brought together the women who'd competed at the World Championships as pipers in Grade 1 bands numbered just eighteen in total. The percentage of women is high among the tenor drummers, but sometimes there's a condescending, if unspoken sense that their contribution is more decorative than musical. That the tenor drummer's dexterous actions are known as 'flourishing' cannot help here, nor the fact that the tenor drum is the only instrument that the RSPBA does not require for a band to compete.

It's probably true that overt sexism is largely a thing of the past. You could no longer have a band—as there was until at least the 1990s—who had an explicit 'nae birds' policy, for instance. Nor would you find a man looking in surprise at a female piper when she said she'd performed in a Grade 1 competition, and asking, 'Really? All the way through?'[31] But while this kind of openly insulting language is no longer present, there remains much that is covertly offensive and downright unjust. In March 2024, the Canadian piper Eilidh MacDonald asked a group of 100 female pipers and drummers what their hopes were for twenty years hence in terms of women in the world of piping and drumming. The sixty women who responded—which included those from Scotland, Canada, Ireland, Australia and the United States—expressed hopes that, as MacDonald puts it, 'are heartbreaking descriptions of the present'.[32] Here are some examples:

- They wonder how many women could've played at the highest level but couldn't deal with the misogyny. So they hope that by 2044 the culture of piping organisations will shift to foster feelings of safety, belonging, and uncapped potential for women who belong to them.
- They describe feeling hopeful that men will support and *believe* women when they disclose harassment, assault, or abuse in our community.
- They hope for a future in which pipe band 'status' and the power of 'social celebrity' will no longer be justifications for unjustifiable actions.

- They describe a future in which we will be able to choose to play in pipe bands without feeling that doing so lowers our tolerance or compromises our standards for how we want to be treated and respected.
- They hope that in the future, we won't hear 'she's the best woman piper I've ever heard' or 'she's really good for a girl', as those specifications will not exist.
- They hope that we look back only to say, '*remember when ...*' and shake our heads in disbelief over what we used to put up with.[33]

Even the world of traditional music, usually hailed for its softer, more inclusive culture, made headlines in 2020 for going through its own #MeToo moment, with a former BBC Scotland Young Traditional Musician of the Year, Rona Wilkie, claiming 'endemic sexual abuse patterns' were evident across the scene.[34] This may partly account for why—despite healthy proportions of young women in the Fèis movement, and at Plockton—the numbers are just not translating into the professional 'trad' world.

While this is worrying, the trad scene has at least not shackled itself to a clichéd picture of the culture for which it sings and sounds. It is not clear, however, that the same could be said about the competitive world of Highland bagpiping. The requirement for solo competitors to wear kilts, hats and jackets when performing suggests that a sense of spectacle remains an important element of the art. While there are players who enjoy the spectacle element, there are plenty who do not, especially those who find their bag sliding away from their arm because of their slippery kilt jacket material. One well-respected figure in the piping world tells me he hates having to don his kilt constantly, saying: 'I just don't feel comfortable, I feel like a freak.' He sees such demands as symptomatic of a childish outlook that insists on pipers conforming to a stereotype. His view is simple: 'We need to grow up in piping!'

In this sense, the language of 'national instrument' could well be a negative contributing factor, putting anachronistic constraints on what should ultimately be about music, not look. The irony here is that, for the most part, audience attendance at the top solo contests is abysmally low. Very often, there are more performers than there are audience members. One exception is the Glenfiddich championship at Blair Castle (see Chapter 6), where you might easily think the piping world has played up to stereotypes—with its grand Highland setting among the hills and the antlers and armour upon the wall. Is this a repeat of that old pattern we've detected before in this book: the Scots being just as much in thrall to their own romantic image as any misty-eyed outsider? Or, more cynically, is this the organisers exploiting that image for financial gain? There are obvious ripostes to these questions—not least the fact that, as far as competitions go, the Glenfiddich is undeniably a magnificent one—but there's enough in them to take a less than bright view of the piping scene.

* * *

Now for the optimistic case. What other instrument in Scotland can boast of its own National Centre devoted to its practice and promotion? And just look at the degree courses in traditional music, with options to specialise in the bagpipes, offered by the Royal Conservatoire of Scotland and the University of the Highlands and Islands' Sabhal Mòr Ostaig, which delivers the course entirely in Gaelic, the language so intimately connected to the music of the Highland pipe. Look, too, at the accredited courses that are now available in piping and the instruction of piping, which have not only been raising the general standard of playing but also the understanding of the theory behind the music. It seems a nonsense to think in our contemporary setting, as some have done in the past, that pipers are not also musicians.[35]

Along with musical understanding, accessibility to the music of the bagpipe has grown too. Even when it comes to piobaireachd, surrounded for much of its recent history by an air of mystique and exclusiveness, recent initiatives have pushed against the grain, whether that be the Pibroch Network, with its online publication of musical scores long held behind paywalls, or the Big Music Society, which has brought bold new arrangements of piobaireachd to audiences unfamiliar with the art.[36] But it's not just piobaireachd: every branch of the music is accessible like never before. Look at the wealth of settings—far from the competition stage or the military parade ground—that are bringing exposure to the bagpipes, from Celtic Connections to Piping Live! And with organisations such as

Fèisean nan Gàidheal, the umbrella organisation for the Fèis movement, and Hamish Moore's Ceòlas—devoted to Gaelic culture, heritage and arts, based on South Uist—there are now numerous avenues through which the Highland bagpipes can be reconnected with the culture out of which they sprang. Ceòlas is especially worthy of note for its keenness to foster strong links with the Cape Breton tradition of piping, ensuring there is nothing parochial about its vision.

In all these settings, instrumental diversity is taken for granted: smallpipes, Lowland pipes, Highland pipes, even uilleann and Northumbrian pipes—these are just part of the natural fabric of the Scottish scene now. And technological advances have meant new instruments too. The pipe maker Donald Lindsay, for example, has developed the Lindsay System Chanter for Scottish smallpipes using 3D printing, creating an instrument capable of preserving the traditional fingering system while extending the range downwards and upwards and allowing players to access semitones as well as a second octave. What's so refreshing about Lindsay's approach is his consciously 'open source' design, so that everything he does is open to collaborative development. One person to join in that collaboration is piper, pipe maker, fiddler and composer Malin Lewis, who became the first person to make a wooden chanter based on the Lindsay System. Malin's open celebration of their queer identity suggests that it's not only instrumental diversity that's becoming an accepted part of the trad scene.

That is a clear healthy development; and on that point, it's interesting that questions concerning health are becoming more commonly connected to the bagpipes. Alastair Campbell, the former Downing Street press secretary and now a chart-topping podcaster, with 1.1 million followers on X, is arguably Britain's best-known bagpiper and has not been shy in linking his piping to his mental health. As he said on the 2019 BBC documentary 'Alastair Campbell: Depression and Me':

> My brother Donald, who had schizophrenia, was a Glasgow University piper for 20-odd years. Since he and my dad died, I get this extraordinary connection with them through the pipes. Quite often I play laments and sometimes I'll be in tears. It's an emotional release. At other times, I get a nice, reflective feeling. And

playing with other people can give you a happy feeling. I get so much out of it.[37]

Concerted efforts are now beginning to be made to promote the health benefits of piping. The Piping for Health initiative, for example, was launched in 2023 by the King's Foundation and the National Piping Centre and offers an introduction to playing the chanter and the bagpipes, among other activities, to those suffering from lung conditions that hamper breathing. The Pibroch Network has taken another angle, working in partnership with the Scotland Singing for Health Network in an attempt to bring the mysterious joys of canntaireachd—sung piobaireachd—to people managing serious health conditions. And if the testimony of seventeen-year-old Katie Robertson from Carnoustie is anything to go by, the bagpipes can even save lives. Katie, who goes by the name 'the Wheeled Piper', is wheelchair-bound and suffers from chronic pain, scoliosis and arthritis but attributes her remarkable recovery from near organ failure to her piping and the effect it has on her lungs.[38] She does not seem to know the meaning of adversity: not only did she have a chanter specially made for her by G1 Reeds that allows her to play unencumbered in her wheelchair but she also skipped over the challenge of an immobile right index finger by learning to play with her hands reversed, so that her right hand pinky covers the E hole. For Katie, her piping has brought a sense of inclusion like never before: 'This is the community I get accepted in. I don't get accepted in other walks of life because I'm different.'[39]

Part of that acceptance is her membership of the National Youth Pipe Band of Scotland, and that, too, is a reminder of what pipe bands can do for young people. Stories abound of the positive effect of playing in a pipe band. Where money has been invested—as it has been at Preston Lodge High School in East Lothian, for instance, thanks to the Scottish Schools Pipes and Drums Trust—the results are quick and life-changing, as the Preston Lodge headteacher, Gavin Clark, has confirmed:

It is impossible to overestimate the impact that piping and drumming has had in Preston Lodge High School in recent years. The Preston Lodge Pipe Band has grown quickly from a tentative group of new players into the flourishing figurehead of our school and its community. Young people of all ages and abilities, across the primary and secondary sector, have benefited immeasurably from the skill development and self-esteem building that piping and drumming can provide.[40]

It's the individual stories that make the impact really come to life. One little girl from Dumfries, who started chanter tuition over Skype during lockdown through the South West Scotland Piping and Drumming Academy, was so shy to begin with that she hid behind the sofa. A year later, she was literally running into band practice. According to her parents, 'her whole behavioural pattern has changed'.[41] A fourteen-year-old boy with Down's Syndrome from Birmingham was facing considerable structural barriers in life, but his grandparents had heard about the academy's summer school and enrolled him, knowing he had a brilliant sense of rhythm. The boy enjoyed it so much, he came back the next year, and before long he was part of the drum corps of the Birmingham Irish Pipes and Drums. As the chair of the academy, Andy McCartney, puts it: 'Things like that you can't put a value on.'[42]

Numerous benefits have been reported for adults too. Though pipe bands are sometimes pejoratively likened to sports teams in their obsession with competitions, where they clearly do differ is in their intergenerational aspect, with old and young, and everything in between, playing together. It is also seen as a social leveller, uniting the accountant and the postal worker, the doctor and the builder, all geared towards one goal. The unity and discipline that brings is generally good for everyone, but it is especially good for those who've recently come out of highly structured organisations such as the military or the police, offering a healthy alternative to the structures they've left behind. The wider community benefits as well: the local pipe band's presence at gala days and festivals is often the high point of the day. Some bands make the decision not to compete at all, and thus service to the community becomes their fundamental *raison d'être*.

One thing that causes some concern is the drinking culture that still goes with pipe bands, and the same concern has been registered about the traditional music scene, with so much of it focused on pubs. But when it comes to the solo circuit, a definite change has been detected. A few decades ago, if you visited Oban for the

Argyllshire Gathering, the Tartan Tavern would be packed with people the night before, including competitors due to play the following morning, who would stumble back to their hotel rooms in the middle of the night rather the worse for wear. Now, the bar is deserted. There's a steely professionalism about the top solo performers of today. Though that's not necessarily always a good thing, it has meant that certain patterns of behaviour that were once common are now unheard of.

For some famous pipers of the past, a large measure of alcohol was simply part of their routine before going on stage. When one competitor in the 1990s found himself parched and without water before a performance, he looked around the competitors' backstage room and saw a fellow performer's water bottle. It looked to be half full of water. Feeling desperate, he took the bottle and drank a great gulp of it. It was down the hatch before he could do anything to remedy the fact that he'd just consumed about three shots of vodka. As Chapter 8 suggested, this reliance on alcohol was most common among those who were either serving soldiers or had left the army. There are not many of those around anymore at the highest level of the competition circuit, with army piping greatly reduced in numbers as it follows the general shrinkage of the military. That is sad in many ways, but the elimination of a booze-reliant culture cannot be a bad thing.

While that culture was still strong, the famous pipers of the day were almost all competing pipers. That is how you made a name for yourself. And here again the optimists, who would like to see a broader field of opportunity, can find fodder for their hope. Some of the most well-known pipers today are not competitors at all. I've mentioned a few of them already: Ross Ainslie, Ali Hutton, Brìghde Chaimbeul. That these musicians have commercialised their output has led to some uncomfortable observations about the disconnect between the communal folk world of the past, with its apparent resistance to the logic of capitalism, and the folk world of the present, where its marketing strategies and performance contexts place it 'easily within the context of neo-liberalism'.[43] But as Finlay MacDonald of the Piping Centre has pointed out, this now means that if you want to turn your love of the pipes into a career, you no longer have to join the army or even become a piping instructor.[44]

What's so exciting about the examples I've given is their unwillingness simply to rehash the tried and tested old favourites and their keenness to play with the tradition, though not abandon it. At first, when you watch a performance by the supergroup known as Treacherous Orchestra, of which Ainslie and Hutton are founding members, you might think a metal band has accidentally misplaced its classic instruments and taken up—with outstanding success—the classic folk instruments instead. With their black outfits and mosh-pit inducing riffs, it is incredibly hard to categorise their project. But as scholar and composer Meghan McAvoy has argued:

> Treacherous Orchestra can also be identified with a long-established aim within Scottish folk music: to recast the national in the context of modernity, using the motifs and signifiers of the tradition in order to continue the process of combining the indigenous with the modern, the local with the global, in a continually self-renewing process of tradition.[45]

Chaimbeul has been equally inventive but in an altogether different direction. Traditionally, the emphasis within bagpipe music falls upon what the chanter is doing, and the drones only really come into focus when they are out of tune and discordant. Chaimbeul's genius is to arrange her music in such a way that the luxurious texture of the smallpipe drones is as noticeable as the notes that are played on the chanter, creating a trance-like atmosphere that brings to mind eastern musical traditions while remaining distinctly connected to Chaimbeul's own Gaelic heritage.

In yet another direction, a band such as the Red Hot Chilli Pipers have proved—through their various appearances on primetime television and radio—that the bagpipes need not be a fringe instrument. Their music and attitude have not been without controversy, however. Why? Some suggest that their move away from the cultural fringe towards the cultural centre has only been made possible by a pitiful capitulation to the banalities of pop music, and that the Chilli Pipers' 'bagrock' sound is an abomination to an instrument that should naturally associate itself with the humanising arts, not with light entertainment for the masses. For one of the founding members of the band Stuart Cassells, however, the response to this is obvious and takes us back to the opening of the chapter:

Music is music at the end of the day and there's no such thing as right and wrong. There is good music and bad music but that's not the same. It can be to your taste or not to your taste. I don't mind if people don't like our music personally, or my style of playing. I suppose I was a generation after Fred Morrison, Gordon Duncan and Allan MacDonald who very much changed the way pipes were played by adopting a style similar to uillean [sic] pipes, and they weren't respected at all for that by their peers.[46]

Cassells' comparison between the reactions to what the Chilli Pipers have attempted to do and the reactions to what Gordon Duncan and like-minded peers attempted in the '90s invites an interesting question. Have the Chilli Pipers pioneered yet a new era for the pipes, or are they just an extension of what the previous generation opened up? And if through them we get a glimpse of the instrument's future, is that a cause for despair or for hope? As we'll see in our conclusion, it's only by looking at the global scene that we can gauge an answer to these questions and unpack their deeper implications.

* * *

One last word on Scotland before we do that. I suggested earlier that the legacies of Gordon Duncan and Martyn Bennett could be seen as useful guides to a healthy piping culture. They seem to show the need for an environment where those who play the instrument, and those who hear it, are open to the past, the present and the future in all their rich abundance all at once. Now that we have seen what a pessimist and an optimist might say to someone considering the health of the bagpipes in contemporary Scotland, where should our judgement fall?

I spoke to many people in preparation for this chapter, and it has to be acknowledged that there was not one among those who expressed concerns to me who was actually a pessimist overall. There was always balance, always much to be hopeful about. And even the concerns imply hope. The very fact that a sizable body of people *care* when funding isn't what it should be, *care* when pipe bands turn their music into sport, *care* when women aren't afforded the respect they deserve within the piping and drumming world, *care* when their art and their land fall victim to their own stereotypes—

this concern for the imperfections of the culture, when coupled with all the things that clearly *are* going well, suggests a community that is deeply attentive to the present and one that is as thoughtful and passionate about progress as it is about preservation.

So forget pessimism; forget optimism for that matter. Stick with realism. My sense is that the real, on balance, is good. It could be better, of course, and the drive to make it better must go on. But perfection in such human matters does not exist.

CONCLUSION

A GLOBAL INSTRUMENT WORTHY OF MYSTERY

One person who knows a fair bit about the state of bagpiping around the globe is Ross O'Connell Jennings, a young man of Irish and British ancestry with an international upbringing who calls himself 'The First Piper'. Having made it his ambition some years ago to be the first person to have played his Highland bagpipes in every country in the world, he has now, at the time of writing, piped in 115 out of the 193 UN countries. His very first destination was Tunisia in 2014. Speaking to someone on the flight over, he was told that a droneless, two-chantered bagpipe was in fact the national instrument of Tunisia and went by the name of *mezoued*. This was a surprise but not something Ross thought overly about for the rest of the flight.

Unsure of the public transport system, Ross decided to hire a car and spend some time driving around the country. But for every town he wished to enter, there was a police checkpoint. He initially thought it would be a good idea to wave to the police as he went by, in the hope he'd make a good impression and they'd wave him on through. Not so. It turned out to be a sure-fire way of getting pulled over. Knowing only a few words of Arabic, this was not a pleasurable prospect, all the more so because the policemen were inclined to be gruff and unfriendly. At one checkpoint, they were especially unwelcoming, going through Ross's stuff, demanding documentation, raising their voices. In the glove compartment, they discovered papers that showed the car registration to be out of date by two years. Now things were getting really uncomfortable, and there was no way that Ross could placate them. Or was there?

It was then that they discovered Ross's pipe case. Opening it, their faces changed. '*Mezoued! Mezoued!*' they started shouting. This,

183

Ross did understand. The men encouraged Ross to play, and he struck up his pipes, at which point the policemen erupted with joy. There was dancing, cries of glee and beaming smiles. All of a sudden, Ross was their best friend. After he finished playing, the policemen tossed back his car keys and bid him farewell with the utmost courtesy and warmth. Over the next few days, Ross discovered that, though the instrument was rather looked down upon by the urban elite, the *mezoued* was everywhere: on the televisions, on the radio, at social gatherings. For the people of Tunisia, this small droneless instrument was *the* bagpipe. They loved to hear the Highland bagpipe, that's for sure, but their minds were a million miles from John MacDonald of Inverness.

In many other countries, however, Ross has discovered that the Highland bagpipe seems to be better known than the indigenous pipes of the people. This is partly because the playing of indigenous pipes is often the preserve of ethnic minorities, who tend to be poorer than the dominant ethnicity or ethnicities and socially outcast to some extent. Of course, the impact of colonialism also bears much of the responsibility for the visibility of the Highland pipes, but it's also interesting to note that even in places where the pipes did not hang around as a cultural legacy, there's been a growing appetite to introduce them into the culture. A fascinating example of this is Nigeria, where pipe bands have been slowly on the rise ever since the presidency of Umaru Yar'Adua (2007–10), who'd been inspired by what he'd discovered in other countries. The next but one of his successors, Muhammadu Buhari, liked the instrument so much that he asked to be piped to the podium whenever he spoke in public. The pipe major of Scottish Power Nigeria, Chukwu Oba Kala, has praised the instrument's capacity to build 'team work and harmony' and revels in their ceremonial usefulness. The instrument has even been pressed into the service of state-building, with the repertoire consciously encompassing Christian and Islamic tunes, so much so that this classically martial instrument is now seen as a harbinger of peace.[1]

Interestingly, there does not seem to be an indigenous bagpipe in Nigeria, but according to Ross Jennings such a lack seems to be an exception not the rule. Despite the bagpipe's near-universal presence, the Highland form of the instrument can elicit the most remarkable responses, as it did in the Tunisian policemen. Some responses have been even more remarkable than theirs. In Bahrain— where the droneless jirba is the indigenous bagpipe—Ross was in his kilt and, having just piped for some locals, was about to get into the car when he was stopped by two women wearing niqabs, whose faces were thus covered except for their eyes. Seeing he had camera equipment, they pleaded with him to take a photo of them standing next to him. This was frowned upon within the culture, but Ross was with his aunt—who lives in Bahrain—and she encouraged him to go ahead and take the photo anyway. So he set up his tripod and camera and took the snap. The women were thrilled. As they were turning to leave, one of them turned back to Ross and grabbed him by his shirtsleeves. As if from a film scene, she pulled back her niqab, stared deep into his eyes and said, 'Remember my face', before disappearing back into the crowd. Ross's aunt summed up the moment well: 'I think you've just been flashed.'[2]

* * *

What emerges from all this is a pretty complex picture, a complexity that mirrors so much of what we've encountered in the instrument's history. As we've seen repeatedly, the minute you try to speak in uniform terms about the bagpipe you face problems, and the narrative all too easily becomes ahistorical. Ubiquity, particularity, multiplicity: this is the confusing concoction of words that blends deep into our awareness. But to register that global complexity is, I would say, a major step forward. The rise of organisations such as the Bagpipe Society and the International Bagpipe Organisation, founded in 1986 and 2012 respectively, has done the instrument a great service in this respect. Their journals and conferences have helped shift the focus away from mono-cultural narratives that have so long pervaded bagpipe speak, in which the whole story is reduced to Scotland and the Great Highland Bagpipe.

Even in this book, where Scotland has taken the focal point of the story, we have continually seen how a much wider international dimension presses itself upon the narrative, with so many of the most significant developments originating beyond Scotland itself— just think of the pioneering approach to women in piping taken by

Australia (a country that continues to produce innovators, such as the piper and experimental composer Lincoln Hilton), or the radical musicality that came out of Canada with the 78th Fraser Highlanders, or, one I have not yet mentioned, the first university degree course specifically devoted to the bagpipe, which was created at Carnegie Mellon University in Pittsburgh, United States, in 1985. In fact, America is particularly interesting in the story of the bagpipes, because so much of the country's awareness of bagpiping comes back, not to Scotland, but to Ireland, with the great processions of the St Patrick's Day celebrations. Indeed, one of the country's most famous pipe bands, the New York City Fire Department Emerald Society Pipes and Drums, was founded in 1962 from Irish rather than Scottish impulses.[3] The band's central role in responding to the terrorist attacks of 9/11 and dealing with the aftermath has endeared them to the nation and raised them to hero status. All of this is to say, the bagpipe's story, even when limited purely to the Great Highland Bagpipe, cannot be told with genuine integrity if it takes a purely Scottish focus.

The rise of social media is now making such narrow-mindedness truly hard to maintain. America is key here again. Arguably, at the time of writing, the most famous bagpiper in the world is not a Scotsman but an American woman. 'Ally the Piper' (real name Allyson Crowley-Duncan) came to prominence over TikTok, and though she plays the Great Highland Bagpipe and has competed to high levels on the solo and pipe band circuits, it is her reimagined versions of film themes and classic rock tunes for the bagpipes, even transposing their intricate guitar solos on to her chanter, that have captured the public's imagination. There is clearly a similarity between what Ally is doing and what the Red Hot Chilli Pipers have done before her, but Ally's approach seems to have been arrived at quite independently, and the range of her success online has taken matters to the next level. Her YouTube videos are gaining hundreds of thousands of views every day. She has over 3 million followers across her social media channels. How are we to account for this?

Despite the bagpipe's long connection to sex (see Chapter 1), Ally is probably one of the first pipers in history to have made the act of bagpiping sexy. She is not the only one, because another internet sensation, this time from India, known as The Snake

Charmer (real name Archy Jay), is simultaneously pulling the instrument into this light, and in her case, it's an electric, two-droned, dragon-headed bagpipe! In Ally's case, the short tartan skirts and tight bodices are undoubtedly part of the appeal for many of her viewers, as are her rhythmic dance moves. If such things were the only reason for her success, it might be tempting to write her off as superficial—though a marketing genius—and we might expect her success to be short-lived. But Ally is also an exceptional musician, a classically trained multi-instrumentalist and singer who not only understands music but has an intuitive feel for it. It is too early to say what kind of longevity her career will have, but if it's of significant length, it will be her musicianship that secures it. The question then becomes, what does her current success mean for the future of the instrument?

Principally, it means visibility for the bagpipes like never before. This visibility is tied to Ally's stated desire 'to break stereotypes about the bagpipes and introduce new audiences to the instrument'.[4] There is no doubt she is achieving this on an unprecedented scale, as her viewing statistics and the comments beneath her videos prove. For those who dislike her music, her success can still be considered a positive: opening people's eyes to the instrument will inevitably lead some, perhaps many, of her listeners to the established repertoire.

While it would be possible to see Ally as yet another innovator standing within a long tradition of innovation, there is one key difference, which could also apply to the Chilli Pipers and The Snake Charmer: that is, their apparent lack of rootedness in the piping music that came before them. Gordon Duncan may have riffed upon the music of AC/DC, but his bread and butter was the fast-paced reel and the leg-flaring jig. Given the weight that the past bears upon the instrument, it was Gordon's deep and audible connection to what preceded him that ensured the wider uptake of his music and his style of playing. Millions may be listening to Ally the Piper's music, but there are still very few other bagpipers doing anything like it, and that is likely to remain the case. It may be that the most globally popular pipers will always be the greatest outliers when it comes to the piping community itself.

This has a lot to do with that community's fierce loyalty to music that is more or less specific to a particular people or peoples, in contrast to rock and pop's transcendent disconnect from geographical boundaries (hence their global popularity). This also means that some of the most exciting and entertaining cross-cultural ventures are likely to remain sideshows in the consciousness of pipers themselves. The extraordinary output of American jazz musician Rufus Harley Jr (1936–2006), the first person to make bagpipes his principal instrument in that realm, is a case in point,[5] as is the music of Afro Celt Sound System, which notably includes the Gaelic hip-hop artist and bagpiper Griogair Labhruidh. They've had popularity, absolutely, but such ventures will never hold the centre ground. Their rarity is part of the enjoyment, of course; few would want such performers to be ten a penny.

Precedent truly does weigh heavily upon the instrument and will to a large extent determine its future course. Psychology plays an important role here. To learn the instrument, to step into its community of performers, is to load oneself, consciously or unconsciously, with a baggage that is very hard to shake off. This is surely partly to do with the bagpipe's tendency to link itself so closely with the identity of a people. When someone deviates from the norm, fellow performers can feel that the very roots of their being have been unsettled, and the defences can go up. When Pipes|Drums magazine posted a YouTube interview with Ally the Piper in March 2023 with the title 'A Conversation with Ally the Piper, the World's Most Famous Piping Performer', a comment was posted beneath by the principal channel for Scottish traditional music, handsupfortrad. It reads: 'The most famous piper in the world? Don't think so …'[6] Such blank denial in the face of the demonstrable facts is fascinating. It's as if the most famous piper *has* to fit the pre-established pattern or else their fame must be a chimera.

Identity is unsettled for further reasons still. It is not just that the pipes so often become synonymous with a people but that an individual set of pipes can become, in a sense, synonymous with a player. There is something about the bodily connections between the piper and their pipes—the arm tucked so tightly around the bag, the blowpipe in the mouth, the drones expansive on shoulder, arm or lap—that blurs the boundaries between the performer and the performed. And with the instrument so often composed out of the remains of another living being—whether goat, sheep or whatever—its earthy materialness only heightens the sense of connection. I have heard devotees of the instrument say their music is their body, and that piping is not a hobby but a way of life, as if they live *through* their bagpipes. For many, criticism of their playing is received as a criticism of their being. And when they witness others using their pipes in a way that is unrecognisable to them, it's probably not an exaggeration to say that it's like they've witnessed an act of abuse.

If these intimacies felt at both communal and individual levels are sometimes considered to be under threat by novel approaches, the intimacy between piping teacher and pupil is also viewed as vulnerable to recent developments. Past chapters have shown just how vital that relationship has been within the piper's psyche—from Josef Režný, who prized beyond all measure the 'family where the tradition is passed on from the older generation to the younger ones', to Angus MacPherson, who proudly boasted of having 'a direct line with the MacCrimmons, for now at least five generations'. The immense popularity of online learning platforms such as the Dojo University (established 2011) and the easy online accessibility of prize-winning performances have now started to disrupt these human to human exchanges. Grey is again insightful here. As he sees it, many contemporary pipers are

> not connecting with a personality and getting inspired and engaged by that teacher and so they're being very opportunistic, they're simply following recordings of the last Gold Medal winners. So they don't get those touches, those little things that take a player from being very good to excellent. I think technology has created this swathe of very good pipers but there are so few people that slavishly visit a teacher every week and talk about piping things and play through tunes and get inspired by that teacher. I think that is generally missing due to technology and modern twenty-first-century life.[7]

But on the flip side, technological advance has also meant that the bagpipes have never been so popular, with more pipers than ever before. It is a hugely exciting time to be involved in piping: the possibilities for collaboration, the instrumental diversity, the accessibility of the music would have been unthinkable just a couple of generations ago. When it comes to the Great Highland Bagpipe,

189

people not connected in any obvious way to Scotland or its diaspora communities are picking up the instrument and giving it a go. Grey again, this time on Canada:

> I can feel the piping culture changing in Ontario and, from recent trips to Vancouver, in British Columbia too, where we're seeing more non-Scots or people that don't have Scots ancestry playing. We're seeing Sikhs coming in, South Asian folks and people from communities that are more reflective of the general immigration waves. Now it's small, but it shows promise.[8]

As for other indigenous bagpipes, there seems to have been no abating in popularity since the era of revival in the 1970s and '80s. People who want to buy a Galician *gaita* or a set of uilleann pipes are sometimes having to join waiting lists that can stretch up to six years.[9] Carlos Núñez has achieved pop star status with his Galician pipes; the French Navy's Breton pipe band can generate 3.8 million views for a single video on X;[10] the Latvian band Auļi, featuring six bagpipers, five on Latvia's native dūda and one on the Estonian torupill, can gather 7.5 million views on YouTube for their collaboration with—most superb of choices—the Mongolian throat singer Batzorig Vaanchig.[11] That at least fifty of those views have come from my mesmerised five-year-old son hardly undermines the point: there is a hunger for piping that tears up the kilt-wearing clichés.

Technology also wards against a narrow taste in music. We rarely now consume music album by album. With Spotify and YouTube, it's more like a pick and mix—a track here from one artist, a track there from another—so that it would take a concerted effort to sustain a rigidness of taste. Gary West reports that he once received mounds of messages complaining about the choice of tunes for *Pipeline* from conservative-minded pipers who disliked what they termed 'plonky plonky' music.[12] In the programme's latter years, however, and now in his new podcast 'Enjoy Your Piping!', such messages have all but dried up. The prevailing approach among those who demur today, he says, is to say, 'that's your taste, it's not mine, but you're more than welcome to listen to what you like'. The changes to the way we consume music have played a large part in this.

With the internet so key in modern piping, does that threaten the myth-making capacity of the instrument? If the wealth of stories that sprung up around the MacCrimmons is anything to go by, geographical particularity and human to human contact has much to do with that capacity. The internet may perpetuate established myths, but insofar as it pulls players and listeners into an indeterminate and impersonal space, it is unlikely to create abiding new ones. But in reality, myths have not been generated on any significant scale for many decades, if not centuries, and their heyday had much to do with the oral nature of past cultures, who had storytelling at their heart. You might think that loss of legend a good thing, taking us ever further into the realm of 'truth'. But there is a deeper truth behind the legends. The bagpipe's readiness to accumulate myth suggests that the instrument speaks of mystery, of a capacity to transcend the analysable, of a tendency to escape our categories. One way of putting it is to say there is something *excessive* about the pipes; not just in their noise, but in their very essence.

Perhaps this explains, in part, the bagpipe's continued potency as an instrument of protest. It must be said that this has actually not been a noticeable feature of the instrument in modern Scotland. Though bagpipes are often played at independence rallies, they are not considered the preserve of one particular political identity—it is the national instrument, not the nationalists' instrument. The Scottish National Party itself has wisely eschewed the bagpipes and other stereotypical Scottish signifiers, knowing it would only fuel the derision of their detractors, who would read the invocation of such symbols as a lack of political seriousness. But the situation is, and has been, very different elsewhere. In Ireland, the large mouth-blown pipe—whether the pipe patented as the Brian Boru pipe with a complete chromatic scale, or what is essentially the Great Highland Bagpipe, or again pipes with only two drones, a form which later became synonymous with the term 'warpipe'—was only really introduced into the culture at the advent of the twentieth century (though, of course, as we've seen, a version of it had been played centuries earlier in Ireland). But, once established, the instrument swiftly took on social, political and military significance in the context of the struggles around English rule; in the words of the Irish Pipe Band Association, the performances of pipe bands, especially in the years immediately preceding the Easter Rising of 1916, 'quite literally, mobilised national identity'.[13] It was in fact the Great Pipe, not the uilleann pipes, that 'became the instrument on which the ideological movement of cultural nationalism was most readily articulated'.[14] Interestingly, the origins of one of Ireland's most celebrated contemporary bands, St Laurence O'Toole, can be traced back to these days of ferment.[15]

This politicising of the pipes has carried on into more recent times. In Tunisia, the *mezoued* players were some of the few musicians who dared to sing, in a time of general censorship, about the harshness of life under the dictatorships of Bourguiba and Ben Ali (1956–2011).[16] In Galicia, the song '¡Eu quero ser gaiteiro!'—'I want to be a bagpiper!'—by Os Diplomáticos de Monte Alto, which came out in 1995, has become 'a war cry of sorts'.[17] In Palestine, despite Britain's own role in creating the problems in the first place, members of the local Scout troop pipe bands—relics of the British occupation during the First World War—'insist the bagpipes' Scottish heritage translates perfectly to the Palestinian struggle for their own independence'.[18] The bagpipe's particular suitability in these contexts is not simply to do with sheer aural power but with the unruly associative web that opens up when the listener encounters the instrument, a web that seems to brook no domestication. It's as if the pipes have the ability to say: 'You, the authorities, are dealing here with something you cannot control; this is an instrument that speaks for us as a people in a way that cannot be brought under your legislation.'

It is this strength of feeling that it evokes that makes the instrument so fascinating. And it is not only the politically oppressed who feel it keenly. The *only* thing for which Queen Elizabeth II is known to have broken the rules of the constitution is the bagpipe. The British monarch is categorically not to intervene in matters political, yet it was thanks to her direct approach to George Osborne, Chancellor of the Exchequer between 2010 and 2016, that the Army School of Bagpipe Music and Highland Drumming did not face major financial cuts during that decade.[19] It's only too well known that some people can't stand the instrument. Just recently, I was at a wedding in England that featured a piper, where I heard the church warden asking: 'When will the music of the pipes begin, if you can call it music?' But the opposite reaction is far more common. The actress Miriam Margolyes, whose father was Scottish, puts her finger on it when she says: 'The music of the bagpipe carries such emotion, it speaks to you … Oh when I hear that sound my heart sings, and that's what you want when you listen to music.'[20] A final quote from Grey feels apposite here:

> It's funny that most of the pipes that anyone hears in the world are not in tune and yet people still love them. What other instrument can be so loud? It's the same as a pneumatic drill. What other instrument can be played out of tune and people still love it? I mean that is black magic at its loudest and most deep and mystical.[21]

I think that's part of the reason why, if I can make an admission, I have found this conclusion so hellishly difficult to write. Only now, as I bring these paragraphs to a close, do I understand my struggles. I am convinced, more than ever, after all these many chapters, that the bagpipe transcends our capacity to speak of it; or, to put it another way, that it brings us to the point of speechlessness. Of clean definitions, of linear histories, of easy explanations, there is none. That is the reason, even after the scholars have cleared the myths away, that the bagpipe retains its romance. Its history, its connotations, are anything but prosaic. For all the music of the instrument, for all the Great Pipe's excessive noise, this book must therefore ultimately end—if it's not too grand to say it—in the silence of mystery. If its pages have advanced your knowledge of the bagpipe to some important extent, that is excellent; but it is even more important that they have stamped upon you a deeper sense of unknowing. This strange animal-like conflation of skin and wood will never be fully understood. It can only lead, finally, to wonder.

NOTES

INTRODUCTION: MORE THAN AN INSTRUMENT

1. 'Angus MacPherson, Invershin: A 1957 Visit with a Great Tradition-Bearer', Dunaber Music, available at http://www.dunaber.com/2022/07/15/angus-macpherson-invershin-a-1957-visit-with-a-great-tradition-bearer/#more-5219, last accessed 20 August 2024. For a full account of MacPherson's life, see his autobiography *A Highlander Looks Back* (Oban: Oban Times, 1955).

2. Thankfully, I don't think the MacPherson quote in question can be accused of carrying the 'powerful strain of bookish mysticism' that the scholar William Donaldson identifies in him. See Donaldson, *The Highland Pipe and Scottish Society 1750–1950: Transmission, Change and the Concept of Tradition* (Edinburgh: John Donald, 2008), p. 191.

3. The impact of James Macpherson's eighteenth-century 'rediscovery' of the ancient poetry of Ossian made a similar impact on the perception of Scotland and, as we'll see, on the understanding of the bagpipe and its music.

4. It would be easy to set Scott's novel writing in opposition to the activities of Scotland's Enlightenment figures, but his 'historical obsessions and antiquarian curiosity' actually aligned him with them. See David Allan, *Virtue, Learning and the Scottish Enlightenment* (Edinburgh: Edinburgh University Press, 2020), p. 10. See also Murray Pittock, 'Enlightenment, Romanticism and the Scottish Canon: Cosmopolites or Narrow Nationalists?', in Gerard Carruthers and Liam McIlvanney (eds), *The Cambridge Companion to Scottish Literature* (Cambridge: Cambridge University Press, 2012), pp. 86–102.

5. Marinell Ash, *The Strange Death of Scottish History* (Edinburgh: Ramsay Head, 1980). See also Colin Kidd, *Subverting Scotland's Past: Scottish Whig Historians and the Creation of an Anglo-British Identity 1689–1830* (Cambridge: Cambridge University Press, 1993), which sheds 'light from an eighteenth-century vantage point on the dissolution of Scottish historical confidence in the nineteenth century' (p. 7).

6. See Murray Pittock, *The Road to Independence? Scotland since the Sixties* (London: Reaktion Books, 2008), p. 22.

7. See especially William Laird Manson, *The Highland Bagpipe: Its History,*

195

Literature, and Music, with Some Account of the Traditions, Superstitions, and Anecdotes Relating to the Instrument and Its Tunes (Paisley: A. Gardner, 1901); Alexander Duncan Fraser, *Some Reminiscences and the Bagpipe* (Falkirk: Wm. J. Hay, 1907); and William H. Grattan Flood, *The Story of the Bagpipe* (London: Walter Scott Publishing Co., 1911).

8. Vivien Williams, 'The Cultural History of the Bagpipe in Britain, 1680–1840', PhD thesis, University of Glasgow, September 2013, p. 10, available at https://theses.gla.ac.uk/5085/1/2013williamsphd.pdf, last accessed 9 February 2024. The literature review within her Introduction (pp. 11–20) is excellent and highly relevant to the issues in question here.

9. The works of Roderick Cannon, Hugh Cheape and William Donaldson typify the approach. The earlier figures of Anthony Baines and Francis Collinson were, perhaps, the transitional figures between the two phases.

10. Quoted in Hugh Cheape, *Bagpipes: A National Collection of a National Instrument* (Edinburgh: NMSE, 2008), p. 75. Wilson McLeod, *Divided Gaels: Gaelic Cultural Identities in Scotland and Ireland, c.1200–c.1650* (Oxford: Oxford University Press, 2004).

11. Williams, 'Cultural History of the Bagpipe in Britain', p. 16.

12. Important books/catalogues that keep a wider perspective throughout are Anthony Baines, *Bagpipes* (Oxford: Oxford University Press, 1960) and Zoltán G. Szabó, *A Duda: The Bagpipe*, Catalogue of the Museum of Ethnography 9 (Budapest: Museum of Ethnography, 2004). On European piping specifically, see Bayerischer Landesverein Für Heimatplege E.V., *Der Dudelsack in Europa* (Munich: n.p., 1996). The work of the Bagpipe Society, founded in 1986, and the International Bagpipe Organisation, established in 2012, have done, and continue to do, marvellous work to give non-Scottish piping traditions their proper due. Valuable, too, is the collection of International Bagpipe Festival lectures given between 1994 and 2002 and edited by Irena Novotnà, titled *Mezinàrodní Dudàckà Sympozia 1994–2002* (Strakonice: Muzeum středního Pootaví Strakonice a MěKS Strakonice, 2004).

13. Michael is also a prolific composer and wrote one of my favourite hornpipes, the supremely titled 'Sergeant Malkie Bow's Consternation'. In addition, he is the current Pipe Major of the grade 1 pipe band, the 78th Fraser Highlanders.

14. My thanks to Vivien Williams for reminding me in conversation of the riches that a contemporary history of the pipes would reveal.

15. As told to me by Sir Charles Fraser, to whom Menuhin said these words in the early 1970s. The description also appears without attribution in Seumas MacNeill, *Piobaireachd: Classical Music of the Highland Bagpipe* (Edinburgh: BBC, 1968), p. 18; it is, however, attributed to Ian Whyte, the founder of the Scottish Symphony Orchestra, in MacNeill and Frank

Richardson's *Piobaireachd and Its Interpretation* (Edinburgh: John Donald, 1987), p. 22. The virtuoso violinist Jascha Heifetz once heard the tune being played by Pipe Major Robert Reid in Glasgow and visited him the next day to ask if he could hear 'this wonderful music' again. See Alistair Campsie, *The MacCrimmon Legend: The Madness of Angus Mackay* (Edinburgh: Canongate, 1980), p. 84.

1. ORIGINS: FROM THE PROFANE TO THE SACRED AND BACK AGAIN

1. Available at https://www.youtube.com/watch?v=fBwwWFGd9qE, last accessed 14 June 2024.
2. Cassandre Balosso-Bardin, 'Hidden Bagpipes of The Met', The Met, available at https://www.metmuseum.org/perspectives/articles/2023/3/hidden-bagpipes#footnote1, last accessed 19 April 2023.
3. See Hugh Cheape, 'The Bagpipes: Perceptions of a National Instrument', PhD thesis, University of Edinburgh, 2008, p. 108, available at https://era.ed.ac.uk/handle/1842/2591, last accessed 22 April 2024.
4. 'The Goat Bagpipes with Huge Horns—gaida gajda гајда гайда Pajdusko oro', YouTube, 15 April 2010, available at https://www.youtube.com/watch?v=ImtjPPBSr8I, last accessed 26 November 2024.
5. Karl Partridge, 'The Maltese Żaqq: Introduction', *Chanter* (Winter 2016), available at https://www.bagpipesociety.org.uk/articles/2016/chanter/winter/maltese-zaqq/, last accessed 31 May 2023. '"If you want to be a Piper …": Celebrating the Duda', *Common Stock* 30, no. 1 (June 2003), pp. 39–46.
6. Michael Peter Vereno, *The Voice of the Wind: A Linguistic History of Bagpipes* (Lincoln, England: International Bagpipe Organisation, 2021), p. 158.
7. Ibid., p. 159.
8. Michael Peter Vereno, 'Bagpipes in Austria: A Story of Diversity', *Chanter* (Summer 2016), available at https://www.bagpipesociety.org.uk/articles/2016/chanter/summer/bagpipes-in-austria/, last accessed 5 February 2024.
9. Hugh Cheape, *The Book of the Bagpipe* (Belfast: Appletree Press, 1999), p. 30.
10. Vereno, *Voice of the Wind*, p. 22.
11. Ibid., pp. 13–25.
12. Dio Chrysostom, *Logoi*, 71.9.
13. See, for instance, Balosso-Bardin, 'Hidden Bagpipes of The Met' and Cheape, *Book of the Bagpipe*, p. 30.
14. Tacitus, *Annals*, 15.39; Suetonius, *The Life of Nero*, 38; Cassius Dio, *Roman History*, 62b.18.
15. Vereno, *Voice of the Wind*, pp. 38–9.

16. This lack of clear differentiation continues until perhaps as late as the thirteenth century, so to use the term 'bagpipe' to designate an entirely separate instrument prior to this date is probably anachronistic, though we will continue to use it here to indicate that we are speaking of a pipe with bag scenario.

17. Ibid., p. 29.

18. See Vivien Williams, 'Cultural History of the Bagpipe in Britain', p. 28. See also Emanuel Winternitz, 'Bagpipes and Hurdy-Gurdies in Their Social Setting', *The Metropolitan Museum of Art Bulletin* 2, no. 1 (1943), pp. 56–83, at p. 61.

19. Vereno, *Voice of the Wind*, pp. 27–8.

20. See Cheape, 'Bagpipes: Perceptions of a National Instrument', pp. 107–8. See also Henry George Farmer, *A History of Music in Scotland* (London: Hinrichsen, 1947) for a full account of the Islamic influence on European music.

21. Quoted in Vereno, *Voice of the Wind*, p. 59.

22. For an example of abundant instrumental variety, see the E codex of the El Escorial manuscript of the thirteenth century *Cantigas de Santa Maria*, one of the largest collections of solo songs from the Middle Ages.

23. Cheape, *Book of the Bagpipe*, p. 32.

24. See G. Fenwick Jones, 'Wittenwiler's "Becki" and the Medieval Bagpipe', *The Journal of English and Germanic Philology* 48, no. 2 (1949), pp. 209–28.

25. Kathleen L. Scott, 'Sow-and-Bagpipe Imagery in the Miller's Portrait', *The Review of English Studies* 18, no. 71 (1967), pp. 287–90, at 289.

26. https://twitter.com/MxComan/status/1049224835069595649/photo/1, last accessed 31 May 2023.

27. Isambard Wilkinson, 'Visions of Hell Prove Bigger Draw than Paradise in Bosch Masterpiece', *The Times*, available at https://www.thetimes.co.uk/article/visions-of-hell-prove-bigger-draw-than-paradise-in-bosch-masterpiece-cc6x3ppx9, last accessed 26 July 2023.

28. For a selection of images, see Williams, 'Cultural History of the Bagpipe in Britain', pp. 79–80.

29. On Burns' complex relationship to the pipes see Vivien Williams, 'The National Poet and the National Instrument', Bagpipe News, 25 January 2024, available at https://bagpipe.news/2024/01/25/robert-burns-and-the-bagpipe/, last accessed 20 December 2024.

30. Ian Pittaway, '"The berray develes officers": Minstrels and the Medieval Church', Early Music Muse, available at https://earlymusicmuse.com/minstrels-and-the-medieval-church/, last accessed 2 June 2023.

31. Ian Bostridge, *Schubert's Winter Journey: Anatomy of an Obsession* (London: Faber & Faber, 2015), pp. 477–8.

32. David Stephens, 'History at the Margins: Bagpipers in Medieval Manuscripts', *History Today* 39 (August 1989), pp. 42–3.

33. 'The Nativity: Duc de Berry Paintings', Jesus-Story, available at https://www.jesus-story.net/nativity/, last accessed 28 July 2023.

34. Jürgen Müller, 'Albrecht Dürer's Peasant Engravings: A Different *Laocoön*, or the Birth of Aesthetic Subversion in the Spirit of the Reformation', *Journal of Historians of Netherlandish Art* 3, no. 1 (Winter 2011), available at DOI: 10.5092/jhna.2011.3.1.2, last accessed 28 July 2023.

35. Incidentally, the vulgarity of the bagpipes, and their association with male genitalia, would have been obvious to anyone in Germany familiar with Sebastian Brandt's satirical allegory *Ship of Fools* of 1494, in which a Fool is depicted blowing away on his phallic bagpipes while a lute and a harp lie unused on the ground, symbolising his neglect of the intellectual and spiritual dimensions of music

36. For a fine selection of Bruegel's bagpipes, see 'Bagpipe Paintings: The Bruegel Files', Prydein, available at https://www.prydein.com/pipes/paintings/brueghel/brueghelspage.html, last accessed 30 May 2024.

2. GETTING TO SCOTLAND: RESISTING NATIONAL BOUNDARIES

1. 'Josef Režný: A písničky žijí dál', YouTube, 4 March 2012, available at https://www.youtube.com/watch?v=KmBZQsyzxQU, last accessed 5 February 2024. Scots, when they see this, may be reminded of Calum Maclean and Hamish Henderson, who carried out similar activities in Scotland across the twentieth century.

2. Mike Patterson, 'Strakonice, Where the Pipes Play', *Chanter* (Spring 2016), available at https://www.bagpipesociety.org.uk/articles/2016/chanter/spring/strakonice-where-the-pipes-play/, last accessed 5 February 2024.

3. Michael Peter Vereno, 'Bagpipes in Austria: A Story of Diversity', *Chanter* (Summer 2016), available at https://www.bagpipesociety.org.uk/articles/2016/chanter/summer/bagpipes-in-austria/, last accessed 5 February 2024.

4. I am discounting a single reference to a 'chorus', which some scholars translate as a droneless bagpipe, in the twelfth-century Latin of the churchman Giraldus Cambrensis, as the meaning of this remains highly contested.

5. On the Skirling date, see Pete Stewart, 'Scotland's Oldest Piper?', available at https://lbps.net/j3site/index.php/history/carvings/314-scotland-s-oldest-piper, last accessed 10 July 2024.

6. See Cassandre Balosso-Bardin, 'A Short Overview of the Bagpipes from

the Iberian Peninsula', *Chanter* (Summer 2017), available at https://
www.bagpipesociety.org.uk/articles/2017/chanter/summer/iberian-
overview/, and Susana Morneno Fernández, 'Gaitas-de-fole in Portugal
and Their Connection to Galicia', *Chanter* (Summer 2017), available at
https://www.bagpipesociety.org.uk/articles/2017/chanter/summer/
gaitas-de-fole/, last accessed 22 July 2024. The idea that these pipes and
the Highland pipes are connected through an 'Atlantic corridor' is
explored in Cheape, 'Bagpipes: Perceptions of a National Instrument',
p. 35 and his article 'Celtic Connections on an Atlantic Corridor', *Piping
Times* 67, no. 5 (February 2015), pp. 37–45.

7. Jenny Wormald, *Court, Kirk, and Community: Scotland 1470–1625*
(Edinburgh: Edinburgh University Press, 2018), p. 228.

8. Kylie Murray, 'The European History of Medieval and Renaissance
Scotland: A Post-Brexit Reflection', Medium, available at https://
medium.com/european-union-and-disunion/the-european-history-of-
medieval-and-renaissance-scotland-a-post-brexit-reflection-fa055cdab-
d4b, last accessed 23 February 2024.

9. Wormald, *Court, Kirk, and Community*, p. 69.

10. Ibid., pp. 69–70.

11. Roderick D. Cannon, 'What Can We Learn about Piobaireachd?', *British
Journal of Ethnomusicology* 4 (1995), pp. 1–15, at pp. 11–12. See also
Allan MacDonald, 'The Relationship between Pibroch and Gaelic Song:
Its Implications on the Performance Style of the Pibroch Urlar', p. 10,
available at https://www.cl.cam.ac.uk/~rja14/musicfiles/manu-
scripts/allanmacdonald/, last accessed 16 April 2024.

12. I'm grateful to Hugh Cheape for sharing with me the talk he gave to the
Royal Society of Edinburgh in April 2023 entitled '"The folk who did
all the business"—*a' mhuinntir do rinn an t-seirbhis uile*: Revisiting the Past
in the Islands', where he points out John of Fordun's introduction of
this concept.

13. Wormald, *Court, Kirk, and Community*, pp. 46–8. Examples of this type
of flow in operation can be found in Martin MacGregor, 'The Campbells:
Lordship, Literature, and Liminality', *Textual Cultures* 7, no. 1 (2012),
pp. 121–57.

14. T. M. Devine, 'Preface', *The Scottish Historical Review* 73 (1994),
pp. 1–3.

15. For an excellent early summary of this topic, see Derick S. Thomson,
'Gaelic Learned Orders and Literati in Medieval Scotland', *Scottish
Studies* 12 (1968), pp. 57–78, at p. 75.

16. See especially Hugh Cheape, 'Traditional Origins of the Piping
Dynasties', in his *Bagpipes*, pp. 57–77. The essay was first presented at
the RSAMD Research Seminar on 31 May 2007. It can also be found in

Joshua Dickson (ed.), *The Highland Bagpipe: Music, History, Tradition* (Farnham, Surrey: Ashgate, 2009), pp. 97–126.

17. Iain MacInnes, 'The Highland Bagpipe: The Impact of the Highland Societies of London and Scotland, 1781–1844', M. Litt diss., University of Edinburgh, 1988, p. 5, available at https://www.cl.cam.ac.uk/~rja14/musicfiles/manuscripts/macinnes/imthesis1.pdf, last accessed 22 April 2024.

18. Samuel Johnson and James Boswell, *A Journey to the Western Islands of Scotland*, and *The Journal of a Tour to the Hebrides* (New York: Everyman's Library, 2002), p. 86.

19. Cheape, *Bagpipes*, p. 61. Cheape is conscious, however, of the dangers of over-emphasising the unitary nature of the relationship, dangers noted especially by Wilson McLeod in his *Divided Gaels: Gaelic Cultural Identities in Scotland and Ireland, c.1200–c.1650* (Oxford: Oxford University Press, 2004). Note, too, that pipers could be bards as well. See MacInnes, 'Highland Bagpipe', p. 10.

20. The letter can be found in Henry Mackenzie, 'Report of the Committee of the Highland Society of Scotland Appointed to Inquire into the Nature and Authenticity of the Poems of Ossian' (Edinburgh, 1805), appendix no. I, p. 6.

21. Trevor-Roper's claims first received wide recognition through his chapter 'The Invention of Tradition: The Highland Tradition of Scotland', in Eric Hobsbawm and Terence Ranger (eds), *The Invention of Tradition* (Cambridge: Cambridge University Press, 1983), pp. 15–42.

22. William Ferguson, 'Review of *The Invention of Scotland: Myth and History*, by H. Trevor-Roper & J. J. Cater', *The Scottish Historical Review* 90, no. 229 (April 2011), pp. 166–9, at p. 166. To 'prove' his point, Trevor-Roper deconstructs the celebrated Scottish humanist George Buchanan's sixteenth-century account of the ancient Whig constitution of Scotland, James Macpherson's eighteenth-century 'rediscovery' of the ancient poetry of Ossian and the Hay Allen brothers' (or, as they wished to be called, Sobieski Stewarts') nineteenth-century assertions concerning the antiquity of traditional Highland dress, notably the origins of the kilt and clan tartans. Each is found guilty of gross mythologising.

23. See Roger A. Mason, 'Review of *The Identity of the Scottish Nation: An Historic Quest*, by W. Ferguson', *The Scottish Historical Review* 79, no. 208 (2000), pp. 240–2, at p. 241.

24. Editor's Foreword to Hugh Trevor-Roper, *The Invention of Scotland: Myth and History* (New Haven: Yale University Press, 2008), p. xiv.

25. Quoted in John G. Gibson, *Traditional Gaelic Bagpiping 1745–1945* (Montreal: McGill–Queen's University Press, 1998), p. 140.

26. Cheape, *Bagpipes*, p. 61.
27. Ibid.
28. Cheape, 'Celtic Connections on an Atlantic Corridor'.
29. Winternitz, 'Bagpipes and Hurdy-Gurdies', p. 62.
30. 'History of the Uilleann Pipes', NPU, available at https://pipers.ie/about/history/?_gl=1*aikbew*_up*MQ..*_ga*NDYzNTg4MzczLjE3MjExNDQ3MTQ.*_ga_8BBP57V9FE*MTcyMTE0NDcxMy4xLjAuMTcyMTE0NDcxMy4wLjAuMA, last accessed 16 July 2024. See also: 'A Statute of the Fortieth Year of King Edward III., Enacted in a Parliament Held in Kilkenny, A.D. 1367, before Lionel Duke of Clarence, Lord Lieutenant of Ireland', Celt, Article XV, available at https://celt.ucc.ie/published/T300001–001.html, last accessed 12 June 2024.
31. There is a reference to '[m]ouths of harps and bags and pipes' in the fifteenth-century manuscript the *Second Battle of Moytura*, though John Purser says this document 'is clearly a great deal older'. See Purser, *Scotland's Music: A History of the Traditional and Classical Music of Scotland from Early Times to the Present Day* (Edinburgh: Mainstream Publishing, 1992), p. 75. In terms of material evidence from the sixteenth century, one is a wood carving of a piper that belonged to Woodstock Castle, County Kilkenny; the other is a picture of a young man playing the pipes that was drawn in the margin of a missal once belonging to the Abbey of Rosgall, County Kildare. See 'History of the Uilleann Pipes'.
32. Craig Williamson, *The Old English Riddles of the Exeter Book* (Chapel Hill: University of North Carolina Press, 1977), pp. 86–7.
33. This is Vivien Williams' translation of 'cuidam garcioni cum una bagepipa pipanti coram rege'. See Williams, 'Cultural History of the Bagpipe in Britain', p. 36.
34. Ibid.
35. Cheape, *Book of the Bagpipe*, p. 28.
36. Geoffrey Chaucer, *The Riverside Chaucer*, ed. Larry Dean Benson (Oxford: Oxford University Press, 2008), p. 32.
37. *General Prologue*, ll.560–1.
38. Scott, 'Sow-and-Bagpipe Imagery in the Miller's Portrait', p. 289. See also Edward A. Block, 'Chaucer's Millers and Their Bagpipes', *Speculum* 29, no. 2 (1954), pp. 239–43. The absurdity and cacophony of the Miller is heightened in the Ellesmere manuscript of c. 1405, compiled five years after Chaucer's death. Here, the Miller is shown blowing away at his bagpipes while astride a horse, which, as any player of the instrument will tell you, would not be conducive to a sweet and steady sound. Despite this, when a company of the 91st Regiment (the Argyll and Sutherland Highlanders) was converted into a mounted infantry com-

pany in South Africa in 1883, their piper was no exception to this equestrian turn. He made the newspapers when the public got wind of his horseback playing. See C. A. Malcolm, *The Piper in Peace and War* (London: Hardwicke Press, 1993), p. 176. Today, Oman and Pakistan can boast of camel-mounted military bands. See Chapter 6.

39. *General Prologue*, II.552–6.

40. Cheape, *Book of the Bagpipe*, p. 42, and Vivien Williams, 'Bagpipe Bandits: How the English Blew Scotland's National Instrument First', The Conversation, available at https://theconversation.com/bagpipe-bandits-how-the-english-blew-scotlands-national-instrument-first-55403, last accessed 17 June 2024.

41. Sandra Sider, *Handbook of Life in Renaissance Europe* (Oxford: Oxford University Press, 2007), p. 169.

42. F. W. Galpin, *Old English Instruments of Music* (London: Methuen, 1965), p. 131. See also R. D. Cannon, 'The Bagpipe in Northern England', *Folk Music Journal* 2, no. 2 (1971), pp. 127–47.

43. Mike O'Connor, 'Altrarnun Revisited: Some Notes on Bagpipe Iconography in Cornwall', Cornish National Music Archive, available at https://cornishnationalmusicarchive.co.uk/content/altarnun-revisited-some-notes-on-bagpipe-iconography-in-cornwall/, last accessed 8 March 2024.

44. A caution often repeated by James Merryweather—see, for example, the opening paragraphs of his essay 'Henry Halewood Bagpiper and Liverpool Town Wait 1571–1589', *Chanter* (Spring 2004), pp. 18–20.

45. Iain MacInnes, 'Taking Stock: Lowland and Border Piping in a Highland World', in Dickson, *Highland Bagpipe*, pp. 169–91, at p. 172.

46. This is Pete Stewart's view, as expressed in 'Once Upon a Time in the Lowlands', *Piping Today*, no. 21 (April 2006), pp. 26–9, at p. 27. See Pete Stewart, *The Day It Daws* (Leicestershire: White House Tune Books, 2005), p. 3.

47. Thomas Dickson (ed.), *Accounts of the Lord High Treasurer of Scotland, Volume 1: A.D. 1473–1498* (Edinburgh: HM General Register House, 1877), pp. 115, 180, 362, 375, 383.

48. There is at least one earlier reference. The 1487 Canongate burgh records of Edinburgh mention 'the commoun pyperis of the Toune'. John MacKay, *History of the Burgh of the Canongate* (Edinburgh, 1900), p. 73. See also MacInnes, 'Taking Stock', p. 178.

49. But note this from Pete Stewart: 'One of the most revealing tunes I came across in terms of the beginnings of what we now think of as the Lowland piping repertoire is from a bass viol manuscript of about 1630 in the Cheshire Records Office. It includes about nine tunes in a section for the instrument "tuned in the bagpipe way"'; 'Once Upon a Time in the Lowlands', p. 28.

50. Alan Radford, 'Bagpipers at the Tudor Court', *Chanter* (Spring 2018), available at https://www.bagpipesociety.org.uk/articles/2018/chanter/spring/bagpipes-at-tudor-court/, last accessed 14 February 2024.

51. As seen in Theseo Ambrogio Albonesi's *Introductio in Chaldaicam linguam* (Cremona, 1539). See also p. 58 of Frances W. Galpin's 'The Romance of the Phagotum', *Proceedings of the Musical Association* 67 (1940), pp. 57–72. The next reference comes in 1619 in Michael Praetorius's *Syntagma Musicum*. This is sometimes assumed to be the first reference to the bellows. See Anthony Baines, *Bagpipes* (Oxford: Oxford University Press, 1960), p. 125; Julian Goodacre, 'Bagpipes in the Scottish Borders: An Emerging Jigsaw', *Common Stock* 17, no. 2 (December 2002), p. 24 and MacInnes, 'Taking Stock', p. 172.

52. James B. Kopp, 'The French Court Musette to 1672: Further Notes', *The Galpin Society Journal* 64 (2011), pp. 243–7.

53. Paul Roberts, 'Lincolnshire, Lancashire and Scotch Bagpipes: Regional and Pastoral Bagpipes in 17th Century England', *Chanter* (Winter 2017), available at https://www.bagpipesociety.org.uk/articles/2017/chanter/winter/lincolnshire-lancashire-scotch-bagpipes/, last accessed 17 June 2024.

54. Purser, *Scotland's Music*, p. 76.

55. Jeannie Campbell, *Pipe Bands* (n.p. [Scotland]: n.p., 2021), p. 2.

56. Quoted in Francis Collinson, *The Bagpipe: The History of a Musical Instrument* (London: Routledge & Kegan Paul, 1975), p. 140.

57. See p. 55 of Jean de Beaugué, *The History of the Campagnes 1548 and 1549: Being an Exact Account of the Martial Expeditions Perform'd in Those Days by the Scots and French on the One Side, and by the English and Their Foreign Auxiliaries on the Other; Done in French, under the Title of, the Scots War, by Monsieur Beague, a French Gentleman* (1707).

58. Williams, 'Cultural History of the Bagpipe in Britain', p. 39. Note, Williams interprets the passage as referring to the Battle of Pinkie. But that battle was in 1547. The confusion is due to the way the facts are presented in Collinson, *Bagpipe*, p. 140.

3. YOU'LL TAKE THE HIGH ROAD AND I'LL TAKE THE LOW ROAD: A DIVERSE AND FLUCTUATING CULTURE: 1500–1700

1. Erskine Beveridge (ed.), *The Burgh Records of Dunfermline, Transcribed from the Original Manuscript Volume Courts, Sasines, etc, 1488–1584* (Edinburgh: William Brown, 1917), p. 152. Funnily enough, a shepherd breaking his own pipe, in an act of despair, was something of a trope in sixteenth-century English literature. See Cannon, 'Bagpipe in Northern England', p. 128.

2. By Lowland, I mean the whole sweep of non-Highland land from the south of Scotland up through Angus and Aberdeenshire.

3. See MacInnes, 'Highland Bagpipe', p. 10.

4. Scott's uncle, Thomas Scott, was a 'gentleman piper' (see Chapter 5) from Monklaw near Jedburgh who was clearly knowledgeable about the history of town pipers, given what he was able to relay to the musicologist and collector Alexander Campbell. See MacInnes, 'Taking Stock', p. 181.

5. Walter Scott, *Minstrelsy of the Scottish Border*, vol. 1 (Kelso, 1802), p. ci.

6. See Chapter 10 of Gibson, *Traditional Gaelic Bagpiping*, entitled '*Ceòl Baeg* and Dance-Music Piping', pp. 133–54.

7. MacDonald, 'Relationship between Pibroch and Gaelic Song'. See also Gibson, *Traditional Gaelic Bagpiping*, pp. 144–8.

8. Cheape, *Bagpipes*, p. 33.

9. See Cannon, 'Bagpipe in Northern England', p. 133. See also Merryweather, 'Henry Halewood Bagpiper and Liverpool Town Wait 1571–1589', p. 18–20.

10. Cannon, 'Bagpipe in Northern England', pp. 133–4.

11. See Brian McCandless, 'Town Pipers: A European Continuity', *Journal of the North American Association of Lowland and Border Pipers* 2 (February 1991), pp. 17–25. McCandless does not, however, address the question of whether a piper is always a bagpiper. Timothy A. Collins does not include the bagpipes within his list of examples of German *Pfeife* as played by the *Stadtpfeife* of the post-Reformation era. See his 'Hora decima: The Musical Theology of the Stadtpfeifer', *Cross Accent: The Journal of the Association of Lutheran Church Musicians* 2, no. 1 (Spring 2003), pp. 27–38, at p. 32. His examples do include crumhorns, Shreyerpfeifen, Rauschpfeifen, dulcians, recorders and flutes. Collins adds an 'etc.' to his list, and one wonders it it's capacious enough for bagpipes.

12. Wormald, *Court, Kirk, and Community*, p. 224.

13. Cheape, *Bagpipes*, pp. 33, 89.

14. Wormald, *Court, Kirk, and Community*, p. 224. Yet, see Cheape, *Bagpipes*, p. 93, where he points to a great musical event of 1695 that 'seems to belie absolutely any sense of Scotland falling behind in the arts'.

15. Gibson, *Traditional Gaelic Bagpiping*, p. 137. See also Donaldson, *Highland Pipe and Scottish Society*, p. 270.

16. MacInnes, 'Highland Bagpipe', p. 16.

17. 'Haddington Pipers Tales', Odd Scotland, available at https://www.oddscotland.com/pipers-tales-haddington, last accessed 20 August 2024.

18. John Leyden, *The Complaynt of Scotland: Written in 1548; With a Preliminary Dissertation, and Glossary* (Edinburgh: Archibald Constable, 1801), p. 142.

19. Ibid., p. 150.

20. Paul Roberts, 'The Border Bagpipe in 17th Century Art: The First Images', *Common Stock:* 28, no. 2 (2011), pp. 22–34.

21. Roberts, 'Lincolnshire, Lancashire and Scotch Bagpipes'.

22. David Johnson, 'The Lost History of the Lowland Scottish Pipes', *Early Music* 34, no. 3 (August 2006), pp. 497–8.

23. See Hugh Cheape, 'The Piper to the Laird of Grant', *Proceedings of the Society of Antiquaries of Scotland* 125 (1995), pp. 1163–73. Three drone bagpipes may be perceptible on a painting of 1684 entitled *The Destruction of the Mole at Tangier*, but the four bagpipers are very hazy indeed, and they may be a later addition due to their inconsistency of scale compared to the other figures in the painting. See David Murray, *Music of the Scottish Regiments* (Edinburgh: Mercat Press, 1994), p. 49.

24. Barry Shears, '"Old Days" of Dance and Diversity', *Piping Today* 35 (August 2008), pp. 27–31.

25. 'Once Upon a Time in the Lowlands', p. 28.

26. This is from p. 12 of Ramsay's essay 'Of the Influence of Poetry and Music upon the Highlanders', which can be found, with no mention of Ramsay's name, in Patrick MacDonald (spelt McDonald in the original publication), *A Collection of Highland Vocal Airs* (n.p., 1784). Interestingly, Ramsay's words are quoted almost word for word, without acknowledgement, in Thomas Newte, *Prospects and Observations: On a Tour in England and Scotland; Natural, Oeconomical, and Literary* (London, 1791), p. 275, available at https://archive.org/details/bim_eighteenth-century_prospects-and-observatio_thomson-william-lld_1791/mode/2up, last accessed 16 April 2024.

27. Cheape, *Bagpipes*, p. 42.

28. Derick S. Thomson, 'Niall Mór MacMhuirich', *Transactions of the Gaelic Society of Inverness* 49 (1977), pp. 9–25, at p. 20–1; Colm Ó Baoill, *Bàrdachd Chloinn Ghill-Eathain: Eachann Bacach and Other Maclean Poets* (Edinburgh: Scottish Gaelic Texts Society, 1979), p. 221. See also R. D. Cannon, 'Who Got a Kiss of the King's Hand? The Growth of a Tradition', available at https://www.cl.cam.ac.uk/~rja14/musicfiles/preprints/kingshand.pdf, last accessed 14 May 2024.

29. See p. 36 of Alexander Hume, *Hymns, or Sacred Songs* (n.p., 1599).

30. See Collinson, *Bagpipe*, p. 141.

31. Murray, *Music of the Scottish Regiments*, p. 47.

32. If we discount the C- and F-naturals employed from the late twentieth century.

33. The words of Joshua Dickson are worth noting: '[Canntaireachd's] popular historiography since the nineteenth century suggests it was fixed and highly formulaic in structure and therefore formal (as befitting its connection to *ceòl mór*), its use the preserve of the studied elite.

However, field recordings of pipers and other tradition-bearers, collected and archived since the 1950s in the School of Scottish Studies,
present a vast trove of evidence suggesting that *canntaireachd* as a living,
vocal medium was (and remains) a dynamic and flexible tool, adapted
and refined to personal tastes by each musician; and that it was (is)
widely used in the transmission of the vernacular *ceòl beag* idiom—pipe
music for dancing and marching—as well.' 'Piping Sung: Women,
Canntaireachd and the Role of the Tradition-Bearer', *Scottish Studies* 36
(2013), pp. 45–65, at p. 46.

34. Roderick Cannon writes: '[W]e can … see in the variant readings the
kind of latitude which the great pipers of the past were prepared to allow
themselves in forming their own personal styles. At present all players
are agreed as to settings, and every last grace note is held sacred.' *A
Bibliography of Bagpipe Music* (Edinburgh: John Donald, 1980), p. 49.

35. Gibson, *Traditional Gaelic Bagpiping*, p. 142.

36. I have taken the phrase 'community piper' from Gibson's *Traditional
Gaelic Bagpiping*. See especially pp. 240–1.

37. Campsie, *MacCrimmon Legend*, p. 118.

38. See Gibson, *Traditional Gaelic Bagpiping*, p. 140.

39. MacDonald, 'Relationship between Pibroch and Gaelic Song', p. 16.

40. Donaldson, *Highland Pipe and Scottish Society*, p. 31.

41. A full rebuttal can be found in Gibson, *Traditional Gaelic Bagpiping*, especially pp. 133–54.

42. On the origins of this view, see Donaldson, *Highland Pipe and Scottish
Society*, p. 156.

43. MacNeill, *Piobaireachd*, p. 18.

44. Bill Livingstone, *Preposterous: Tales to Follow* (Victoria, Canada: Friesen
Press, 2017), p. 112. Livingstone's father's words are reminiscent of
what Charles Bannatyne had written in the *Oban Times* in 1920: 'Even a
lament … need not be a crawl.' 'Piobaireachd Playing', *Oban Times*
(10 July 1920), p. 3.

45. Cheape, *Bagpipes*, p. 48.

46. Cheape, *Bagpipes*, p. 36 and MacDonald, 'Relationship between Pibroch
and Gaelic Song'. See also Peter Cooke, 'Problems of Notating Pibroch:
A Study of "Maol Donn"', in Dickson, *Highland Bagpipe*, pp. 5–22. On
the impact of harp music on piobaireachd, see especially Barnaby Brown,
'What Do 1s and Os Mean?', *Piping Today* 71 (2014), pp. 38–43. For
thoughts on the links to skaldic poetry, see the three essays by Bridget
MacKenzie on the possible origins of *ceòl mòr* that appear in the *Piping
Times* across March, May and August 1980.

47. Donaldson, *Highland Pipe and Scottish Society*, p. 37. It is interesting to
note Bill Livingstone's words on the piobaireachd teaching of the great

Donald MacLeod (1916–82): 'He used his knowledge of the Gaelic language and song to extract the full beauty of the melody.' *Preposterous*, p. 113.

48. Ibid.

49. Donald Mòr MacCrimmon, who served as the fifteenth chief of the MacLeods, is believed to have attended a school of piping in Dún Dealgan (Dundalk), County Louth, Ireland. See MacInnes, 'Highland Bagpipe', p. 7.

50. See William Donaldson's chapter '"Return from the Cave of Gold": The Creation of the MacCrimmon Metaphor', in his *Highland Pipe and Scottish Society*, pp. 401–23. It's worth noting, however, that references to the MacCrimmons as the pre-eminent Highland pipers can be found in the Wardlaw MS of the 1680s ('All the pipers in the army gave John Macgurmen the van, and acknowledged him for their patron in chiefe') and in John MacCodrum's poem of 1760, *Dimoladh Pìoba Dhomhnaill Bhàin*, 'Dispraise of Donald Bàn's Pipes', where we read that '[o]f all pipers MacCrimmon was king ...' See Cannon, 'Who Got a Kiss', pp. 2, 15. In the much-cited (by piping historians) Indenture prepared for Lord Lovat's piper, David Fraser, in 1743, Fraser is commanded to journey to Skye 'to have him perfected a Highland Pyper by the famous Malcolm Mcgrimon'. The full text can be found here: Stuart Letford, 'The 1743 Lord Lovat-David Fraser Piping Indenture', Bagpipe News, 24 April 2020, available at https://bagpipe.news/2020/04/24/the-1743-lord-lovat-david-fraser-piping-indenture/, last accessed 17 May 2024. Finally, there is this reference to the capture of Malcolm MacCrimmon in an anonymous but contemporary account of the Jacobite rebellion of 1745, 'Memoirs of the Rebellion in Aberdeen and Banff': 'McLeod's own piper, McGruman, happened also to be taken, and the piper is always looked on as a person of importance in a Highland Chief's retinue, but McGriman especially was a respected person being esteemed the best piper in the Highlands, having had most of the Clan pipers as his scholars, and being looked on by them as a kind of chief.' Quoted in Ruaraidh Halford MacLeod, 'The MacCrimmons and the '45', *Piping Times* 29, no. 6 (March 1977), pp. 11–13, at p. 13.

51. The claim that the college never existed was first made in Alistair Campsie's controversial book *The MacCrimmon Legend*; the case is put more tactfully in Donaldson, *Highland Pipe and Scottish Society*, p. 180: 'The MacCrimmon pipers had always moved around, sometimes on one farm, sometimes on another, and teaching must have taken place wherever they happened to be at the time.' Ruari Halford-MacLeod's very detailed address to the Piobaireachd Society in 2001, entitled 'Donald Ruadh MacCrummen', puts it thus: 'Later tradition stated that there

was a piping college at Boreraig and certainly there are records, from 1698, that the MacCrummens were teaching piping in Skye. It is now difficult to assess how many pupils were taught at any one time.' The address is available to members on the Piobaireachd Society website and the quote is on p. 7. Halford-MacLeod clearly believed that the college did indeed exist; see p. 18, especially during the discussion after his paper.

52. Iain MacInnes is, however, right to remind us that 'piping was not the preserve of a select group of families concentrated in the Western Isles … Throughout the *Gaidhealtachd*, from the Uists to Sutherland, to Kintyre and Perthshire, the piper was a major constituent of clan society. The records of any Highland clan from the sixteenth century will bear testimony to the presence of a piper in the ranks.' MacInnes, 'Highland Bagpipe', p. 6.

53. Cheape, *Bagpipes*, p. 45.

54. Ibid., p. 44.

55. Cannon, 'Who Got a Kiss of the King's Hand?', p. 1.

56. Hugh Cheape has pointed out to me that the words literally mean 'A kiss was got of the King's claw.'

57. James Fraser, *Chronicles of the Frasers: The Wardlaw Manuscript Entitled 'Polichronicon seu policratica temporum, or, The True Genealogy of the Frasers' 916–1674*, ed. William MacKay (Edinburgh: T. and A. Constable, 1905), pp. 379–80. Interestingly, C. A. Malcolm tells of another piper who was captured at Worcester and who 'discovered to his amazement that he was regarded by his captors as an object of wonder and admiration; he was encouraged to play his pipes and a post was given him in Bath, where he prospered'. *Piper in Peace and War*, p. 54.

58. Though later than the period under discussion here, it's notable that the pipes in the eighteenth century were used to accompany work, both in the Highlands and the Lowlands. See MacDonald, 'Relationship between Pibroch and Gaelic Song', p. 16.

59. Donaldson, *Highland Pipe and Scottish Society*, p. 19.

60. Paul Elmer More (ed.), *The Complete Poetical Works of Byron* (Boston: Houghton Mifflin Company, 1933), p. 39.

61. See Victoria Henshaw, *Scotland and the British Army, 1700–1750: Defending the Union* (London: Bloomsbury, 2014), pp. 17–18.

62. See 'The Highland Clearances', *In Our Time*, BBC, 8 March 2018, at around 7:50, available at https://www.bbc.co.uk/programmes/b09tc4tm, last accessed 8 May 2024. But as Hew Strachan has also pointed out, 'the kingdom of Scotland had acquired by the early modern period … a social structure appropriate to the production of warriors. Nonetheless, its battlefield record in the sixteenth and early sev-

enteenth centuries was abysmal.' The Highlanders were in some cases to blame. Their apparent ill-discipline at Flodden (1513) was said to have been a major factor in defeat, and at Pinkie (1547) the Highlanders were the first to abandon the field. See Hew Strachan, 'Scotland's Military Identity', *The Scottish Historical Review* 85, no. 220 (2006), pp. 315–32, at p. 317.

63. Strachan, 'Scotland's Military Identity', p. 318.

64. See Murray, *Music of the Scottish Regiments*, p. 40.

65. Steve Murdoch, 'James VI and the Formation of a Scottish and British Military Identity', in Steve Murdoch and Andrew MacKillop (eds), *Fighting for Identity: Scottish Military Experience c. 1550–1900* (Leiden: Brill, 2002), pp. 3–31.

66. Michael Roberts, 'The Military Revolution 1560–1660', in Roberts, *Essays in Swedish History* (Minneapolis: University of Minnesota Press, 1967), pp. 195–225.

67. See Murray, *Music of the Scottish Regiments*, pp. 40–1.

68. A look at the roll books for these companies suggest that the pipers were held in some regard, appearing alongside the names of officers. Their payment of 10 shillings Scots was, according to C. A. Malcolm, 'exactly half the pay of an ensign and more than thrice the three shillings paid to a private or sentinel'. Malcolm, *Piper in Peace and War*, p. 92

69. Ibid.

70. Bruce Seton and John Grant, *The Pipes of War: A Record of the Achievements of Pipers of Scottish and Overseas Regiments during the War, 1914–18* (Glasgow: MacLehose, Jackson & Co., 1920), p. 14.

71. Ibid.

72. Gibson, *Traditional Gaelic Bagpiping*, p. 68.

73. Ibid., p. 73.

74. Wormald, *Court, Kirk, and Community*, p. 195.

4. PIPING IN JACOBITE TIMES: THE SOUND OF DIVIDED LOYALTIES: 1700–46

1. Rob Reid, 'Hollywood's Top Piper: I've Played on Lots of Big Films but I Still Get Grief for Using Irish Pipes in Braveheart', *Daily Record*, available at https://www.dailyrecord.co.uk/entertainment/celebrity/hollywoods-top-piper-ive-played-5274903, last accessed 28 March 2024.

2. 'Outlandish', Pipes|Drums, 30 September 2014, available at https://www.pipesdrums.com/outlandish/, last accessed 28 March 2024.

3. The exact date of publication has been disputed, ranging from 1740 to 1746, but most likely it was around 1743. See Séan Donelly, 'A Publication Date for John Geoghegan's *Compleat Tutor*', *An Píobaire* 4,

no. 47 (2008), pp. 26–7. See also Christoph Heyl, 'The Pastoral Pipes', *Chanter* (Autumn 2021), available at https://www.bagpipesociety.org. uk/articles/2021/chanter/autumn/the-pastoral-pipes/, last accessed 30 April 2024.

4. In other words, mouth-blown pipes with drones leaning on the shoulder. Pastoral or union drones rested across the arm or the lap.

5. Thomas E. Kaiser, 'The Drama of Charles Edward Stuart: Jacobite Propaganda and French Political Protest, 1745–1750', *Eighteenth-Century Studies* 30, no. 4 (1997), pp. 365–81, at p. 366.

6. Viccy Coltman, *Art and Identity in Scotland: A Cultural History from the Jacobite Rising of 1745 to Walter Scott* (Cambridge: Cambridge University Press, 2019), p. 10. See also Murray Pittock, *The Myth of the Jacobite Clans* (Edinburgh: Edinburgh University Press, 1995), pp. 149–50.

7. Allan MacInnes, *Clanship, Commerce and the House of Stuart* (East Linton: Tuckwell Press, 1996), p. 175.

8. *Compleat Theory*, p. 97.

9. Donaldson, *Highland Pipe and Scottish Society*, p. 88.

10. Campsie, *MacCrimmon Legend*, p. 118.

11. To reinforce the diversity of Highland piping, it is worth consulting Bridget Mackenzie's valuable series of books with the title beginning *Piping Traditions of the ...*, e.g., *Piping Traditions of the North of Scotland* (Edinburgh: John Donald, 1998) and *Piping Traditions of the Inner Isles* (Edinburgh: John Donald, 2012).

12. John Slavin, '18th Century Heirloom in TNPC Museum', Bagpipe News, 3 March 2022, available at https://bagpipe.news/2022/03/03/ 18th-century-heirloom-in-tnpc-museum/, last accessed 28 March 2024.

13. *Piping Times* 71, no. 9 (June 2019), pp. 19–20.

14. That's not exactly the same as saying that British Army pipers were paid for out of the public purse. If a regiment wanted a piper, it was an expense the officers had to bear. This was a practice that would last a long time. See Murray, *Music of the Scottish Regiments*, p. 116.

15. 'Keeping It Real with Outlander's Historical Advisor', British Heritage, available at https://britishheritage.com/art-culture/outlander-historial-advisor, last accessed 28 March 2024.

16. Angela Wright, 'The History of the Unfortunate Lady Grange: Gothic Exhumations of a Concealed Scottish Fate', *Gothic Studies* 24, no. 1 (2022), pp. 31–43.

17. Quoted in David Laing, 'An Episode in the Life of Mrs Rachel Erskine, Lady Grange: Detailed by Herself in a Letter from St Kilda, January 20, 1738, and Other Original Papers', *Proceedings of the Society of Antiquaries of Scotland* 11 (1875), pp. 593–608, at p. 602, available at http://journals.socantscot.org/index.php/psas/article/view/5777, last accessed 29 March 2024.

18. These are helpfully collected and entertainingly retold in Stuart McHardy, *The Silver Chanter: Historical Tales of Scottish Pipers* (Edinburgh: Birlinn, 2004), pp. 24–66.

19. Quoted in Ruairidh Halford MacLeod, 'Everyone Who Has an Intrigue Hopes It Should Not Be Known: Lord Loudoun and Anne Mackintosh; An Intrigue of the '45', *Transactions of the Gaelic Society of Inverness* 55 (1986–8), pp. 256–323, at p. 263, available at https://archive.org/details/tgsi-vol-lv-1986–1988/page/285/mode/2up?view=theater, last accessed 3 April 2024.

20. 'Of the Influence of Poetry and Music upon the Highlanders', p. 14.

21. We do know that Malcolm was freed by the prince, having been brought before him at Stirling. See Halford-MacLeod, 'Donald Ruadh MacCrummen', p. 8.

22. Ibid., p. 283.

23. Ibid, pp. 256–323.

24. Locals subsequently referred to Fraser as *Caiptin nan Coig*, meaning the Captain of the Five. See Hugh Cheape, 'Dr I F Grant (1887–1983): The Highland Folk Museum and a Bibliography of Her Written Works', *Review of Scottish Culture* 2 (1986), pp. 113–24, at p. 116.

25. 'The Rout of Moy (1746)', Calum I Maclean Blogspot, available at http://calumimaclean.blogspot.com/2013/02/the-rout-of-moy-1746.html, last accessed 2 April 2024.

26. To Sir John Cope, quoted in MacLeod, 'Everyone Who Has an Intrigue', p. 276.

27. The tune, with a different title, 'Cha till mi tuil(le)', was in fact in existence before 1745. See Campsie, *MacCrimmon Legend*, p. 155.

28. There were certainly Gaelic bards who had to side with the government due to their chief's allegiance who nonetheless made songs in honour of the prince and his cause. Examples include Duncan Bàn MacIntyre and Rob Donn MacKay.

29. John MacLellan, 'The Hereditary Pipers: The MacCrimmons', *The International Piper* 3, no. 1 (May 1980), pp. 2–3.

30. C. A. Malcolm reports that the King's Own Scottish Borderers—known then as the 25th or 'Edinburgh' Regiment—played their troops off the field, 'just as their predecessors had played their companies off Sheriffmuir in 1715'. *Piper in Peace and War*, pp. 74–5.

31. Thomas Brown, 'Letters from the Dead to the Living, and from the Living to the Dead, Both Serious and Comical', in *The Works of Thomas Brown*, 5th edn, vol. 2 (London: Printed for Sam Briscoe, 1719), p. 298. I am particularly indebted here to Vivien Williams' wonderful article 'The Scottish Bagpipe: Political and Religious Symbolism in English Literature and Satire', available at https://www.thebottleimp.org.

uk/2013/05/the-scottish-bagpipe-political-and-religious-symbolism-in-english-literature-and-satire/, last accessed 4 April 2024.

32. Brown, *Works of Thomas Brown*, p. 300.

33. Edward Ward, *Nuptial Dialogues and Debates: Or, an Useful Prospect of the Felicities and Discomforts of a Married Life*, vol. 2 (London: Printed for C. Hitch et al., 1759), p. 199.

34. Williams, 'Scottish Bagpipe'. In her PhD thesis, Williams makes it clear that the connection between Scotland and Catholicism was not universal, giving John Arbuthnot's *The History of John Bull* (1727) as an example of where the country is associated principally with Presbyterianism. See Williams, 'Cultural History of the Bagpipe in Britain', pp. 82–3.

35. Charles Edward Steuart Chamber, *The Woodhouselee MS: A Narrative of Events in Edinburgh and District during the Jacobite Occupation* (London: W. & R. Chambers, 1907), pp. 26–7.

36. Ibid., p. 39.

37. Ibid., 93.

38. The quote does not appear in any of Scott's published works but has long been attributed to him.

39. John Lorne Campbell (ed.), *Highland Songs of the Forty-Five* (Edinburgh: Scottish Gaelic Texts Society, 1984), pp. 18–19. My thanks to Vivien Williams, whose PhD thesis drew this and the following poems to my attention.

40. Colm Ó Baoill (ed.), *Poems and Songs by Sileas MacDonald* (Edinburgh: Published by the Scottish Academic Press for the Scottish Gaelic Texts Society, 1972), pp. 22–3.

41. Campbell, *Highland Songs of the Forty-Five*, pp. 52–3.

5. PIPES, POWER AND PATRONAGE: THE ENLIGHTENED REIMAGINING OF THE HIGHLANDS: 1746–1830s

1. Quoted in Donaldson, *Highland Pipe and Scottish Society*, p. 79.

2. Ibid.

3. See Campsie, *MacCrimmon Legend*, p. 116.

4. See the chapter by James H. Jamieson, 'Social Assemblies of the Eighteen Century', in *The Book of the Old Edinburgh Club, Nineteenth Volume* (Edinburgh: T & A Constable, 1933), pp. 31–91, especially p. 66.

5. There is an irony here insofar as the Select Society was a vehicle for a certain Anglicising force entering Scottish society, not least when it came to the written language. See Nicholas T. Phillipson, 'Culture and Society in the 18th Century Province: The Case of Edinburgh and the Scottish Enlightenment', in Lawrence Stone (ed.), *The University in Society* (Princeton: Princeton University Press, 1975), pp 407–48, and by the same author,

'Politics, Politeness and the Anglicisation of early Eighteenth-Century Scottish Culture', in Roger A. Mason (ed.), *Scotland and England 1286–1815* (Edinburgh: John Donald, 1987), pp. 226–46.

6. Donaldson, *Highland Pipe and Scottish Society*, p. 67.

7. Arthur Herman (New York: Crown Publishing Group, 2001).

8. Murray, *Music of the Scottish Regiments*, p. 114.

9. Pittock, 'Enlightenment, Romanticism and the Scottish Canon', p. 91.

10. Such composers included Lully, Rameau and Boismortier, Chédeville and Hotteterre.

11. See Hugh Cheape, 'Raising the Tone: The Bagpipe and the Baroque', in M. J. Grant (ed.), *Hearing Heritage: Selected Essays on Scotland's Music from the Musica Scotica Conferences* (Glasgow: Musica Scotica Trust, 2020), pp. 3–18, at pp. 8f. The following article is also enlightening: Pieterjan Van Kreckhoven, 'Bourdon Collectif', *Chanter* (Spring 2017), available at https://www.bagpipesociety.org.uk/articles/2017/chanter/spring/bourdon-collectif/, last accessed 29 April 2024.

12. On the French origins of Northumbrian pipes, see Cannon, *Bibliography of Bagpipe Music*, p. 14.

13. Having said that, the very first pictorial representation of the image is in a burlesque version of John Gay's *The Beggar's Opera* from 1728, and it accompanies an orchestra of 'rude instruments'—a dulcimer, a humthrum (i.e., a bladder and bow-string) and a salt box. See Cheape, *Bagpipes*, p. 90.

14. A. D. Fraser, *Some Reminiscences and the Bagpipe*, p. 144.

15. The question of how *uilleann* arrived out of 'union' remains obscure, as does the original reason for the use of union in the first place. See Cheape, *Bagpipes*, pp. 106–7, and Dave Rowlands, 'The Gentleman Piper', *Chanter* (Winter 2003), pp. 4–11.

16. Ross Anderson suggests this may account for why the pastoral pipe did not survive beyond the first half of the nineteenth century, and why union or uilleann piping did: 'If playing on the knee become fashionable because of the staccato, the improved dynamics and the greater range of tone colour—in short, as it made the instrument more eloquent—then in time the instruments would be tuned for performance on the knee rather than off, and the foot joint [the bottom section of the pastoral chanter] would fall into disuse.' 'The Pastoral Pipe Repertoire, Rediscovered', *Common Stock* 20, no. 2 (December 2005), available at https://www.cl.cam.ac.uk/~rja14/music/pastoral.pdf, last accessed 8 May 2024.

17. 'Pastoral Pipes'.

18. John Geoghegan, *The Compleat Tutor for the Pastoral or New Bagpipe* (London: n.p., n.d.), p. 1.

19. See Hugh Cheape, 'Patron as Performer: Lament for the "Gentleman-Piper"', in Wilson McLeod et al. (eds), *Bile ós Chrannaibh: A Festschrift for William Gillies* (Ceann Drochaid, Perthshire: Clann Tuirc, 2010), pp. 57–78, especially pp. 61–3.

20. Though note this from Gibson: '[T]he notion that one's family was gentlemanly, a characteristic of so many Highlanders in Scotland after Culloden, extended to what is left of Gaelic Cape Breton and now crops up time and again in what appear to be materially unprepossessing surroundings.' *Traditional Gaelic Bagpiping*, p. 240.

21. He would not have been alone in looking so grand. In a 2001 address to the Piobaireachd Society, entitled 'Donald Ruadh MacCrummen', Halford-MacLeod stated: 'In 1714, Patrick Morrison, merchant in Edinburgh, was paid 57 merks 6s "for livery Cloathes to MacCrummen, MacLeod's pyper" ... MacCrimmon's clothes were probably an elaborate blue coat and vest embroidered with silver lace—the livery colours of the MacLeod chief whose coat of arms is a silver castle on a blue shield.' The address is available to members on the Piobaireachd Society website and the quote can be found on p. 6.

22. Donaldson, *Highland Pipe and Scottish Society*, p. 185.

23. Halford-MacLeod, 'Donald Ruadh MacCrummen', pp. 4, 12. See p. 18 for fuller discussion of the issue after Halford-MacLeod had read his paper. Halford-MacLeod, who is about as knowledgeable as anyone can be on the MacCrimmons, unambiguously refers to them as 'gentlemen', who would not have done any work other than fulfil their minimal piping duties and, as was appropriate for a gentleman, deal in black cattle. See p. 19.

24. Hugh Cheape names a number on p. 110 of *Bagpipes* and again in 'Patron as Performer', pp. 63f.

25. Later, in the late 1830s, of the 245 predominantly landed and titled subscribers to Angus Mackay's *A Collection of Ancient Piobaireachd*, there were at least twenty pipers among them. See Donaldson, *Highland Pipe and Scottish Society*, p. 148.

26. Brown, 'What Do 1s and Os Mean?', p. 38.

27. Iain MacInnes utters a word of caution here: 'The celebrated Border piper James Allan was once described as having played a "port pibroch" at Elsdon Court Baron in Northumberland (in about 1797); this designation might seem fanciful, but the sentiment is understandable; some of the Border music is indeed "big music".' 'Taking Stock', pp. 183, 186. There was also a long-standing fashion for 'pibrochs' played on the fiddle.

28. Quoted in Donaldson, *Highland Pipe and Scottish Society*, p. 80.

29. K. N. MacDonald, *The Oban Times* (4 January 1913). See also MacInnes, 'Taking Stock', p. 171.

30. David Johnson, 'The Lost History of the Lowland Scottish Pipes', *Early Music* 34, no. 3 (August 2006), pp. 497–8; Roberts, 'Lincolnshire, Lancashire and Scotch Bagpipes'.

31. See Seton Gordon, 'The Bagpipe', in John Hadfield (ed.), *The Saturday Book 15* (London: Hutchinson & Co., 1955), pp. 188, 193. For further comment, see MacInnes, 'Taking Stock', pp. 169–90, at pp. 171–4.

32. Cheape, 'Raising the Tone', p. 13.

33. Cheape, *Bagpipes*, p. 78.

34. Ibid.

35. See MacInnes, 'Taking Stock', pp. 182–3.

36. 'Pastoral Pipes'.

37. See MacInnes, 'Taking Stock', p. 187.

38. David Johnson, *Music and Society in Lowland Scotland in the Eighteenth Century* (Oxford: Oxford University Press, 1972), p. 111. For that recent scholarship, see Cheape, 'Raising the Tone'.

39. 'The Piper's House: The Musical Heritage of the Mackays of Raasay', Bagpipe News, 28 December 2023, available at https://bagpipe.news/2023/12/28/the-pipers-house-the-musical-heritage-of-the-mackays-of-raasay/, last accessed 30 April 2024.

40. Gibson, *Traditional Gaelic Bagpiping*, p. 139; Donaldson, *Highland Pipe and Scottish Society*, p. 101.

41. Hugh Cheape, 'The Pipe of Fluent Chanters', *Piping Today* 26 (2013), pp. 34–40, at p. 40.

42. The Highland Society of Scotland almost seemed to show an apathy to the instrument when compared to the London Society. See Donaldson, *Highland Pipe and Scottish Society*, pp. 64–5.

43. Quoted in ibid., p. 58.

44. Ibid., p. 90.

45. Tom Devine has convincingly shown that we ought to resist the idea that 1746 represented a sudden rupture with the social and commercial developments that had already been taking place for decades previously in the Highlands. In fact, such change continued for about fifteen to twenty years after 1746. See T. M. Devine, *Clanship to Crofters' War: The Social Transformation of the Scottish Highlands* (Manchester: Manchester University Press, 1994). And as Matthew P. Dziennik has written: 'The century preceding the battle of Culloden saw the preservation of land-based hierarchies but also the decline of the clan system, as elites came to rely on commercial enterprise and the exploitation of rent-paying tenants rather than retaining large retinues of clansmen.' *The Fatal Land: War, Empire, and the Highland Soldier in British America* (New Haven: Yale University Press, 2015), p. 29.

46. See the section entitled 'The Myth of Proscription', in Gibson, *Traditional Gaelic Bagpiping*, pp. 28–35, and MacInnes, 'Highland Bagpipe', p. 15.

47. Murray Pittock, 'In Our Time: The Jacobite Rebellion', BBC Sounds, originally aired 8 May 2003, around minute 38, https://www.bbc.co.uk/sounds/play/p00548y0, last accessed 21 November 2024.

48. Strachan, 'Scottish Military Identity', p. 325.

49. Murray, *Music of the Scottish Regiments*, p. 48.

50. Strachan, 'Scottish Military Identity', pp. 324–5. Strachan's account of what drove recruitment is seriously qualified by Dziennik in *The Fatal Land*, especially his excellent chapter 'A Perfect Purgatory: Recruitment in the Scottish Highlands', where he writes: 'Many Highland landlords feared this not-inconsiderable drain on their labor force and sought to shield their tenants from the recruiters' (p. 45).

51. Murray, *Music of the Scottish Regiments*, p. 48. For evidence of how hard it was to recruit pipers in the earliest days of recruitment after the '45, see Halford-MacLeod, 'Donald Ruadh MacCrummen', pp. 8–9.

52. Gibson, *Traditional Gaelic Bagpiping*, p. 75.

53. Murray, *Music of the Scottish Regiments*, p. 50. C. A. Malcolm, with perhaps some exaggeration, writes: 'Highlanders with a reputation as pipers were wont to choose the 25th as the best unit for their genius.' *Piper in Peace and War*, p. 76.

54. Murray, *Music of the Scottish Regiments*, p. 50.

55. See Colin Kidd, 'North Britishness and the Nature of Eighteenth-Century British Patriotisms', *The Historical Journal* 39 (1996), pp. 361–82.

56. Malcolm, *Piper in Peace and War*, p. 96.

57. Ibid., p. 113.

58. Strachan, 'Scottish Military Identity', p. 325. See also John Cookson, *The British Armed Nation 1793–1815* (Oxford: Oxford University Press, 1997), pp. 126–7.

59. Strachan, 'Scottish Military Identity', p. 325.

60. Colin Kidd, 'Review of *The King's Jaunt: George IV in Scotland, August 1822*, by J. Prebble', *The Scottish Historical Review* 81, no. 211 (2002), 141–42, at p. 142. Robert Pirrie, the present chief executive to an exclusive body of Scottish lawyers known as Writers to the Signet, has shown in an MA dissertation of 2019 that some of the claims, most notably made by John Prebble in *The King's Jaunt* (London: Collins, 1988), around the 'stage management' of Scott and the excesses of the royal visit are overstated. See Pirrie, 'Edinburgh's Urban Enlightenment and George IV: Staging North Britain, 1752–1822', MA diss., Open University, 2019, available at https://oro.open.ac.uk/60286/3/Pirrie_R%20Pirrie%20A826%20-%20REDACTED_Dissertation.pdf, last accessed 9 May 2024.

61. Quoted in 'Royal Visit 1822: Pipers and the Clan Chiefs', Bagpipe News, 18 July 2022, available at https://bagpipe.news/2022/07/18/royal-

visit-1822-pipers-and-the-clan-chiefs/#:~:text=According%20to%20
the%20Notices%20of,the%20contingent%20from%20the%20Society,
last accessed 18 June 2024.

62. Donaldson, *Highland Pipe and Scottish Society*, pp. 153–4. See also the classic works of John Telfer Dunbar, *History of Highland Dress* (Philadelphia: Dufour Editions, 1964) and *The Costume of Scotland* (London: Batsford, 1981). Further insights can be found in Hugh Cheape, *Tartan: The Highland Habit* (Edinburgh: NMSE, 1990).

63. Campsie, *MacCrimmon Legend*, p. 54.

64. Donaldson, *Highland Pipe and Scottish Society*, p. 81.

65. Gibson, *Traditional Gaelic Bagpiping*, p. 177.

66. Donaldson, *Highland Pipe and Scottish Society*, p. 96.

67. Ibid., p. 46.

68. MacDonald, 'Preface', *Collection of Highland Vocal Airs*, p. 1. Interestingly, Donaldson quotes these words too (*Highland Pipe and Scottish Society*, p. 27), but he clearly sees them in quite a different category from anything expressed by Ramsay. In a poem of 1784, perhaps the most preeminent Gaelic poet of the time, Duncan Bàn MacIntyre, gave to the Prize Pipe at that year's Highland Society competition a prehistoric and mythical ancestry, claiming it to be the pipe of Fionn Mac Cumhail, who produced with it 'the first music that ever was on earth'. See Cheape, 'Pipe of Fluent Chanters', p. 39.

69. Gibson, *Traditional Gaelic Bagpiping*, p. 25.

70. Ibid., p. 61.

71. Quoted in 'Royal Visit 1822: Pipers and the Clan Chiefs'.

72. Quoted in Cheape, 'Piper to the Laird of Grant', p. 1164.

73. Ibid., p. 1166.

74. Murray, *Music of the Scottish Regiments*, pp. 116–17.

75. On Scott's influence on romantic nationalism, see Murray Pittock (ed.), *The Reception of Sir Walter Scott in Europe* (London: Bloomsbury, 2007). The quote is from Graeme Morton, *Ourselves and Others: Scotland 1832–1914* (Edinburgh: Edinburgh University Press, 2012), p. 12.

76. See T. M. Devine, *The Scottish Clearances: A History of the Dispossessed, 1600–1900* (London: Allen Lane, 2018). It's also worth noting that the victim narrative needs to be balanced with the mentality of the Highlanders when it came to soldiers acquiring land in America after having served there. As Dziennik points out: '[W]hile many English commentaries envisaged America as a pristine land waiting to be cultivated, Highland texts tended to emphasize the existing indigenous population. One writer would later express the view that "the most desirable holding of any for a Highlander" was to conquer land from the Indians by the sword. The righteousness of Gaels acquiring land in

America, even at the expense of the indigenous or white settler population, not only arose unquestioned but was clearly fundamental to the achievement ... From [the Gaels'] point of view, the Highland regiments had displaced the Indians and it was only right that the Gaels would reap the benefits.' *Fatal Land*, pp. 162–3.

77. Morton, *Ourselves and Others*, p. 247.
78. Ibid., p. 10.
79. Donaldson, *Highland Pipe and Scottish Society*, p. 194.
80. It is interesting to note the few attempts that were made to place Highland pipers into Lowland towns to take over the office of 'town piper'. This happened in Hawick in 1803 and in Haddington in 1824. As Iain MacInnes has suggested, the latter might be taken 'as an early attempt at conscious revival' ('Taking Stock', p. 176). In other words, the authorities may have felt that the only way to keep the town piper tradition alive would be to put a Highland piper into the role. Telling indeed.
81. 'History of the Uilleann Pipes'.
82. 'History', Northumbrian Pipers' Society, available at https://www.northumbrianpipers.org.uk/the-society/history/, last accessed 16 July 2024.

6. A TIME FOR GIANTS: DEVELOPING A TRADITION OF INNOVATION (AND MADNESS): 1830s–1900s

1. Campsie, *MacCrimmon Legend*, p. 1.
2. 'Writer Tries to End MacCrimmon Recriminations', *The Herald*, available at https://www.heraldscotland.com/news/12129002.writer-tries-to-end-maccrimmon-recriminations/, last accessed 27 May 2024.
3. Robert Wallace, 'Famous Pipers: Angus MacKay, Life and Times of a True Piping Genius', Piping Press, available at https://pipingpress.com/famous-pipers-angus-mackay-life-and-times-of-a-true-piping-genius/, last accessed 24 May 2024.
4. Notwithstanding the editorial liberties Archibald Campbell of Kilberry may or may not have subsequently taken editing Mackay's versions. See Donaldson, *Highland Pipe and Scottish Society*, pp. 374–400.
5. Wallace, 'Famous Pipers'.
6. Ibid.
7. Quoted in Hugh Cheape and Decker Forrest, 'The Piper's House on Raasay: Taigh a' Phìobaire; Part 2', *Piping Today* 50 (February 2011), pp. 14–19, at pp. 14–15.
8. It's not clear why Halford-MacLeod varies his spelling of the name.
9. Halford-MacLeod, 'Donald Ruadh MacCrummen', p. 15.

10. Ibid., p. 17.

11. William Donaldson, *Pipers: A Guide to the Players and Music of the Highland Bagpipe* (Edinburgh: Birlinn, 2005), p. 95.

12. Ibid., p. 94.

13. Angus Mackay, *A Collection of Ancient Piobaireachd and Highland Pipe Music* (Aberdeen: Logan & Company, 1838), p. 3, available at https://ceol-sean.net/content/MacKay/MacKay_TOC.html, last accessed 27 May 2024.

14. Captain John MacLellan, 'History of Piping: The Mackenzies', *The International Piper* 4, no. 2 (June 1981), pp. 11, 14, at p. 11.

15. Jeannie Campbell, *Highland Bagpipe Makers* (Edinburgh: Magnus Orr Publishing, 2001), p. 41.

16. See Donaldson, *Highland Pipe and Scottish Society*, pp. 97–122, especially p. 120.

17. Gibson, *Traditional Gaelic Bagpiping*, pp. 239–50, and Barry Shears, *Dance to the Piper: The Highland Bagpipe in Nova Scotia* (Sydney, Nova Scotia: Cape Breton University Press, 2008), *passim*.

18. Donaldson, *Highland Pipe and Scottish Society*, p. 198.

19. Gibson, *Traditional Gaelic Bagpiping*, pp. 223–38.

20. This purpose is one of the fundamental points highlighted throughout Gibson's *Traditional Gaelic Bagpiping*.

21. *Oban Times* (4 April 1942), p. 5.

22. Malcolm, *Piper in Peace and War*, p. 96.

23. See Donaldson, *Highland Pipe and Scottish Society*, pp. 193–4.

24. Cheape, 'Patron as Performer', p. 57.

25. N. A. Malcolm Smith (ed.), *The First Hundred Years: A History of the Royal Scottish Pipers' Society* (Edinburgh: Royal Scottish Pipers' Society, 1983), p. 2.

26. It's said the great John MacDougall Gillies left the employment of Lord Breadalbane, having been asked by her Ladyship to sweep the drive. See Donaldson, *Highland Pipe and Scottish Society*, p. 194.

27. Ibid., p. 359.

28. Campbell, *Pipe Bands*, p. 5. Campbell's book, at 850 pages, is by far and away the most exhaustive account of the pipe band world ever produced.

29. See '065: Dr William (Willie) Donaldson; The Interview', Pipers' Persuasion, at around 1:05, available at https://www.piperspersuasion.com/dr-williamwillie-donaldson-the-interview/, last accessed 30 May 2023. See also Donaldson, *Highland Pipe and Scottish Society*, p. 194, and his *Pipers*, p. 100.

30. See Keith Sanger's comments below the article: 'History of the Pipe Band and the Worlds', Piping Press, available at https://pipingpress.

com/history-of-the-pipe-band-and-the-worlds/#:~:text=The%20
1880s%20saw%20the%20emergence,first%20ever%20civilian%20
pipe%20band, last accessed 19 June 2024. Lonach also have a claim to
the title of possessing the first civilian pipe band, but the 1868 reference
to the pipes and drums playing together appears to be a one-off. See
Campbell, *Pipe Bands*, p. 35.

31. 'The Influence of the Boys Brigade on Piping', RSPBA, available at
https://rspba.org/the-associations-history/the-influence-of-the-boys-
brigade-on-piping/, last accessed 20 June 2024.

32. *Oban Times* (4 April 1942), p. 5.

33. Strachan writes that Scots in the mid-nineteenth century 'appropriated
the paraphernalia of the Highland soldier as a universal symbol of
Scotland. Kilts and broadswords, dirks and pipes, which to the eighteenth century beacons of the Scottish Enlightenment represented a barbaric and even alien form of life, became the embodiment of nationalism. Like so many selfdeceptions, they became self-perceptions, and
ultimately self-fulfilling perceptions.' 'Scotland's Military Identity',
p. 327.

34. Murray, *Music of the Scottish Regiments*, p. 119.

35. Ibid., p. 120.

36. Archibald Campbell, 'The Highland Bagpipe', part II, *Piping Times* 14,
no 2 (August 1962), pp. 6–9, at pp. 8–9.

37. By which I mean Malcom's *Piper in Peace and War*.

38. Ibid., p. 127.

39. Ibid. As for pipers to the sovereign, it was not unknown for them to
continue playing while waist deep in a river. Queen Victoria especially
commissioned painter Carl Haag to capture the moment that pipers John
MacPherson and Aeneas Rose forded the River Tarf, playing the whole
time. See 'Playing Waist Deep in a River: All Part of Royal Duty for
Pipers', Bagpipe News, 4 September 2019, available at https://bag-
pipe.news/2019/09/04/playing-waist-deep-in-a-river-all-part-of-
royal-duty-for-pipers/, last accessed 12 June 2024.

40. Henry Lytton Bulwer, *The Life of Henry John Temple, Viscount Palmerston*,
vol. 1 (London: Richard Bentley, 1870), p. 400.

41. Quoted in Malcolm, *Piper in Peace and War*, p. 145.

42. Not until 1888 were the pipers of the Scottish Rifles allowed to play
with the drums; the band of the Highland Light Infantry did not get
drummers until 1905. See ibid., pp. 88, 117.

43. Quoted in Richard Cannon, *Historical Records of the 72nd Regiment, or the
Duke of Albany's Own Highlanders* (London: Parker, Furnivall & Parker,
1848), p. 32, fn 15.

44. Strachan, 'Scotland's Military Identity', p. 326.

45. L. E. Ruutz Rees, *The Personal Narrative of the Siege of Lucknow* (London: Longman, Brown, Green, Longmans & Roberts, 1858), p. 224.

46. Quoted in Malcolm, *Piper in Peace and War*, p. 131.

47. Ibid., pp. 37, 99.

48. Ibid., p. 66.

49. William Munro, *Reminiscences of Military Service with the 93rd Sutherland Highlanders* (London: Hurst and Blackett, 1883), p. 318.

50. Ibid., pp. 318–19.

51. Julian Goodacre, 'Highland Pipemaking in India', *Chanter* (Autumn 2017), available at https://www.goodbagpipes.com/index.php/about-me/writings/pipe-making/148-highland-pipemaking-in-india, last accessed 10 June 2024.

52. Ibid.

53. Peter Cooke, 'Bagpipes in India', *InterArts* (Spring 1987), pp. 14–15, at p. 14.

54. Ibid., p. 14.

55. Quoted in Mike Paterson, 'Return of the Drone: A "Folk" Thing?', in Dickson, *Highland Bagpipe*, p. 249.

56. Etan Smallman, 'Inside the Bizarre, Ruthless World of Competitive Bagpiping', *The Telegraph*, 3 July 2024, available at https://www.telegraph.co.uk/tv/2024/07/03/battle-of-the-bagpipes-sky-arts/, last accessed 3 July 2024.

57. See for instance 'Thirsty for Fame: Pakistan's Camel-Mounted Military Bagpipe Band', YouTube, 24 November 2015, available at https://www.youtube.com/watch?v=bAi7dsv9SyA, and 'LADAKH SCOUTS SKATING PIPE BAND || UNIQUE PIPE BAND', YouTube, 10 February 2021, available at https://www.youtube.com/watch?v=LDJ-4DRzbtE, last accessed 6 June 2024.

58. See for instance 'Indian Military Pipe Band Award Winning Performance', YouTube, 12 June 2015, available at https://www.youtube.com/watch?v=9fkT6SdD9LQ and 'SUMI BAND AT NORTH POINT FOR ANNUAL SPORTS 2019', YouTube, 11 October 2019, available at https://www.youtube.com/watch?v=BeEF_L2q7K0, last accessed 10 June 2024.

59. My thanks to Prof. Joshua Dickson of the Royal Conservatoire of Scotland for alerting me to this interview.

60. 'Shyopat Julia | The Tale of a Rajasthani Bagpiper | Mashak | I Believe Art Matters: Folk Edition', YouTube, 26 August 2022, available at https://www.youtube.com/watch?v=hSFJsZyrOsM, last accessed 6 June 2024. See also Peter Cooke, 'India 1986', available at https://www.drpetercooke.uk/india-1986/, and 'Post-colonial Bagpiping: Nigeria in Context', Soundyngs, 10 July 2023, available at https://soun-

dyngs.wp.st-andrews.ac.uk/2023/post-colonial-bagpiping-nigeria-in-context/, last accessed 10 June 2024.

61. Andrew Alter, 'Garhwali Bagpipes: Syncretic Processes in a North Indian Regional Musical Tradition,' *Asian Music* 29, no. 1 (1997), pp. 1–16, at p. 1.

62. Ibid.

63. Lady Wilson (Anne Campbell MacLeod), *Letter's from India* (Edinburgh: William Blackwood and Sons, 1911), p. 174.

64. Alter, 'Garhwali Bagpipes', p. 5.

65. H. S. Bhatia, *Military History of British India (1607–1947)* (New Delhi: Deep and Deep, 1977), p. 89.

66. Cooke, 'Bagpipes in India', p. 14.

67. Details on Findlater's life have been taken from Edward M. Spiers, 'Findlater, George Frederick (1872–1942)', *ODNB*, published online 4 October 2008, available at https://www.oxforddnb.com/display/10.1093/ref:odnb/9780198614128.001.0001/odnb-9780198614128-e-96873, last accessed 22 November 2024.

68. Strachan, 'Scotland's Military Identity', p. 328.

7. EVERYTHING CHANGES: THE GREAT WAR, WOMEN AND THE STANDARDISATION OF TRADITION: 1903–39

1. p. 11449.

2. Murray, *Music of the Scottish Regiments*, p. 292. Three pages earlier, Murray wrote: 'Estimable as his action was, Findlater was to motivate a host of would-be imitators, many of whom were to die emulating his example in the hope of winning the coveted award, the first at the Battle of Atbara in the Sudan the very next year.'

3. Seton and Grant, *Pipes of War*, pp. vii, 46.

4. I have relied upon Malcom's *Piper in Peace and War* of 1927 for casualty statistics rather than Seton and Grant's *Pipes of War* of 1920. Though Malcolm is not always accurate in his historical tales, he had the benefit of seven extra years to confirm these more verifiable facts, whereas Seton and Grant are perfectly clear that, publishing in 1920, their records were 'not, in all cases, complete' (p. 71). Malcolm's preface shows he consulted officials of the War Office, Public Record Office and Canadian Headquarters, among other sources of authority.

5. 'Voices from the Past: Daniel Laidlaw VC, Piper of Loos', YouTube, 29 October 2014, available at https://www.youtube.com/watch?v=CHYbYdfuyNs, last accessed 13 June 2024.

6. For the sources on Richardson's service, see Tim Stewart, '"The pipes play on": Canadian Pipers at War, 1914–1918; An Inspired Tradition',

Canadian Military History 9, no. 4 (2000), pp. 57–64, and 'James Richardson VC and His Pipes', Bagpipe News, available at https://bag-pipe.news/2022/10/09/james-richardson-vc-and-his-pipes/#_ftn-ref7, last accessed 13 June 2024. The 'coolness' quote below comes from the announcement of his VC in *The London Gazette* (Supplement), 22 October 1918, p. 12488.

7. H. M. Urquhart, *The History of the 16th Battalion (The Canadian Scottish), Canadian Expeditionary Force, in the Great War: 1914–1919* (Toronto: Macmillan, 1932), p. 182.

8. Robert Neal Rudmose Brown, R. C. Mossman, and J. H. Harvey Pirie, *The Voyage of the 'Scotia': Being the Record of a Voyage of Exploration in Antarctic Seas* (Edinburgh: W. Blackwood and Sons, 1906), p. 241. The penguin was in fact tied to Kerr's foot.

9. Details have been taken from 'World War 1 and an Unsung Piping Hero Comes to Light: Pipe Major David Anderson', Piping Press, 22 December 2020, available at https://pipingpress.com/2020/12/22/world-war-1-and-an-unsung-piping-hero-comes-to-light-pipe-major-david-anderson/, last accessed 13 June 2024.

10. 'War or Peace (Cogadh no Sith)', Piobaireachd Society, available at https://www.piobaireachd.co.uk/wp-content/uploads/2017/02/War-or-Peace-article.pdf, last accessed 19 August 2024.

11. Seton and Grant, *Pipes of War*, p. 43.

12. Quoted in Malcolm, *Piper in Peace and War*, p. 40.

13. 'Bagpipes in War: Part 1', YouTube, 6 March 2023, at 3:07, available at https://www.youtube.com/watch?v=Xlab5ADVP_s, last accessed 24 June 2024.

14. 'The Day the Guns Fell Silent: Armistice 1918', The Old Front Line, posted 7 November 2020, from minute 28, available at https://old-frontline.co.uk/2020/11/07/the-day-the-guns-fell-silent/, last accessed 25 November 2024.

15. Seton and Grant, *Pipes of War*, p. vii.

16. Gibson, *Traditional Gaelic Bagpiping*, p. 220.

17. Donaldson, *Highland Pipe and Scottish Society*, p. 282.

18. Ibid., p. 325.

19. Ibid., p. 330. Donaldson's book provides (though not without polemic) many of the details around the controversial past of the society.

20. See especially Chapter 17 in ibid., pp. 354–73.

21. Ibid., p. 430.

22. Ibid., p. 364.

23. From MacDonald's Foreword for the 1993 edition of Malcolm's *Piper in Peace and War*.

24. Michael Grey, 'Survey: 100 Year Evolution of Pipe Bands', Bagpipe

News, 6 December 2019, available at https://bagpipe.news/2019/12/06/survey-100-year-evolution-of-pipe-bands/, last accessed 20 June 2024.

25. An excellent short history of the Army Class, by Diana Henderson, is provided in the June and July editions of the 1989 *Piping Times*, with the title 'From Humble Beginnings: The Story of The Army School of Piping' (pp. 19–20, 37–45).

26. 'The Greatest 10 Pipe Band Drummers in History', Pipes|Drums, available at https://www.pipesdrums.com/article/the-greatest-10-pipe-band-drummers-in-history/, last accessed 20 June 2024.

27. Quoted in 'The Influence of the Boys Brigade on Piping'.

28. 'The MacLean Pipe Band, Champions of the World, 1927–30–35', *Piping and Dancing* 2 (September 1935), p. 18.

29. Donaldson, *Highland Pipe and Scottish Society*, p. 431. I have taken the costs from there too.

30. Interview with the author.

31. 'The Association's History', RSPBA, available at https://rspba.org/the-associations-history/, last accessed 21 November 2024.

32. John Johnston, 'Dr. K. N. MacDonald and Bagpipe Playing', *The Oban Times* (12 September 1896), p. 3.

33. J. F. Campbell (ed.), *Canntaireachd: Articulate Music* (Glasgow: Archibald Sinclair, 1880), pp. 33–4.

34. Ibid., p. 34.

35. Donaldson, *Pipers*, pp. 66–7.

36. 'Clan Chattan's Gathering', Pipes|Drums, available at https://www.pipesdrums.com/wp-content/docengines/E9A514380639413999544 56FB4832434.pdf?escape=1, last accessed 29 July 2024.

37. Donaldson, *Pipers*, p. 68.

38. Quoted in Jeannie Campbell, 'How Women Gained Equal Status in the Professional Piping World: Part 1', Bagpipe News, 8 March 2020, available at https://bagpipe.news/2020/03/08/how-women-gained-equal-status-in-the-professional-piping-world-part-1/, last accessed 21 June 2024.

39. Edgar Johnson, *Sir Walter Scott: The Great Unknown*, vol. 1 (London: Hamish Hamilton, 1970), p. 683.

40. See Donaldson, *Pipers*, pp. 67–8, and 'Lizzie Higgins', Hands Up for Trad, available at https://projects.handsupfortrad.scot/hall-of-fame/lizzie-higgins/, last accessed 20 June 2024.

41. 'Women & Democracy: The West Lothian Story', West Lothian Council, p. 14, available at https://news.westlothian.gov.uk/media/33057/Women-Democracy-the-West-Lothian-story/pdf/Women_and_Democracy_booklet_-_digital.pdf, last accessed 29 July 2024.

42. Jeannie Campbell names Elspeth Campbell (1873–1942), founder mem-

ber of the Piobaireachd Society, as the very first, playing for the Inveraray Pipe Band, which her father, Lord Archibald Campbell, had founded in the 1880s. See *Pipe Bands*, p. 495.

43. 'The Thread about Bessie Watson, the Incredible Life Story of the "Suffragette Piper Girl"', Threadinburgh, available at https://threadinburgh.scot/2023/08/31/the-thread-about-bessie-watson-the-incredible-life-story-of-the-suffragette-piper-girl/, last accessed 29 July 2024.

44. Jeannie Campbell, 'The Australian Ladies Pipe Band: The Definitive History Part 1', Piping Press, available at https://pipingpress.com/2023/07/13/the-australian-ladies-pipe-band-the-definitive-history-part-1/, last accessed 20 June 2024.

45. Campbell, *Pipe Bands*, p. 499.

46. The Victoria Street Girls' Pipe Band may have started some ten years prior to the Dagenham Girls, but little is known of their history. See ibid., p. 502.

47. 'The Dagenham Girl Pipers Pipe Band', RSPBA, available at https://rspba.org/the-associations-history/ladies-pipe-bands/, last accessed 20 June 2024. I'm grateful to this article for the other information contained in these paragraphs.

48. Ibid.

49. Jeannie Campbell, 'Ladies' Pipe Bands: A History Part 1', Piping Press, 18 January 2019, available at https://pipingpress.com/2019/01/18/ladies-pipe-bands-a-history-part-1/, last accessed 21 June 2024. The first Ladies' band in Canada was formed in Vancouver in 1927. See Campbell, *Pipe Bands*, p. 502.

50. Campbell, 'How Women Gained Equal Status in the Professional Piping World—Part 1'.

51. Ibid.

52. Ibid.

53. Quoted in Jeannie Campbell, 'Ladies' Pipe Bands: A History Part 2', Piping Press, 21 January 2019, available at https://pipingpress.com/2019/01/21/ladies-pipe-bands-a-history-part-2/, last accessed 24 June 2024.

8. PIPING CHARACTERS OF THE OLD WORLD ON THE CUSP OF THE NEW: ROUSING THE ROMANCE FROM WITHIN: 1939–1970s

1. Brett Tidswell, 'Piping in World War Two', Bagpipe News, 31 May 2020, available at https://bagpipe.news/2020/05/31/piping-in-world-war-two/, last accessed 1 July 2024.

2. Said in a speech at the Lord Mayor's Day Luncheon, 10 November 1942. See Winston Churchill, *The End of the Beginning: The Third Volume of Winston Churchill's War Speeches* (London: Cassell, 1943).

3. '5th Camerons Company Piper, Donald Macpherson, El Alamein, October 42', 51 HD, available at https://51hd.co.uk/accounts/camerons_piper_donald_macpherson, last accessed 1 July 2024.

4. Details from Jeannie Campbell, 'Piping in WW2: Prisoners of War Keep Their Music Alive', Piping Press, 24 January 2022, available at https://pipingpress.com/2022/01/24/piping-in-ww2-prisoners-of-war-keep-their-music-alive/, last accessed 3 July 2024.

5. Jeannie Campbell, 'WW2 Piping: John Wilson "Not Dead" and the Reel of the 51st Highland Division', Piping Press, 2 February 2022, available at https://pipingpress.com/2022/02/02/ww2-piping-john-wilson-not-dead-and-the-reel-of-the-51st-highland-division/, last accessed 3 July 2024.

6. Beth Roars, 'The Truth about Bagpipes', 26 January 2021, available at https://www.bethroars.com/singing-blog-tips/the-truth-about-bagpipes, last accessed 3 July 2024. I have been unable to find the original source of this information.

7. Details from Jeannie Campbell, 'Piping in WW2: The Army School Expands Its Teaching to All Serving Pipers', Piping Press, 17 January 2022, available at https://pipingpress.com/2022/01/17/piping-in-ww2-the-army-school-expands-its-teaching-to-all-serving-pipers/, last accessed 3 July 2024.

8. The following details and quotes are gathered from Robert Barr Smith, 'The Real Story of "Mad Jack" Churchill: A Rare Breed of Warrior', Warfare History Network, July 2005, available at https://warfarehistorynetwork.com/article/mad-jack-churchill-a-rare-breed-of-warrior/, last accessed 4 July 2024, and Miriam Bibby, 'Fighting Jack Churchill', Historic UK, available at https://www.historic-uk.com/HistoryUK/HistoryofBritain/Fighting-Jack_Churchill/, last accessed 4 July 2024.

9. Mini Katana, 'Claybeg Sword: The Techniques Behind Its Legendary Sharpness', 25 February 2024, available at https://minikatana.com/blogs/main/claybeg-sword-the-techniques-behind-its-legendary-sharpness, last accessed 4 July 2024. The actual Gaelic spelling is *claidheamh-beag*.

10. Lord Lovat's father also deserves a place in the annals of piping, for it was through him that Willie Ross's position as the famed instructor at the Army School of Piping was secured. Interestingly, the Rosses were keepers on the Fraser estate for three generations. See 'Willie Ross', Pipe Tunes, available at https://pipetunes.ca/composer/pipe-major-willie-ross/, last accessed 29 July 2023.

11. '"Piper Bill" Millin Played British Commandos from Sword Beach to Pegasus Bridge', War History Online, available at https://www.warhistoryonline.com/world-war-ii/bill-millin.html, last accessed 8 July 2024.

12. 'Obituary: Bill Millin', *The Economist*, 26 August 2010.
13. Ibid.
14. Greg Moodie, 'Bill Millin: The Bagpiper on the Beaches of Normandy', *The National*, 6 August 2023, available at https://www.thenational. scot/culture/23703813.bill-millin---bagpiper-beaches-normandy/, last accessed 8 July 2024.
15. 'Lord Lovat and D-day Piper Bill Millin 1994', YouTube, 11 December 2013, available at https://www.youtube.com/watch?v=TDEO0O IBD8U, last accessed 4 July 2024.
16. 'D-Day 80: Piper Bill Millin', Facebook, available at https://www.face-book.com/BritishMemorial/videos/d-day-80-piper-bill-millin/ 480775561280922/, last accessed 4 July 2024.
17. The details for this story are taken from '043: David Murray', Pipers' Persuasion, available at https://www.piperspersuasion.com/davidmur-ray/, last accessed 4 July 2024. Murray says it was the end of March, but Iain MacFadyen, one of the three pipers involved, remembers it as February. My thanks to Dougie Pincock for confirming this with Iain.
18. For other modern piobaireachd composers, see Donaldson, *Highland Pipe and Scottish Society*, p. 442.
19. Ibid., p. 445.
20. It was Pearston who came up with the name 'The College of Piping' and it was he who laid down the initial objects of the College. Listen from minute 28 to Seylan Baxter, 'Hillwalkers, Long Distance Melodeon Players and Gangrels', available at https://www.seylanbaxter.com/ blog/2018/2/15/hillwalkers-long-distance-melodeon-players-and-gan-grels, last accessed 19 August 2024.
21. For other modern piobaireachd composers, see *Donaldson, Highland Pipe and Scottish Society*, p. 436.
22. Ibid., p. 438.
23. Quoted in Jeannie Campbell, 'The Piping Times Championed the Cause of Women as Pipers', *Piping Times* 59, no. 6 (March 2007), pp. 23–33, at pp. 25–7.
24. Seumas MacNeill, 'Heather MacKenzie or a Defence of Lady Pipers', *Piping Times* 10, no. 3 (December 1957), pp. 9, 17.
25. Fergus Muirhead (ed.), *A Piper's Tale: Stories from the World's Top Pipers* (Glasgow: Cargo Publishing, 2013), p. 125.
26. Jeannie Campbell, 'Piping during WW2: The Founding of the College of Piping, Dunkirk and "Mad" Jack Churchill', Piping Press, 6 January 2022, available at https://pipingpress.com/2022/01/06/piping-dur-ing-ww2-the-founding-of-the-college-of-piping-dunkirk-and-mad-jack-churchill/, last accessed 19 August 2024.
27. 'College Membership', *Piping Times* (November 2017), p. 14. See also Duke University Libraries, 'Constitution of Fianna na h-Alba (Scottish

Youth Association)', available at https://repository.duke.edu/dc/broadsides/bdsbi15005, last accessed 19 August 2024.

28. College of Piping, 'Obituary: James "Jimmy" Jennett, 1928–2018', *Piping Times* 70, no. 6 (March 2018), pp. 49–52, at p. 49.

29. 'Constitution of Fianna na h-Alba (Scottish Youth Association)'.

30. Seylan Baxter, 'Hillwalkers, Long Distance Melodeon Players and Gangrels.'

31. Nick Brooke, *Terrorism and Nationalism in the United Kingdom* (London: Palgrave Macmillan, 2018), p. 18.

32. T. K. Wilson, *Killing Strangers: How Political Violence Became Modern* (Oxford: Oxford University Press, 2020), p. 66.

33. *Birmingham Mail* (31 January 1944), p. 4.

34. Listen to 'Hillwalkers, long-distance melodeon players and gangrels', at around minute 17.

35. *Scotsman* (10 January 1944), p. 3.

36. Seumas MacNeill and Thomas Pearston, *The College of Piping Tutor for the Highland Bagpipe Part 1* (Glasgow: College of Piping, 1953), p. 44.

37. See David Francis, 'The Emergence of the "Traditional Arts" in Scottish Cultural Policy', in Simon McKerrell and Gary West (eds), *Understanding Scotland Musically: Folk, Tradition and Policy* (London: Routledge, 2018), pp. 44–50.

38. Quoted in Campbell, *Pipe Bands*, p. 11.

39. MacNeill, *Piobaireachd*, p. 15.

40. Ibid., pp. 15–16.

41. Seumas MacNeill, 'The Argyllshire Gathering', *Piping Times* 26, no. 1 (October 1973), p. 10.

42. Bridget Mackenzie, 'MacNeill, Seumas [Seamas, James]', *ODNB*, published online 23 September 2004, available at https://www.oxforddnb.com/display/10.1093/ref:odnb/9780198614128.001.0001/odnb-9780198614128-e-65735, last accessed 25 November 2024.

43. Dougie Pincock in conversation with the author.

44. Seumas MacNeill, 'Editorial', *Piping Times* 9, no. 4 (January 1957), p. 5.

45. Max Arthur, 'Obituary: Maj-Gen Frank Richardson', *The Independent*, 16 September 1996, available at https://www.independent.co.uk/news/people/obituary-majgen-frank-richardson-1363613.html, last accessed 8 July 2024.

46. Frank Richardson, *Mars with Venus: A Study of Some Homosexual Generals* (Edinburgh: W. Blackwood, 1981), p. 4.

47. Ibid., p. 5.

48. 'Call Me Susan, Says the Pipe Major', *Daily Mail* (18 November 1976).

49. Quoted in Jeannie Campbell, 'Sue MacIntyre 1929–2010', *Piping Times* 62, no. 11 (August 2010), pp. 50–1, at p. 51.

50. 'Call me Susan, Says the Pipe Major'.

51. Campbell, 'Sue MacIntyre 1929–2010', p. 51.

52. Andra Noble, 'Famous Pipers: Roddy Ross, a Capital Character', *Piping Times* 72, no. 4 (January 2020), pp. 33–8, at p. 37.

53. This is taken from a brief biography found beneath the above article; it is not clear who wrote it.

54. 'When Malcolm Passed Away', Piobaireachd Society, available at https://www.piobaireachd.co.uk/wp-content/uploads/2014/03/When-Malcolm-passed-away.pdf, last accessed 9 July 2024.

55. My thanks to Michael Grey for supplying me with this brilliant anecdote.

56. Taken from Colonel David Murray's eulogy at Burgess's funeral, available at http://www.pmjohndburgess.com/eulogy2.html, last accessed 9 July 2024.

57. Ibid. Burgess's stint with the Invergordon Distillery Pipe Band between 1965 and 1967 cannot have helped matters.

58. James Burnet in conversation with the author.

59. '093: Allan W. Hamilton', Pipers' Persuasion, available at https://www.piperspersuasion.com/093-allan-w-hamilton/, last accessed 24 July 2024. It was a privilege to be asked by Allan to interview him for this episode.

60. 'Seumas MacNeill and John D Burgess', YouTube, 10 January 2023, available at https://www.youtube.com/watch?v=_yf9vqaKZcg, last accessed 10 June 2024.

9. BREAKING FREE FROM THE SHACKLES OF CONVENTION: THE BAG-PIPES REDEFINED: 1970s–1994

1. J. Quigg and P. Glendinning, 'Gail Force Piping: An Interview with Gail Brown', *The Voice* (Spring 2002), p. 27.

2. 'Editorial', *Piping Times* 23, no. 8 (May 1971), p. 7.

3. Campbell, 'Piping Times Championed the Cause of Women', pp. 23–33.

4. Bill Livingstone in conversation with the author. The incident is also related on p. 120 of Livingstone's memoirs *Preposterous*.

5. This was Margaret Houlihan (now Dunn), from Ireland, who won the Argyllshire Gathering's 'A' grade Strathspey and Reel that year.

6. Dougie Pincock points this out in Muirhead, *Piper's Tale*, p. 127.

7. MacLeod was also the first piper in a folk group to play other instruments, mainly whistle and bodhran.

8. 'Seumas MacNeill and John D Burgess'.

9. Quoted in Steve Winick, 'Blows-a-Bellows #2', *Dirty Linen* 61 (December 1995/January 1996), available at https://www.rootsworld.com/rw/feature/dlbag2.html, last accessed 18 July 2024.

10. As quoted to me by Dougie Pincock.

11. Dougie Pincock in conversation with the author.

12. '057: Iain MacDonald of Neilston', Pipers' Persuasion, available at http://www.piperspersuasion.com/iainmacdonaldneilston/, last accessed 20 July 2024.

13. See Kate Martin (ed.), *Fèis: The First Twenty-Five Years of the Fèis Movement* (Portree, Skye: Fèisean nan Gàidheal, 2006), pp. 12, 17.

14. Gary West in conversation with the author.

15. 'Colin Ross Remembered', Bagpipe Society, available at https://www.bagpipesociety.org.uk/articles/2019/chanter/autumn/colin-ross-remembered/, last accessed 19 July 2024.

16. The two players, whose names have been given to me by Hugh Cheape, were Jimmy Wilson and Cedric Clarke.

17. The details of Wallace's adventures are taken from '056: Robert Wallace', Pipers' Persuasion, available at https://www.piperspersuasion.com/robertwallace-2/, last accessed 19 July 2024.

18. 'The Whistlebinkies', Hands Up for Trad, available at https://projects.handsupfortrad.scot/hall-of-fame/the-whistlebinkies/, last accessed 19 July 2024.

19. Gordon Mooney, 'A Memoir of the Early Days of the Lowland and Border Pipers Society and Reviving "*The Auld Loveable Use*"', Odd Scotland, available at https://www.oddscotland.com/lowland-and-border-pipers-society-history, last accessed 19 July 2024. Subsequent details are taken from this account.

20. According to Rab Wallace in his Pipers' Persuasion interview.

21. According to Moore, 'Jimmy Anderson had [also] worked on the development of ... Border [or Lowland] Pipes and The Scottish Small Pipes by adapting oboe reeds for his small pipes chanter ... It was Colin, however, who had the idea of using the Northumbrian chanter reed technology in the design and production of the modern Scottish Small Pipe chanter. This improved the sound and created a "standard" chanter and reed for The Scottish Small Pipes.' 'Colin Ross Remembered'.

22. Rab Wallace, 'A Far Cry from the MacCrimmons: Scotland's Forgotten Bagpipes', *Chanter* (1986), pp. 35–6, at p. 36.

23. Details taken from '057: Iain MacDonald of Neilston'.

24. Other examples might include Czechoslovakia, Romania, Bulgaria, Hungary, Germany, Austria, Sweden, Portugal, Italy; the list could go on!

25. Mano Panferreteiro, 'Pipes and Pipers: Galician Symbols of Ever Evolving Meaning', *Chanter* (Summer 2017), available at https://www.bagpipesociety.org.uk/articles/2017/chanter/summer/pipes-and-pipers, last accessed 22 July 2024.

26. Ibid.

27. It should be noted that the ideas behind the word 'Celtic' are highly contested. See Cheape, 'Celtic Connections on an Atlantic Corridor'.

28. Quoted in Michael Moll, 'More Pipers than Priests: Carlos Núñez on the Spanish Celtic Scene and Touring in the World', Folk World, available at http://www.folkworld.de/5/carlos3.html, last accessed 22 July 2024.

29. 'Piping among the Bretons: A History, Part 1', Piping Press, 30 July 2021, available at https://pipingpress.com/2021/07/30/piping-among-the-bretons-a-history-part-1/, last accessed 22 July 2024.

30. The contested history is outlined in Jean-François Allain, 'The Acculturation of the Great Highland Bagpipe in Brittany', Piping Times (February 1995), pp. 30–9.

31. For the development of the marching band tradition within Brittany and Galicia, see '057: Iain MacDonald of Neilston'.

32. Santiago Caneiro, 'A Asociación de Gaiteiros Galegos e as memorias dun conflicto', December 1995, available at http://gaiteirosgalegos.gal/xoops/uploads/agg-memorias-conflicto.pdf#page=3&zoom=auto,-275,811, last accessed 22 November 2024, and 'Colectivo en Defensa da Gaita (CDG)', CD Gaita, available at https://cdgaita.wixsite.com/cdgaitagal, last accessed 22 November 2024.

33. 'More Pipers than Priests'. See also José Colmeiro, 'Bagpipes, Bouzoukis, and Bodhráns: The Reinvention of Galician Folk Music', in Colmeiro, Peripheral Visions/Global Sounds: From Galicia to the World (Liverpool: Liverpool University Press, 2018); online edn, Liverpool Scholarship Online, 24 May 2018, available at https://doi.org/10.5949/liverpool/9781786940308.003.0011, last accessed 24 July 2024.

34. See Gibson, Traditional Gaelic Bagpiping, especially Chapters 14 and 17.

35. Colin MacLellan in conversation with the author.

36. Preposterous, p. 118.

37. Ibid., p. 110.

38. Bill Livingstone in conversation with the author.

39. Preposterous, p. 146.

40. Despite this Scottish dominance, between the 1950s and '70s the RSPBA were refreshingly open to holding the contest outside Scotland. The championships were also held in Belfast in 1956 and 1962 and in England on two occasions—Corby in 1975 and Nottingham in 1979. They have been held in Glasgow since 1986.

41. Michael Grey in conversation with the author.

42. Preposterous, p. 149.

43. Ibid.

10. YESTERDAY, TODAY AND FOREVER: THE HEALTH, OR OTHERWISE, OF SCOTLAND'S CONTEMPORARY PIPING CULTURE: 1994 ONWARDS

1. This and any of the following stories that are unattributed are from 'Gordon Duncan Full Documentary: Just for Gordon', YouTube, 30 December 2020, available at https://www.youtube.com/watch?v= VIGFrUju0KU, last accessed 26 July 2024.

2. Gary West, *Voicing Scotland: Folk, Culture, Nation* (Edinburgh: Luath Press, 2012), p. 89.

3. Ibid., p. 84.

4. 'Gordon Duncan Full Documentary: Just for Gordon'.

5. Seumas MacNeill to Ian Green of Greentrax records in response to Green's proposal of an advert in the *Piping Times* for some of his records. The quote was supplied to me by Gary West, who saw the letter.

6. Bob Thomas, my mother's older brother, who played guitar, five-string banjo and mandolin. He left the band in 1979.

7. 'Gordon Duncan Full Documentary: Just for Gordon'.

8. Quoted in 'Just for Seumas', The Session, available at https://thesession.org/recordings/2856, last accessed 26 July 2024.

9. 'Hamish Moore: It Might Lead to Dancing', Bagpipe News, 4 February 2021, available at https://bagpipe.news/2021/02/04/hamish-moore-it-might-lead-to-dancing/, last accessed 26 July 2024.

10. West, *Voicing Scotland*, p. 86.

11. 'Famous Pipers: Gordon Duncan', Bagpipe News, 14 December 2021, available at https://bagpipe.news/2021/12/14/famous-pipers-gordon-duncan/, last accessed 26 July 2024.

12. Ibid.

13. Ibid.

14. 'Gordon Duncan Full Documentary: Just for Gordon'.

15. Martyn Bennett, 'Biography', available at http://www.martynbennett.com/Martyn_Biography.html#, last accessed 26 July 2024. At the point of writing, Gary West is putting the final touches to his comprehensive biography of Martyn, to be entitled *Brave New Music: the Martyn Bennett Story*, which will be published by Luath Press in January 2025.

16. Ibid.

17. Martyn Bennett, 'Timeline', available at http://www.martynbennett.com/Martyn_Timeline.html, last accessed 27 July 2024.

18. Quoted in 'Remembering Martyn Bennett: The Rebirth of Grit', BBC, 16 January 2015, available at https://www.bbc.co.uk/programmes/articles/5l1pTPXFnJfZL61MFkMHbws/remembering-martyn-bennett-the-rebirth-of-grit, last accessed 27 July 2024.

19. 'Martyn Bennett "Grit": The Documentary', YouTube, 23 May 2014,

available at https://www.youtube.com/watch?v=9aJXNN_D07o, last accessed 27 July 2024.

20. Ibid.

21. Gary West in conversation with the author. West recognises, however, the other important attempts in this direction, spearheaded by The Big Music Society. The following performance is especially worthy of note: 'Lord Lovat's Lament: The Big Music Society Featuring Murray Henderson; Live at Cottiers', YouTube, 24 February 2016, available at https://www.youtube.com/watch?v=qqtGWvBUzfE, last accessed 29 July 2024.

22. Martyn Bennett, *GRIT* (2003), sleeve notes.

23. Finlay MacDonald in conversation with the author.

24. For an excellent discussion of 'tradition' understood in these terms, see West, *Voicing Scotland*, pp. 23–49.

25. The Gordon Duncan Memorial Trust, founded in 2006, and the trust's solo piping competition, continue to inspire and entice pipers to approach their music with something of Gordon's flair. The award-winning musical *Thunderstruck*, written and performed by David Colvin, adds another dramatic aspect to his legacy.

26. '"Scotland" in International Sign Language', YouTube, 3 September 2014, available at https://www.youtube.com/watch?v=ZbDbHPmvj 9Y, last accessed 15 August 2024.

27. The founders were Sir Brian and Lady Ivory and Sandy Grant Gordon. The College of Piping remained independent of the centre until the former transferred its charitable and commercial activities to the latter in 2018.

28. 'Piping Live Organisation!', Piping Live!, available at https://pipinglive. co.uk/pages/piping-live-organisation, last accessed 29 July 2024.

29. Information provided by the Scottish Schools Pipes and Drums Trust.

30. 'The BBC Responds to the Piping Press Story on the Future of "Pipeline"', Piping Press, 13 December 2022, available at https://pipingpress. com/2022/12/13/the-bbc-responds-to-the-piping-press-story-on-the-future-of-pipeline/, last accessed 30 July 2024.

31. The recipient of this condescension was Jenny Hazzard. I shall not name the giver.

32. 'Positive Change: A Collective Vision for the Future', Pipes|Drums, 8 March 2024, available at https://www.pipesdrums.com/article/positive-change-a-collective-vision-for-the-future/, last accessed 30 July 2024. While the present book was in production, the National Piping Centre published the results of their own even more comprehensive review, entitled 'Women in Piping and Drumming: Equality, Inclusivity, and Diversity (EDI)'. The results showed similarly worrying concerns.

33. Ibid.
34. Brian Ferguson, 'Campaign Launched to Protect Women from Sexual Abuse and Harassment in Scots Trad Music Scene', *Scotsman*, 22 August 2020, available at https://www.scotsman.com/whats-on/arts-and-entertainment/campaign-launched-to-protect-women-from-sexual-abuse-and-harassment-in-scots-trad-music-scene-2950056, last accessed 30 July 2024.
35. '100: Are Pipers Musicians?', Pipers' Persuasion, available at https://www.piperspersuasion.com/are-pipers-musicians/, last accessed 31 July 2024.
36. Some writers have even metamorphosed piobaireachd into literature. I'm thinking of Kirsty Dunn's novel, *The Big Music* (London: Faber & Faber, 2012) and the poet Jock Stein's collection *The Iolaire/An Iolaire* (Haddington: Handsel Press, 2019).
37. Quoted in Bill Gibb, 'Former Spin Doctor Alastair Campbell on How Bagpipe Music Helps His Mental Health', *The Sunday Post*, 19 May 2019, available at https://www.sundaypost.com/fp/former-spin-doctor-alastair-campbell-on-how-bagpipe-music-helps-his-mental-health/, last accessed 30 July 2024.
38. 'The Wheeled Piper', Facebook, available at https://www.facebook.com/thewheeledpiper/, last accessed 30 July 2024.
39. 'Katie "The Wheeled Piper" Interview: Piping Live! 2023', YouTube, 29 October 2023, available at https://www.youtube.com/watch?v=vUWQCcXI0bw, last accessed 30 July 2024.
40. 'Gavin Clark, PLHS Headteacher', Preston Lodge High School Pipe Band, 23 October 2017, available at https://plhspipeband.com/2017/10/23/gavin-clark-plhs-headteacher/, last accessed 31 July 2024.
41. As told to me by Andy McCartney, chair of the South West Scotland Piping and Drumming Academy.
42. Andy McCartney in conversation with the author.
43. Meghan McAvoy, 'Slaying the Tartan Monster: Hybridisation in Recent Scottish Music', in McKerrell and West, *Understanding Scotland Musically*, pp. 93–108, at p. 103.
44. Finlay MacDonald in conversation with the author.
45. McAvoy, 'Slaying the Tartan Monster', p. 107.
46. Muirhead, *Piper's Tale*, p. 31.

CONCLUSION: A GLOBAL INSTRUMENT WORTHY OF MYSTERY

1. Jane Pettegree, 'Post-colonial Bagpiping: Nigeria in Context', Soundyngs, 10 July 2023, available at https://soundyngs.wp.st-andrews.ac.uk/2023/post-colonial-bagpiping-nigeria-in-context/, last accessed 15 August 2024.

2. Ross O'C Jennings in conversation with the author.

3. See Kerry Sheridan, *Bagpipe Brothers: The FDNY Band's True Story of Tragedy, Mourning, and Recovery* (New Brunswick, NJ: Rutgers University Press, 2004). For all the Irish connections, since 1999 New York City's largest piping event has been the Pipes of Christmas, a celebration of the holiday season through the sound of pipes, an event hosted by the Learned Kindred of Currie, a non-profit organisation explicit about the Scottish ancestry of its members. The organisation exists to preserve and promote Celtic heritage and the arts.

4. 'Ally the Piper' (channel), YouTube, available at https://www.youtube.com/@PiperAlly/featured, last accessed 16 August 2024.

5. My thanks to my friend Dr Alastair Andrew for drawing my attention to this remarkable musician.

6. 'A Conversation with Ally the Piper, the World's Most Famous Piping Performer: Part 1', YouTube, 24 March 2023, available at https://www.youtube.com/watch?v=jitpa6znipA, last accessed 16 August 2024.

7. Michael Grey in conversation with the author.

8. Michael Grey in conversation with the author.

9. '057: Iain MacDonald of Neilston'.

10. https://x.com/EmergencyBod/status/1801560437596602475, last accessed 17 August 2024.

11. 'Hunnu Guren: Batzorig Vaanchig & Auli', YouTube, 4 October 2018, available at https://www.youtube.com/watch?v=vztRqe_CHC0, last accessed 17 August 2024.

12. Gary West in conversation with the author.

13. 'Pipe Band Heritage in the South of Ireland', Irish Pipe Band Association, p. 10, available at https://ipba.ie/wp-content/uploads/2023/06/Chapter-I-Revival.pdf, last accessed 19 August 2024.

14. Ibid., p. 11.

15. Ibid., p. 10.

16. Skander Hannachi, 'Mezoued, the North African Art Form You Never Heard Of …', Medium, 16 October 2019, available at https://medium.com/music-voices/mezoued-the-north-african-art-form-you-never-heard-of-1228b51b3911, last accessed 18 August 2024.

17. Panferreteiro, 'Pipes and Pipers'.

18. 'Palestinian Bagpipers Join Battle Cry for Scottish Independence', *The Guardian*, 16 September 2014, available at https://www.theguardian.com/world/2014/sep/16/palestinian-bagpipers-battle-cry-scottish-independence, last accessed 18 August 2024.

19. 'How Queen Elizabeth Stopped George Osborne from Cutting the Highland Bagpipe School …', YouTube, 7 November 2023, available

at https://www.youtube.com/watch?v=X_dD74uhe40, last accessed 18 August 2024.

20. 'Miriam Margolyes Loves Piping! And Happy Birthday, Bill Livingstone!', YouTube, 20 March 2023, available at https://www.youtube.com/watch?v=ZUD0dg_RIPs, last accessed 19 August 2024.

21. Michael Grey in conversation with the author.

BIBLIOGRAPHY

Books

Albonesi, Theseo Ambrogio, *Introductio in Chaldaican linguam* (Cremona, 1539).

Allan, David, *Virtue, Learning and the Scottish Enlightenment* (Edinburgh: Edinburgh University Press, 2020).

Ash, Marinell, *The Strange Death of Scottish History* (Edinburgh: Ramsay Head, 1980).

Baines, Anthony, *Bagpipes* (Oxford: Oxford University Press, 1960).

Beaugue, Jean de, *The History of the Campagnes 1548 and 1549: Being an Exact Account of the Martial Expeditions Perform'd in Those Days by the Scots and French on the One Side, and by the English and Their Foreign Auxiliaries on the Other; Done in French, under the Title of, The Scots War, by Monsieur Beague, a French Gentleman* (1707).

Beveridge, Erskine (ed.), *The Burgh Records of Dunfermline, Transcribed from the Original Manuscript Volume Courts, Sasines, etc, 1488–1584* (Edinburgh: William Brown, 1917).

Bhatia, H. S., *Military History of British India (1607–1947)* (New Delhi: Deep and Deep, 1977).

Bostridge, Ian, *Schubert's Winter Journey: Anatomy of an Obsession* (London: Faber & Faber, 2015).

Brooke, Nick, *Terrorism and Nationalism in the United Kingdom* (London: Palgrave Macmillan, 2018).

Brown, Robert Neal Rudmose and R. C. Mossman, J. H. Harvey Pirie, *The Voyage of the 'Scotia': Being the Record of a Voyage of Exploration in Antarctic Seas* (Edinburgh: W. Blackwood and Sons, 1906).

Brown, Thomas, *The Works of Thomas Brown*, vol. 2, 5th edn (London: Printed for Sam Briscoe, 1719).

Bulwer, Henry Lytton, *The Life of Henry John Temple, Viscount Palmerston*, vol. 1 (London: Richard Bentley, 1870).

BIBLIOGRAPHY

Campbell, J. F. (ed.), *Canntaireachd: Articulate Music* (Glasgow: Archibald Sinclair, 1880).

Campbell, Jeannie, *Highland Bagpipe Makers* (Edinburgh: Magnus Orr Publishing, 2001).

———— *Pipe Bands* (n.p. [Scotland]: n.p., 2021).

Campbell, John Lorne (ed.), *Highland Songs of the Forty-Five* (Edinburgh: Scottish Gaelic Texts Society, 1984).

Campsie, Alistair, *The MacCrimmon Legend: The Madness of Angus Mackay* (Edinburgh: Canongate, 1980).

Cannon, Richard, *Historical Records of the 72nd Regiment, or the Duke of Albany's Own Highlanders* (London: Parker, Furnivall & Parker, 1848).

Cannon, Roderick D., *A Bibliography of Bagpipe Music* (Edinburgh: John Donald, 1980).

———— *The Highland Bagpipe and its Music* (Edinburgh: John Donald, 2002)

Chamber, Charles Edward Steuart, *The Woodhouselee MS: A Narrative of Events in Edinburgh and District during the Jacobite Occupation* (London: W. & R. Chambers, 1907).

Chaucer, Geoffrey, *The Riverside Chaucer*, ed. Larry Dean Benson (Oxford: Oxford University Press, 2008).

Cheape, Hugh, *Bagpipes: A National Collection of a National Instrument* (Edinburgh: NMSE, 2008).

———— *The Book of the Bagpipe* (Belfast: The Appletree Press, 1999).

———— *Tartan: The Highland Habit* (Edinburgh: NMSE, 1990).

Churchill, Winston, *The End of the Beginning: The Third Volume of Winston Churchill's War Speeches* (London: Cassell, 1943).

Collinson, Francis, *The Bagpipe: The History of a Musical Instrument* (London: Routledge & Kegan Paul, 1975).

Coltman, Viccy, *Art and Identity in Scotland: A Cultural History from the Jacobite Rising of 1745 to Walter Scott* (Cambridge: Cambridge University Press, 2019).

Cookson, John, *The British Armed Nation 1793–1815* (Oxford: Oxford University Press, 1997).

Devine, T. M., *Clanship to Crofters' War: The Social Transformation of the Scottish Highlands* (Manchester: Manchester University Press, 1994).

———— *The Scottish Clearances: A History of the Dispossessed, 1600–1900* (London: Allen Lane, 2018).

Dickson, Joshua (ed.), *The Highland Bagpipe: Music, History, Tradition* (Farnham, Surrey: Ashgate, 2009).

BIBLIOGRAPHY

Dickson, Thomas (ed.), *Accounts of the Lord High Treasurer of Scotland, Volume 1: A.D. 1473–1498* (Edinburgh: HM General Register House, 1877).

Donaldson, William, *The Highland Pipe and Scottish Society 1750–1950: Transmission, Change and the Concept of Tradition* (Edinburgh: John Donald, 2008).

———— *Pipers: A Guide to the Players and Music of the Highland Bagpipe* (Edinburgh: Birlinn, 2005).

Dunbar, John Telfer, *The Costume of Scotland* (London: Batsford, 1981).

————*History of Highland Dress* (Philadelphia: Defour Editions, 1964).

Dziennik, Matthew P., *The Fatal Land: War, Empire, and the Highland Soldier in British America* (New Haven: Yale University Press, 2015).

Farmer, Henry George, *A History of Music in Scotland* (London: Hinrichsen, 1947).

Fraser, Alexander Duncan, *Some Reminiscences and the Bagpipe* (Falkirk: Wm. J. Hay, 1907).

Fraser, James, *Chronicles of the Frasers: The Wardlaw Manuscript Entitled 'Polichronicon seu policratica temporum, or, The True Genealogy of the Frasers' 916–1674*, ed. William MacKay (Edinburgh: T. and A. Constable, 1905).

Galpin, F. W., *Old English Instruments of Music* (London: Methuen, 1965).

Geoghegan, John, *The Compleat Tutor for the Pastoral or New Bagpipe* (London, n.d.).

Gibson, John G., *Traditional Gaelic Bagpiping 1745–1945* (Montreal: McGill–Queen's University Press, 1998).

Grattan Flood, William H., *The Story of the Bagpipe* (London: Walter Scott Publishing Co., 1911).

Henshaw, Victoria, *Scotland and the British Army, 1700–1750: Defending the Union* (London: Bloomsbury Publishing, 2014).

Herman, Arthur, *How the Scots Invented the Modern World: The True Story of How Western Europe's Poorest Nation Created Our World and Everything in It* (New York: Crown Publishing Group, 2001).

Hume, Alexander, *Hymnes, or Sacred Songs* (n.p., 1599).

Jamieson, James H., *The Book of the Old Edinburgh Club, Nineteenth Volume* (Edinburgh: T & A Constable, 1933)

Johnson, David, *Music and Society in Lowland Scotland in the Eighteenth Century* (Oxford: Oxford University Press, 1972).

Johnson, Edgar, *Sir Walter Scott: The Great Unknown*, vol. 1 (London: Hamish Hamilton, 1970).

BIBLIOGRAPHY

Johnson, Samuel and James Boswell, *A Journey to the Western Islands of Scotland* and *The Journal of a Tour to the Hebrides* (New York: Everyman's Library, 2002).

Kidd, Colin, *Subverting Scotland's Past: Scottish Whig Historians and the Creation of an Anglo-British Identity 1689–1830* (Cambridge: Cambridge University Press, 1993).

Leyden, John, *The Complaynt of Scotland: Written in 1548; With a Preliminary Dissertation, and Glossary* (Edinburgh: Archibald Constable, 1801).

Livingstone, Bill, *Preposterous: Tales to Follow* (Victoria, Canada: Friesen Press, 2017).

MacDonald [spelt McDonald in the original publication], Patrick, *A Collection of Highland Vocal Airs* (n.p., 1784).

MacInnes, Allan, *Clanship, Commerce and the House of Stuart* (East Linton: Tuckwell Press, 1996).

Mackay, Angus, *A Collection of Ancient Piobaireachd and Highland Pipe Music* (Aberdeen: Logan & Company, 1838).

MacKay, John, *History of the Burgh of the Canongate* (Edinburgh, 1900).

Mackenzie, Bridget, *Piping Traditions of the Inner Isles* (Edinburgh: John Donald, 2012).

———— *Piping Traditions of the North of Scotland* (Edinburgh: John Donald, 1998).

MacNeill, Seumas, *Piobaireachd: Classical Music of the Highland Bagpipe* (Edinburgh: BBC, 1968).

MacNeill, Seumas and Frank Richardson, *Piobaireachd and Its Interpretation* (Edinburgh: John Donald, 1987).

MacPherson, Angus, *A Highlander Looks Back* (Oban: Oban Times, 1955).

Malcolm, C. A., *The Piper in Peace and War* (London: Hardwicke Press, 1993).

Malcolm Smith, N. A. (ed.), *The First Hundred Years: A History of the Royal Scottish Pipers' Society* (Edinburgh: Royal Scottish Pipers' Society, 1983).

Manson, William Laird, *The Highland Bagpipe: Its History, Literature, and Music, with Some Account of the Traditions, Superstitions, and Anecdotes Relating to the Instrument and Its Tunes* (Paisley: A. Gardner, 1901).

Martin, Kate (ed.), *Fèis: The First Twenty-Five Years of the Fèis Movement* (Portree, Skye: Fèisean nan Gàidheal, 2006).

McHardy, Stuart, *The Silver Chanter: Historical Tales of Scottish Pipers* (Edinburgh: Birlinn, 2004).

McKerrell, Simon and Gary West (eds), *Understanding Scotland Musically: Folk, Tradition and Policy* (London: Routledge, 2018).

McLeod, Wilson, *Divided Gaels: Gaelic Cultural Identities in Scotland and Ireland, c.1200–c.1650* (Oxford: Oxford University Press, 2004).

More, Paul Elmer (ed.), *The Complete Poetical Works of Byron* (Boston: Houghton Mifflin Company, 1933).

Morton, Graeme, *Ourselves and Others: Scotland 1832–1914* (Edinburgh: Edinburgh University Press, 2012).

Muirhead, Fergus (ed.), *A Piper's Tale: Stories from the World's Top Pipers* (Glasgow: Cargo Publishing, 2013).

Munro, William, *Reminiscences of Military Service with the 93rd Sutherland Highlanders* (London: Hurst and Blackett, 1883).

Murray, David, *Music of the Scottish Regiments* (Edinburgh: Mercat Press, 1994).

Newte, Thomas, *Prospects and Observations: On a Tour in England and Scotland; Natural, Oeconomical, and Literary* (London, 1791).

Ó Baoill, Colm, *Bàrdachd Chloinn Ghill-Eathain: Eachann Bacach and Other Maclean Poets* (Edinburgh: Scottish Gaelic Texts Society, 1979).

——— (ed.), *Poems and Songs by Sileas MacDonald* (Edinburgh: Scottish Academic Press for the Scottish Gaelic Texts Society, 1972).

Pittock, Murray, *The Myth of the Jacobite Clans* (Edinburgh: Edinburgh University Press, 1995).

——— (ed.), *The Reception of Sir Walter Scott in Europe* (London: Bloomsbury, 2007).

——— *The Road to Independence? Scotland since the Sixties* (London: Reaktion Books, 2008).

Purser, John, *Scotland's Music: A History of the Traditional and Classical Music of Scotland from Early Times to the Present Day* (Edinburgh: Mainstream Publishing, 1992).

Richardson, Frank, *Mars with Venus: A Study of some Homosexual Generals* (Edinburgh: W. Blackwood, 1981).

Roberts, Michael, *Essays in Swedish History* (Minneapolis: University of Minnesota Press, 1967).

Ruutz Rees, L. E., *The Personal Narrative of the Siege of Lucknow* (London: Longman, Brown, Green, Longmans & Roberts, 1858).

Scott, Walter, *Minstrelsy of the Scottish Border*, vol. 1 (Kelso, 1802).

Seton, Bruce and John Grant, *The Pipes of War: A Record of the Achievements of Pipers of Scottish and Overseas Regiments during the War, 1914–18* (Glasgow: MacLehose, Jackson & Co., 1920).

Shears, Barry, *Dance to the Piper: The Highland Bagpipe in Nova Scotia* (Sydney, Nova Scotia: Cape Breton University Press, 2008).

Sheridan, Kerry, *Bagpipe Brothers: The FDNY Band's True Story of Tragedy, Mourning, and Recovery* (New Brunswick: Rutgers University Press, 2004).

Sider, Sandra, *Handbook of Life in Renaissance Europe* (Oxford: Oxford University Press, 2007).

Szabó, Zoltán G., *A Duda: The Bagpipe; Catalogue of the Museum of Ethnography 9* (Budapest: Museum of Ethnography, 2004).

Trevor-Roper, Hugh, *The Invention of Scotland: Myth and History* (New Haven: Yale University Press, 2008).

Urquhart, H. M., *The History of the 16th Battalion (The Canadian Scottish), Canadian Expeditionary Force, in the Great War: 1914–1919* (Toronto: Macmillan, 1932).

Vereno, Michael Peter, *The Voice of the Wind: A Linguistic History of Bagpipes* (Lincoln, England: International Bagpipe Organisation, 2021).

Ward, Edward, *Nuptial Dialogues and Debates: Or, an Useful Prospect of the Felicities and Discomforts of a Married Life*, vol. 2 (London: Printed for C. Hitch et al., 1759).

West, Gary, *Voicing Scotland: Folk, Culture, Nation* (Edinburgh: Luath Press, 2012).

Williamson, Craig, *The Old English Riddles of the Exeter Book* (Chapel Hill: University of North Carolina Press, 1977).

Wilson, Lady (Anne Campbell MacLeod), *Letter's from India* (Edinburgh: William Blackwood and Sons, 1911).

Wilson, T. K., *Killing Strangers: How Political Violence Became Modern* (Oxford: Oxford University Press, 2020).

Wormald, Jenny, *Court, Kirk, and Community: Scotland 1470–1625* (Edinburgh: Edinburgh University Press, 2018).

Articles, book chapters, pamphlets and reports

Allain, Jean-François, 'The Acculturation of the Great Highland Bagpipe in Brittany', *Piping Times* (February 1995), pp. 30–9.

Alter, Andrew, 'Garhwali Bagpipes: Syncretic Processes in a North Indian Regional Musical Tradition,' *Asian Music* 29, no. 1 (1997), pp. 1–16.

Anderson, Ross, 'The Pastoral Pipe Repertoire, Rediscovered', *Common Stock* 20, no. 2 (December 2005), available at https://www.cl.cam.ac.uk/~rja14/music/pastoral.pdf, last accessed 8 May 2024.

Balosso-Bardin, Cassandre, 'A Short Overview of the Bagpipes from the Iberian Peninsula', *Chanter* (Summer 2017), available at https://www.

bagpipesociety.org.uk/articles/2017/chanter/summer/iberian-overview/, last accessed 22 July 2024.

Block, Edward A., 'Chaucer's Millers and Their Bagpipes', *Speculum* 29, no. 2 (1954), pp. 239–43.

Brown, Barnaby, 'What Do 1s and Os Mean?', *Piping Today* 71 (2014), pp. 3–7.

Campbell, Archibald, 'The Highland Bagpipe', part II, *Piping Times* 14, no. 2 (August 1962), pp. 6–9.

Campbell, Jeannie, 'The Piping Times Championed the Cause of Women as Pipers', *Piping Times* 59, no. 6 (March 2007), pp. 23–33.

———— 'Sue MacIntyre 1929–2010', *Piping Times* 62, no. 11 (August 2010), pp. 50–1.

———— 'How Women Gained Equal Status in the Professional Piping World: Part 1', *Bagpipe News*, 8 March 2020, available at https://bagpipe.news/2020/03/08/how-women-gained-equalstatus-in-the-professional-piping-world-part-1/, last accessed 21 June 2024.

———— 'Ladies' Pipe Bands: A History Part 1', *Piping Press*, 18 January 2019, available at https://pipingpress.com/2019/01/18/ ladies-pipe-bands-a-history-part-1/, last accessed 21 June 2024. The first Ladies' band in Canada was formed in Vancouver in 1927.

———— 'Ladies' Pipe Bands: A History Part 2', *Piping Press*, 21 January 2019, available at https://pipingpress. com/2019/01/21/ladies-pipe-bands-a-history-part-2/, last accessed 24 June 2024.

———— 'Piping during WW2: The Founding of the College of Piping, Dunkirk and "Mad" Jack Churchill', *Piping Press*, 6 January 2022, available at https://pipingpress.com/2022/01/06/piping-during-ww2-the-founding-of-the-college-of-piping-dunkirk-and-mad-jack-churchill/, last accessed 19 August 2024.

———— 'Piping in WW2: Prisoners of War Keep Their Music Alive', *Piping Press*, 24 January 2022, available at https:// pipingpress. com/2022/01/24/piping-in-ww2-prisoners-of-war-keeptheir-music-alive/, last accessed 3 July 2024.

———— 'Piping in WW2: The Army School Expands Its Teaching to All Serving Pipers', *Piping Press*, 17 January 2022, available at https:// pipingpress.com/2022/01/17/pipingin-ww2-the-army-school-expands-its-teaching-to-all-serving-pipers/, last accessed 3 July 2024.

———— 'WW2 Piping: John Wilson "Not Dead" and the Reel of the 51st Highland Division', *Piping Press*, 2 February 2022, available at https://

pipingpress.com/2022/02/02/ww2-piping-john-wilsonnot-dead-and-the-reel-of-the-51st-highland-division/, last accessed 3 July 2024.

Cannon, Roderick D., 'The Bagpipe in Northern England', *Folk Music Journal* 2, no. 2 (1971), pp. 127–47.

———— 'What Can We Learn about Piobaireachd?', *British Journal of Ethnomusicology* 4 (1995), pp. 1–15.

———— 'Who Got a Kiss of the King's Hand? The Growth of a Tradition', available at https://www.cl.cam.ac.uk/~rja14/musicfiles/preprints/kingshand.pdf, last accessed 14 May 2024.

Cheape, Hugh, 'Celtic Connections on an Atlantic Corridor', *Piping Times* 67, no. 5 (February 2015), pp. 37–45.

———— 'Dr I F Grant (1887–1983): The Highland Folk Museum and a Bibliography of Her Written Works', *Review of Scottish Culture* 2 (1986), pp. 113–25.

———— 'Patron as Performer: Lament for the "Gentleman-Piper"', in Wilson McLeod, Abigail Burnyeat, Domhnall Uilleam Stiùbhart, Thomas Owen Clancy, Roibeard Ó Maolalaigh (eds), *Bile ós Chrannaibh: A Festschrift for William Gillies* (Ceann Drochaid, Perthshire: Clann Tuirc, 2010), pp. 57–78

———— 'The Piper to the Laird of Grant', *Proceedings of the Society of Antiquaries of Scotland* 125 (1995), pp. 1163–73.

———— 'The Pipe of Fluent Chanters', *Piping Today* 26 (2013), pp. 34–40.

———— 'Raising the Tone: The Bagpipe and the Baroque', in M. J. Grant (ed.), *Hearing Heritage: selected essays on Scotland's Music from the Musica Scotica conferences* (Glasgow: Musica Scotica Trust, 2020), pp. 3–18.

———— Cheape, Hugh and Decker Forrest, 'The Piper's House on Raasay: Taigh a' Phìobaire', *Piping Today* 49 (December 2010), pp. 14–19.

———— 'The Piper's House on Raasay: Taigh a' Phìobaire; Part 2', *Piping Today* 50 (February 2011), pp. 14–19.

'College Membership', *Piping Times* 7, no. 2 (November 2017), p. 14.

College of Piping, 'Obituary: James "Jimmy" Jennett, 1928–2018', *Piping Times* 70, no. 6 (March 2018), pp. 49–52.

Collins, Timothy A., 'Hora decima: The Musical Theology of the *Stadtpfeifer*', *Cross Accent: The Journal of the Association of Lutheran Church Musicians* 2, no. 1 (Spring 2003), pp. 27–38.

Colmeiro, José, 'Bagpipes, Bouzoukis, and Bodhráns: The Reinvention of Galician Folk Music', in Colmeiro, *Peripheral Visions / Global Sounds: From Galicia to the World* (Liverpool: Liverpool University Press, 2018); online edn, Liverpool Scholarship Online, 24 May 2018, available at https://doi.org/10.5949/liverpool/9781786940308.003.0011, last accessed 24 July 2024.

Cooke, Peter, 'Bagpipes in India', *InterArts* (Spring 1987), pp. 14–15.

———— 'India 1986', available at https://www.drpetercooke.uk/india-1986/, last accessed 10 June 2024.

Devine, T. M., 'Preface', *The Scottish Historical Review* 73 (1994), pp. 1–3.

Dickson, Joshua, 'Piping Sung: Women, Canntaireachd and the Role of the Tradition-Bearer', *Scottish Studies* 36 (2013), pp. 45–65.

Donelly, Séan, 'A Publication Date for John Geoghegan's *Compleat Tutor*', *An Píobaire* 4, no. 47 (2008), pp. 26–7.

Ferguson, William, 'Review of *The Invention of Scotland: Myth and History*, by H. Trevor-Roper & J. J. Cater', *The Scottish Historical Review* 90, no. 229 (April 2011), pp. 166–9.

Fernández, Susana Morneno, 'Gaitas-de-fole in Portugal and Their Connection to Galicia', *Chanter* (Summer 2017), available at https://www.bagpipesociety.org.uk/articles/2017/chanter/summer/gaitas-de-fole/, last accessed 22 July 2024.

Galpin, Frances W., 'The Romance of the Phagotum', *Proceedings of the Musical Association* 67 (1940), pp. 57–72.

Goodacre, Julian, 'Bagpipes in the Scottish Borders: An Emerging Jigsaw', *Common Stock* 17, no. 2 (December 2002).

———— 'Highland Pipemaking in India', *Chanter* (Autumn 2017), available at https://www.goodbagpipes.com/index.php/about-me/writings/pipe-making/148-highland-pipemaking-in-india, last accessed 10 June 2024.

Gordon, Seton, 'The Bagpipe', in John Hadfield (ed.), *The Saturday Book 15* (London: Hutchinson & Co., 1955).

Halford MacLeod, Ruaraidh, 'Everyone Who Has an Intrigue Hopes It Should Not Be Known: Lord Loudoun and Anne Mackintosh; An Intrigue of the '45', *Transactions of the Gaelic Society of Inverness* 55 (1986–8), pp. 256–323.

———— 'The MacCrimmons and the '45', *Piping Times* 29, no. 6 (March 1977), pp. 11–13.

Heyl, Christoph, 'The Pastoral Pipes', *Chanter* (Autumn 2021), available at https://www.bagpipesociety.org.uk/articles/2021/chanter/autumn/the-pastoral-pipes/, last accessed 30 April 2024.

BIBLIOGRAPHY

'Historic Pipes Donated to Museum', *Piping Times* 71, no. 9 (June 2019), pp. 19–20.

Diana, Henderson, 'From Humble Beginnings: The Story of the Army School of Piping; Part 1', *Piping Times* 41, no. 9 (June 1989), pp. 19–29.

———— 'From Humble Beginnings: The Story of the Army School of Piping; Part 2', *Piping Times* 41, no. 10 (July 1989), pp. 37–45.

Johnson, David, 'The Lost History of the Lowland Scottish Pipes', *Early Music* 34, no. 3 (August 2006), pp. 497–8.

Jones, G. Fenwick, 'Wittenwiler's "Becki" and the Medieval Bagpipe', *The Journal of English and Germanic Philology* 48, no. 2 (1949), pp. 209–28.

Kaiser, Thomas E., 'The Drama of Charles Edward Stuart: Jacobite Propaganda and French Political Protest, 1745–1750', *Eighteenth-Century Studies* 30, no. 4 (1997), pp. 365–81.

Kidd, Colin, 'North Britishness and the Nature of Eighteenth-Century British Patriotisms', *The Historical Journal* 39 (1996), pp. 361–82.

———— 'Review of *The King's Jaunt: George IV in Scotland, August 1822*, by J. Prebble', *The Scottish Historical Review* 81, no. 211 (2002), pp. 141–2.

Kopp, James B., 'The French Court Musette to 1672: Further Notes', *The Galpin Society Journal* 64 (2011), pp. 243–7.

Laing, David, 'An Episode in the Life of Mrs Rachel Erskine, Lady Grange. Detailed by Herself in a Letter from St Kilda, January 20, 1738, and Other Original Papers,' *Proceedings of the Society of Antiquaries of Scotland* 11 (1875), pp. 593–608, available at http://journals.socantscot.org/index.php/psas/article/view/5777, last accessed 29 March 2024.

MacGregor, Martin, 'The Campbells: Lordship, Literature, and Liminality', *Textual Cultures* 7, no. 1 (2012), pp. 121–57.

MacKenzie, Bridget, 'The Origins of Ceol Mor: A Theory; Part 1', *Piping Times* 32, no. 6 (March 1980), pp. 13–21.

———— 'The Origins of Ceol Mor: A Theory; Part 2', *Piping Times* 32, no. 8 (May 1980), pp. 32–7.

———— 'The Origins of Ceol Mor: A Theory; Part 3', *Piping Times* 32, no. 11 (August 1980), pp. 30–4.

Mackenzie, Henry, 'Report of the Committee of the Highland Society of Scotland Appointed to Inquire into the Nature and Authenticity of the Poems of Ossian' (Edinburgh, 1805).

'The MacLean Pipe Band, Champions of the World, 1927–30–35', *Piping and Dancing* 2 (September 1935), p. 18.

MacLellan, John, 'The Hereditary Pipers: The MacCrimmons', *The International Piper*, vol. 3, no. 1 (May 1980), pp. 2–3.

———— 'History of Piping: The Mackenzies', *The International Piper* 4, no. 2 (June 1981), pp. 11, 14.

MacNeill, Seumas, 'The Argyllshire Gathering', *Piping Times* 26, no. 1 (October 1973), p. 10.

———— 'Editorial', *Piping Times* 9, no. 4 (January 1957), p. 5.

———— 'Editorial', *Piping Times* 23, no. 8 (May 1971), p. 7.

———— 'Heather MacKenzie or A Defence of Lady Pipers', *Piping Times* 10, no. 3 (December 1957), pp. 9, 17.

Mason, Roger A., 'Review of *The Identity of the Scottish Nation: An Historic Quest*, by W. Ferguson', *The Scottish Historical Review* 79, no. 208 (2000), pp. 240–42.

McCandless, Brian, 'Town Pipers: A European Continuity', *Journal of the North American Association of Lowland and Border Pipers* 2 (February 1991), pp. 17–25.

Merryweather, James, 'Henry Halewood Bagpiper and Liverpool Town Wait 1571–1589', *Chanter* (Spring 2004), pp. 18–20.

Müller, Jürgen, 'Albrecht Dürer's Peasant Engravings: A Different *Laocoön*, or the Birth of Aesthetic Subversion in the Spirit of the Reformation', *Journal of Historians of Netherlandish Art* 3, no. 1 (Winter 2011), available at DOI: 10.5092/jhna.2011.3.1.2, last accessed 28 July 2023.

Murdoch, Steve, 'James VI and the Formation of a Scottish and British Military Identity', in Steve Murdoch and Andrew MacKillop (eds), *Fighting for Identity: Scottish Military Experience c. 1550–1900* (Leiden: Brill, 2002), pp. 3–31.

Noble, Andra, 'Famous Pipers: Roddy Ross, a Capital Character', *Piping Times* 72, no. 4 (January 2020), pp. 33–8.

Panferreteiro, Mano, 'Pipes and Pipers: Galician Symbols of Ever Evolving Meaning', *Chanter* (Summer 2017), available at https://www.bagpipesociety.org.uk/articles/2017/chanter/summer/pipes-and-pipers, last accessed 22 July 2024.

Patterson, Mike, 'Strakonice, Where the Pipes Play', *Chanter* (Spring 2016), available at https://www.bagpipesociety.org.uk/articles/2016/chanter/spring/strakonice-where-the-pipes-play/, last accessed 5 February 2024.

Partridge, Karl, 'The Maltese Żaqq Introduction', *Chanter* (Winter, 2016), available at https://www.bagpipesociety.org.uk/articles/2016/chanter/winter/maltese-zaqq/, last accessed 31 May 2023.

Phillipson Nicholas T., 'Culture and Society in the 18th Century Province: The Case of Edinburgh and the Scottish Enlightenment', in Lawrence Stone (ed.), *The University in Society* (Princeton: Princeton University Press, 1975), pp. 407–48.

———— 'Politics, Politeness and the Anglicisation of early Eighteenth-Century Scottish Culture', in Roger A. Mason (ed.), *Scotland and England 1286–1815* (Edinburgh: John Donald, 1987), pp. 226–46.

Pittock, Murray, 'Enlightenment, Romanticism and the Scottish Canon: Cosmopolites or Narrow Nationalists?', in Gerard Carruthers and Liam McIlvanney (eds), *The Cambridge Companion to Scottish Literature* (Cambridge: Cambridge University Press, 2012), pp. 86–102.

Quigg, J. and P. Glendinning, 'Gail Force Piping: An Interview with Gail Brown', *The Voice* (Spring 2002), p. 27.

Radford, Alan, 'Bagpipers at the Tudor Court', *Chanter* (Spring 2018), available at https://www.bagpipesociety.org.uk/articles/2018/chanter/spring/bagpipes-at-tudor-court/, last accessed 14 February 2024.

Roberts, Paul, 'The Border Bagpipe in 17th Century Art. The First Images', *Common Stock*. vol. 28, no. 2 (2011), 22–34.

———— 'Lincolnshire, Lancashire and Scotch Bagpipes: Regional and Pastoral Bagpipes in 17th Century England', *Chanter* (Winter 2017), available at https://www.bagpipesociety.org.uk/articles/2017/chanter/winter/lincolnshire-lancashire-scotch-bagpipes/, last accessed 17 June 2024.

Rowlands, Dave, 'The Gentleman Piper', *Chanter* (Winter 2003), pp. 4–11.

Scott, Kathleen L., 'Sow-and-Bagpipe Imagery in the Miller's Portrait', *The Review of English Studies* 18, no. 71 (1967), pp. 287–90.

Shears, Barry, '"Old Days" of Dance and Diversity', *Piping Today* 35 (August 2008), pp. 27–31.

Spiers, Edward M., 'Findlater, George Frederick (1872–1942)', *ODNB*, available at https://www.oxforddnb.com/display/10.1093/ref:odnb/9780198614128.001.0001/odnb-9780198614128-e-96873, last accessed 22 November 2024.

Stephens, David, 'History at the Margins: Bagpipers in Medieval Manuscripts', *History Today* 39 (August 1989), pp. 42–3.

Stewart, Pete, 'Once Upon a Time in the Lowlands', *Piping Today* 21 (April 2006), pp. 26–9.

———— 'Scotland's Oldest Piper?', available at https://lbps.net/j3site/index.php/history/carvings/314-scotland-s-oldest-piper, last accessed 10 July 2024.

Stewart, Tim, '"The pipes play on": Canadian Pipers at War, 1914–1918; An Inspired Tradition', *Canadian Military History* 9, no. 4 (2000), pp. 57–64.

Strachan, Hew, 'Scotland's Military Identity', *The Scottish Historical Review* 85, no. 220 (2006), pp. 315–32.

Thomson, Derick S., 'Gaelic Learned Orders and Literati in Medieval Scotland', *Scottish Studies* 12 (1968), pp. 57–78.

———— 'Niall Mór MacMhuirich', *Transactions of the Gaelic Society of Inverness* 49 (1977), pp. 9–25.

Trevor-Roper, Hugh, 'The Invention of Tradition: The Highland Tradition of Scotland', in Eric Hobsbawm and Terence Ranger (eds), *The Invention of Tradition* (Cambridge: Cambridge University Press, 1983), pp. 15–42.

Van Kreckhoven, Pieterjan, 'Bourdon Collectif', *Chanter* (Spring 2017), available at https://www.bagpipesociety.org.uk/articles/2017/chanter/spring/bourdon-collectif/, last accessed 29 April 2024.

Vereno, Michael Peter, 'Bagpipes in Austria: A Story of Diversity', *Chanter* (Summer 2016), available at https://www.bagpipesociety.org.uk/articles/2016/chanter/summer/bagpipes-in-austria/, last accessed 5 February 2024.

Wallace, Rab, 'A Far Cry from the MacCrimmons: Scotland's Forgotten Bagpipes', *Chanter* (1986), pp. 35–6.

West Lothian Council, 'Women & Democracy: The West Lothian Story', available at https://news.westlothian.gov.uk/media/33057/Women-Democracy-the-West-Lothian-story/pdf/Women_and_Democracy_booklet_-_digital.pdf, last accessed 29 July 2024.

Williams, Vivien, 'The Scottish Bagpipe: Political and Religious Symbolism in English Literature and Satire', available at https://www.thebottleimp.org.uk/2013/05/the-scottish-bagpipe-political-and-religious-symbolism-in-english-literature-and-satire/, last accessed 4 April 2024.

———— 'The National Poet and the National Instrument', *Bagpipe News*, 25 January 2024, available at https://bagpipe.news/2024/01/25/robert-burns-and-the-bagpipe/, last accessed 20 December 2024.

Winternitz, Emanuel, 'Bagpipes and Hurdy-Gurdies in Their Social Setting', *The Metropolitan Museum of Art Bulletin* 2, no. 1 (1943), pp. 56–83.

Winick, Steve, 'Blows-a-Bellows #2', *Dirty Linen* 61 (December 1995/January 1996), available at https://www.rootsworld.com/rw/feature/dlbag2.html, last accessed 18 July 2024.

Wright, Angela, 'The History of the Unfortunate Lady Grange: Gothic Exhumations of a Concealed Scottish Fate', *Gothic Studies* 24, no. 1 (2022), pp. 31–43.

Unpublished theses and talks

Cheape, Hugh, 'The Bagpipes: Perceptions of a National Instrument', PhD thesis, University of Edinburgh, 2008, available at https://era.ed.ac.uk/handle/1842/2591, last accessed 22 April 2024.

————— '"The folk who did all the business"—*a' mhuinntir do rinn an t-seirbhis uile*: Revisiting the Past in the Islands', talk at the Royal Society of Edinburgh, April 2023.

Halford-MacLeod, Ruari, 'Donald Ruadh MacCrummen', address to the Piobaireachd Society, 2001.

MacDonald, Allan, 'The Relationship between Pibroch and Gaelic Song: Its Implications on the Performance Style of the Pibroch Urlar', available at https://www.cl.cam.ac.uk/~rja14/musicfiles/manuscripts/allanmacdonald/, last accessed 16 April 2024.

MacInnes, Iain, 'The Highland Bagpipe: The Impact of the Highland Societies of London and Scotland, 1781–1844', M. Litt, University of Edinburgh, 1988, p. 5, available at https://www.cl.cam.ac.uk/~rja14/musicfiles/manuscripts/macinnes/imthesis1.pdf, last accessed 22 April 2024.

Pirrie, Robert, 'Edinburgh's Urban Enlightenment and George IV: Staging North Britain, 1752–1822', student dissertation for Open University module A826 MA History part 2, January 2019, available at https://oro.open.ac.uk/60286/3/Pirrie_R%20Pirrie%20A826%20-%20REDACTED_Dissertation.pdf, last accessed 9 May 2024.

Williams, Vivien, 'The Cultural History of the Bagpipe in Britain, 1680–1840', PhD thesis, University of Glasgow, September 2013, available at https://theses.gla.ac.uk/5085/1/2013williamsphd.pdf, last accessed 9 February 2024.

INDEX

Abbotsford, Borders, 111
Abercromby, Ralph, 68
Aberdeen, Aberdeenshire, 63
AC/DC, 162, 187
Act of Proscription (1746), 65
Act of Settlement (1701), 47
Afghanistan, 89
Afridi tribe, 96
Afro Celt Sound System, 188
Ainslie, Ross, 165, 179, 180
Alba, 141
Albert, Prince Consort, 77
alcohol, 6, 133, 179
'Allo 'Allo! (TV series), 31
Ally the Piper, 186–7, 188
Alnwick Pipers' Society, 147
'Amazing Grace', 120
American colonies (1607–1776),
    51, 66, 68
Anderson, David, 102–3
Anderson, Ian, 157
Anderson, James B., 104
Anderson, Jimmy, 143, 145, 150
'Andy Renwick's Ferret', 162
Antarctica, 102
Argyll and Southerland
    Highlanders, 92
Argyll, John Campbell, 5th
    Duke, 89

Argyllshire Gathering, 84, 129,
    134, 179
Argyllshire Regiment, 91st, 90
Aristophanes, 9
Army Class, 108
Army School of Bagpipe Music,
    108, 122, 192
Ash, Marinell, 4
Assembly Rooms, Edinburgh, 58
Atholl Highlanders, 162
Auļi, 190
Australia, 72, 109, 112, 113,
    172, 173, 186
Australian Ladies Pipe Band, 112
Austria, 18–19, 29, 48
Auxiliary Territorial Service, 112

B flat, 143–4, 146, 155
Bach, Johann Sebastian, 33
Badenoch and Strathspey,
    Highland, 71
Bagpipe Society, 185
bagpipes
    bellows, see bellows
    blowpipes, 8, 20, 34, 35
    chanters, 8, 20, 35, 36, 67, 73,
        143, 155
    Christianity and, 12–15, 33,
        54–5, 152

drones, 8, 11, 20, 35, 36, 48, 60, 73, 95, 144, 155, 180

Highland pipes, *see* Great Highland Bagpipe

Lowland pipes, 34–6, 37, 63–4, 145–6, 176

military use, *see* military

Northumbrian smallpipes, 7, 60, 64, 73–4, 146–8, 150, 176

origins, 9–11

pastoral pipes, 46, 59–61, 63, 65, 149

piobaireachd, see *piobaireachd*

pitches, 60, 62, 143, 146

reeds, 8, 10, 12, 60, 118, 144

regulators, 60

Scottish smallpipe, 147–8, 150, 173, 176

shepherds and, 7, 8, 14, 60

single drone, 20, 35

uilleann pipes, 45–6, 49, 73, 149, 150, 162, 176

union pipes, 46, 59, 61, 63

worldwide, 5, 7, 8, 183–90

written music, 6, 38, 83

Bahrain, 185

'Ballachulish Walkabout, The', 137

Ballymena, County Antrim, 158

'Banks o' the Lee, The' (Bennett and Stewart), 167

bardic tradition, 22–3, 32, 37, 40, 42

baroque movement, 60, 63, 64

Barra, Outer Hebrides, 136, 144

Battle of Ancre Heights (1916), 101

Battle of Auldearn (1645), 97

Battle of the Bagpipes (2024 documentary), 171

Battle of Bannockburn (1314), 127

Battle of Cromdale (1690), 97

Battle of Culloden (1746), 47–9, 54, 56, 70

Battle of El Alamein (1942), 115–17

Battle of Flodden (1513), 28

Battle of Inverlochy (1645), 121

Battle of Inverurie (1745), 53

Battle of Keren (1941), 130

Battle of Loos (1915), 100

Battle of Omdurman (1898), 95

Battle of Porto Novo (1781), 68

Battle of Prestonpans (1745), 55

Battle of Saint Pierre (1813), 103

Battle of Salamanca (1812), 91

Battle of the Somme (1916), 102–3

Battle of Vimiero (1808), 97

Battle of Waterloo (1815), 68, 103–4

Battlefield Band, 141, 143

Batzorig Vaanchig, 190

Bellahouston Park, Glasgow, 158

Belles Heures of Jean de Berry, 14

bellows, 8, 18, 28, 34, 35, 36

boom (1700s), 56, 59–63

decline (1800s), 73

Northumbrian smallpipes, 7, 60, 64, 73–4, 146–8, 150, 176

pastoral pipes, 46, 59–61, 63, 65, 149

revival (1980s), 145–50

uilleann pipes, 45–6, 49, 73, 149, 150, 162, 176

union pipes, 46, 59, 61, 63

'Belly Dancer, The' (Duncan), 164

Ben Ali, Zine El Abidine, 192

Bennett, Kirsten, 166

Bennett, Martyn, 165–8, 171, 181

Bénouville Bridge, Caen Canal, 119–20

Bethlem Royal Hospital, London, 77

Bhatia, H. S., 95

Big Music Society, 175

'Big Nameless', 129

binioù, 151, 153–4

Binneas is Boreraig, 133

Birmingham Irish Pipes and Drums, 178

Black Watch, 43, 91, 116

Blair Castle, Perthshire, 75, 174

Blatchford, Robert, 104

blowpipes, 8, 20, 34, 35

'Blue Bonnets over the Border', 100, 120

'Bobs of Balmoral', 123

bock, 8

Bohemia, 18, 19

bombards, 153–4

Bonnie Prince Charlie, 47, 49, 50, 52

Book of Leinster, 24

Border pipes, 34–6, 37, 63–4

Boreraig, Skye, 40, 76, 78–9, 81

Bosch, Hieronymus, 13, 14

Bostridge, Ian, 14

Bothy Band, The, 141, 162, 163

Bourguiba, Habib, 192

boxwood, 61

Boy Scouts, 170

Boyd, Andrea, 172

Boys' Brigade, 87, 108, 170

Braemar Girls' Pipe Band, 113

Braemar, Aberdeenshire, 112

Bratach Gorm contest, 139

Braveheart (1995 film), 45, 69

Breadalbane, John Campbell, 2nd Marquess, 82

'Break Yer Bass Drone' (Duncan), 164

Brechin, Angus, 87

Brexit, 20

Brian Boru pipe, 191

British Broadcasting Corporation (BBC), 31, 109, 147, 163, 171

British Columbia, Canada, 102, 190

British Heritage Travel, 49

Brittany, 14, 18, 143, 151, 153–4, 190

Broughton High School, Edinburgh, 112

Brown, Barnaby, 62

Brown, Gail, 139

Brown, Robert, 123

Broxburn, West Lothian, 111

Bruce, Sandy, 62

Bruegel the Elder, Pieter, 15

Buchanan, George, 37

Buddha Bar, Paris, 166

Buhari, Muhammadu, 184

Bulgaria, 91

Burgess, John D., 134–7, 141, 142, 168

Burgess, Sheila, 135

Burnet, James, 136
Burns, Robert, 13, 59, 70, 127
busking, 117
Byron, George Gordon, 6th
  Baron, 42

Caddell, Allester, 43
Caledonian Pocket Companion
  (Oswald), 64
Caledonian Society of London,
  The, 110
Cambridge Folk Festival, 167
camels, 93
Cameron Highlanders, 116,
  134–5
Cameron, C. A., 116
Cameron, Donald, 83
Cameron, Sandy, 86
Camerons of Lochiel, 50
Campbell, Alastair, 176–7
Campbell, Archibald, 80
Campbeltown Pipe Band, 145
Campsie, Alistair, 39, 76–9, 80–
  81
Canada, 40, 72, 101–2, 113, 114,
  155–9, 172, 173, 186, 189–90
  Nova Scotia, 83, 124, 128, 155,
  158, 176
Canadian Expeditionary Force,
  101
Cannon, Roderick, 41
canntaireachd, 38, 85, 110, 177
Cantares Gallegos (Castro), 153
cantata, 60
Canterbury Tales, The (Chaucer),
  25–6
Cape Breton, Nova Scotia, 124,
  128, 155, 158, 176

capitalism, 6, 73, 179
Carnegie Mellon University, 186
Cassells, Stuart, 180–81
Castle Grant, Highlands, 71
de Castro, Rosalía, 153
Catholicism, 47–8, 50, 54–5, 152
Celestine III, Pope, 20
Celtic Connections, 161, 175
Celtic Society, 69, 71, 80
ceòl beag, 39–40, 65, 83, 107, 110,
  114
ceòl mòr, 38
Ceòla, 176
'Cha Till MacCriumein', 54
chabrette, 8
Chaimbeul, Brìghde, 173, 179,
  180
'Chanter' (Bennett), 167
chanters, 8, 20, 35, 36, 60, 67,
  73, 143, 155
Charity Band, The, 109
Charles II, King of England,
  Scotland and Ireland, 41
Charles, William, 105
Charles, Young Pretender, 47,
  49, 50, 52
Chaucer, Geoffrey, 25–6
Cheape, Hugh, 12, 24, 36, 41, 75–
  6, 78–9, 148, 149
Chiesa, Giuseppe, 72
Childe Harold's Pilgrimage (Byron),
  42
chorus, 11
Christianity, 12–15, 20, 152
  Catholicism, 47–8, 50, 54–5,
  152
  Episcopalians, 47–8, 50
  Reformation (1517–1648), 15,
  32–3, 152

Church of Scotland, 33
Churchill, Jack, 118–19, 130
Churchill, Winston, 115
cimpoi, 8
Circular Breath, The (Duncan), 164
Clan Donald, 37, 49, 51, 56
Clan Grant, 35, 61, 71
Clan Ranald, 56
Clark, Gavin, 177–8
Clark, George, 97
classical music, 38, 59, 60, 62, 63–4
Clephane, Marianne, 111
Clutha, The, 143, 145
Codex Exoniensis, 25
Colkelbie's Sow, 27
Collection of Ancient Piobaireachd, A (Mackay), 76
Collection of Highland Vocal Airs, A (MacDonald), 69
Collection of Quicksteps, A (MacDonald), 64
College of Piping, Glasgow, 40, 48, 122–30, 137
Collie, Mary, 110
Collier, Jacob, 7
Collinson, Francis, 37, 145
comic pieces, 8, 130, 137
community pipers, 61
competitions, 48–9, 57, 84, 107, 124, 129, 155
 in Canada, 156–7
 Cowal Gathering, 107, 112, 113, 157
 Edinburgh Competition (1784), 57, 62
 Glenfiddich championship, 38, 75, 80, 174

Highland Societies, 48, 57, 58, 62, 65, 67, 69, 76, 82, 93
 Northern Meeting, 84, 117, 134, 142
 Piobaireachd Society, 106
 pipe bands, 109, 113, 139, 151, 171–2
 World Pipe Band Championship, 107, 113, 118, 139, 143, 171, 172
Complaynt of Scotland, The, 34
Compleat Theory, A (MacDonald), 39, 40, 48, 70
Compleat Tutor, The (Geoghegan), 46, 61, 62, 63
Comunn na h-Alba, 125, 126
Connery, Sean, 166
Controversy of Pipers, A, 150
'Cook in the Kitchen', 141
Cooke, Peter, 95
Coote, Eyre, 68
Corrieyairack Pass, Highland, 121
Cowal Highland Gathering, 107, 112, 113, 157
Craigend Pipe Band, 113
Craigievar Castle, Aberdeenshire, 35
Cramb Lecture, 21
Creative Scotland, 169
Crichton Royal Hospital, Dumfries, 77
Crieff, Perthshire, 52, 82
Crimean War (1853–6), 90
Croix de Guerre, 103
Crowley-Duncan, Allyson, 186–7, 188
Crùnluath (BBC Radio), 171
Cuillin, 166

Culross Games, 113

Cum universi (Celestine III), 20

Currie, Alex, 155

Currie, Rosemary and Hazel, 123

Czech Republic, 8, 17–18, 29

Czechoslovakia (1918–92), 19, 151

D-Day landings (1944), 119–21

D'Oyly, Elizabeth Jane Ross, Lady, 92, 110

Dagenham Girl Pipers, 110, 111, 112, 113, 114

Dalziel, John, 81

dance, 15–16, 17, 32, 33, 36, 39, 64, 73, 111, 125, 163
  Highlands, 36, 39, 62, 64, 111, 125

Danse Macabre, 16

Dark Ages (c. 500–1000), 11

David II, King of Scotland, 27

Davies, Peter Maxwell, 144

Day it Daws, The (Stewart), 35

De Caelo, De anima, 12

Death, 16

degree courses 175

Denmark, 42

Devine, Tom, 21, 42

Diderot, Denis, 59

Dio Chrysostom, 9

Diplomáticos de Monte Alto, Os, 192

Dogras, 93

Dojo University, 189

Donaghadee, County Down, 51

Donald Drone, 126

Donaldson, William, 42, 61, 69, 81, 107

drones, 8, 11, 20, 35, 36, 48, 60, 73, 95, 144, 155, 180

drumming, 32, 86, 88, 89, 100, 108, 152, 154, 172, 178

Drysdale, Walter, 164

Dublin, Ireland, 63

dūda, 190

Dudey, 28, 35

Duirinish Churchyard, Skye, 51

Duke of Albany's Own Highlanders, 90

'Dumbarton's Drums', 102

Dumfries and Galloway, Scotland, 170

Dunbar, East Lothian, 35

Duncan, Gordon, 159, 161–5, 168–9, 171, 181, 187

Dunfermline, Fife, 31

Dunn, John, 58

Dunn, Margaret, 172

Dunvegan, Skye, 3, 50, 51

Dürer, Albrecht, 15

Duthart, Alex, 108

Eaglesham, Stuart, 162

East Edinburgh Pipers, 113

Easter Rising (1916), 126, 191

Edinburgh, Scotland, 58, 63
  busker arrests, 117–18
  Castle, 2, 77, 108, 134
  City Police, 103
  Folk Festival, 148–50
  folk pubs, 141
  George IV's visit (1822), 68–9
  Highland Society, 48, 58, 76, 82
  Jacobite occupation (1745), 55
  Military Tattoo, 2, 127

Royal Mile, 3
Summer of Love (1994), 166
University of Edinburgh, 4,
127
Edinburgh Folk Festival, 148–50
Edinburgh Society for
Encouraging the Arts, 58
Edward I, King of England, 25
Eisteddfod, 110
Elizabeth I, Queen of England, 26
Elizabeth II, Queen of the United
Kingdom, 113, 192
emigration, 72–3
England, 16, 25–9, 32, 63
Act of Settlement (1701), 47
Acts of Union (1707), 47, 65,
67
Glorious Revolution (1688),
47
Jacobite conflict (1688–1746),
44, 47
Rough Wooing (1543–51), 28
Union of the Crowns (1603),
20, 42
Enlightenment, Scottish (c.
1740–1800), 57–8, 59, 65, 70
Episcopalians, 47–8, 50
Eritrean campaign (1941), 130
Escola de Gaitas, Ourense, 154
Esra prize, 161
Estonia, 190
Exeter Riddles, 25

Faed, Thomas, 72
Falkirk, Stirlingshire, 113
Faujas de Saint-Fond, Barthélemy,
57–8, 62
Fèis movement, 144, 174, 176

Fèisean nan Gàidheal, 176
Ferguson, Adam, 23
Ferguson, Alex, 166
Fianna na h'Alba, 125–6
fiddle music, 64–5
Field Marshal Montgomery Pipe
Band, 172
Finbar Furey, 147
Findlater, George, 96–7
Findlater/Dargai syndrome, 99,
101, 115, 121
First World War (1914–18), 91,
98, 99–106, 112, 114
fishing, 72
five-fingered organ playing, 21
folk music, 17, 59, 60, 63–4, 141–
59
folk pubs, 141
football, 166
Forbes, Duncan, 52
Forbes, William, 35
Fort Augustus, Highland, 121
Foxo, José Lois, 154
Fraga Iribarne, Manuel, 154
Fragments of Ancient Poetry
(Macpherson), 59
France, 8, 28, 42, 60, 91
Brittany, 14, 18, 143, 151, 153–
4
Catholicism in, 152
First World War (1914–18),
98, 99–106
musette, 28, 60, 91
Napoleonic Wars (1803–15),
68, 72, 88, 97, 103
Second World War (1939–45),
119–21, 153
Franco, Francisco, 153

François I, King of France, 28
Fraser Highlanders, 68, 157–9
Fraser, Donald, 53
Fraser, James, 41
French and Indian War (1754–63), 68

Gabaldon, Diana, 45
Gabriel, Peter, 167
Gaelic, 21–4, 36–7, 38, 40, 41, 45, 125, 144, 175
in Canada, 155, 156
Gaelic League, 73
gaida, 8
Gairloch, Highland, 61
gaita, 20, 151, 152–3, 154–5, 190
Galicia, 18, 20, 151, 152–3, 154–5, 190, 192
Gallipoli campaign (1915–16), 100
Gandy, Bruce, 157
Garden of Earthly Delights (Bosch), 13
Garhwal, India, 94
Garson, Amy, 140
Garvamore, Highland, 121, 122
Gay Gordons, 76
General Strike (1926), 109
gentlemen pipers, 61, 62
Geoghegan, John, 46, 61, 62, 63, 64
George I, King of Great Britain, 47
George II, King of Great Britain, 47
George IV, King of the United Kingdom, 68–9

Germany, 18, 19
First World War (1914–18), 98, 99–106
Second World War (1939–45), 114, 115–21, 153
ghillies, 43
Glasgow, Scotland, 63
College of Piping, 40, 48, 122–30, 137
folk pubs, 141
National Piping Centre, 48, 168, 169, 177, 179
University of Glasgow, 21, 45, 127
Glasgow Police Pipe Band, 136
Glencoe, Highland, 21
Glenfiddich championship, 38, 75, 80, 174
Glenuig, Moidart, 150
Glorious Revolution (1688), 47
Gold Medal, 82, 84, 134, 141, 142, 157, 163
Gordon Highlanders, 89, 96–7, 103–4
Gow, Niel, 64
Grange, Rachel Erskine, Lady, 51
Grant, G. P., 121
Graves, J. W., 112
Great Highland Bagpipe, 1, 5, 7, 21, 29, 35–40, 45–6, 56, 73, 74, 176, 185, 186, 191, 193
classical music and, 64
gentlemen pipers, 61, 62
Glenfiddich championship, 38, 75, 80
global presence, 88
military use, 37, 56, 65
Prize Pipe, 65, 93

Great Pipes of Baleshare, 49
Greece, 91
    ancient, 9, 10
Green Book (MacNeill and
    Pearston), 127
Green, Ian, 164
Greenock Highlanders, 86
'Greensleeves', 27
Greentrax Records, 164
Grey, Michael, 2, 5, 156, 157,
    189, 190, 193
GRIT (Bennett), 166–7
Gurkhas, 93

habanera, 155
Haddington, East Lothian, 33
Halewood, Henry, 32
Halford-MacLeod, Ruari, 80
Hall, Rena, 114
Hamilton, Allan, 136
Hardland, 166
Harley Jr, Rufus, 188
harps, 40
Harris, Outer Hebrides, 51, 52
Hastie, John, 34
'Haughs O'Cromdale, The', 96,
    97
Hazzard, Jenny, 172
'Hector the Hero', 95
'Heights of Dargai, The', 96
Henderson, Hamish, 167
Henderson, Patricia, 140
Henry VII, King of England, 26
Henry VIII, King of England, 26–
    7, 28
Higgins, Donald, 111
Higgins, Lizzie, 111
Highland Armed Association of
    London, 86

Highland Boundary Fault, 67, 145
Highland Games, 84, 140
Highland Great Pipes, 36–8, 40,
    46, 56, 62, 63, 65, 73, 193
Highland Light Infantry, 71st, 90
Highland Regiment, 64th, 52
Highland Societies, 48, 58, 65,
    67, 68, 76, 82
    Gold Medal, 82, 84
    Prize Pipes, 65, 76, 82, 84, 93
Highlanders, 74th, 90
Highlanders, 78th, 91
Highlands, Scotland, 4, 21, 28–
    44, 46
    Clearances (1750–1860), 72
    dance in, 36, 39, 62, 64, 111,
        125
    diversity of pipes, 48–9, 62–3
    dress, 68, 69, 71, 72, 112, 174
    Great Highland Bagpipe, *see*
        Great Highland Bagpipe
    Highland Great Pipes, 36–8,
        40, 46, 56, 62, 63, 65, 73,
        193
    Jacobite uprisings, *see* Jacobite
        movement
    military recruitment in, 66–7
    national identity and, 69–72,
        174
Hilton, Lincoln, 186
Hitler, Adolf, 114
Holbein the Younger, Hans, 16
Holy Roman Empire (962–1806),
    18
Horner, James, 45
House of Stuart, 47
*How the Scots Invented the Modern
    World* (Herman), 58

Hume, Alexander, 37
Hume, David, 58, 65
Hungary, 8
Hutton, Ali, 164–5, 179, 180
Hyde Park, London, 86

I Believe Art Matters, 94
'I Got a Kiss of the King's Hand',
    41
Iberian Peninsula, 18, 20, 151,
    152
ice skating, 93
Imperial Chemicals Industries
    (ICI), 125–6
In Our Time, 42
'Incitement for the Gaels, An'
    (Mac Dhomhnuill), 55
Independent Highland
    Companies, 43, 52
India, 89, 90–98
International Bagpipe Festival, 17,
    151
International Bagpipe
    Organisation, 185
International Piper, The, 77–8, 150
Inverness, Highland, 52, 84, 139,
    146, 157
Inverscotia Nomads, 125
Inverscotia Singers, 125
Ireland, 18, 21–2, 24, 28, 37, 45,
    46, 126, 144, 146, 173
    Easter Rising (1916), 126, 191
    folk music, 141
    Gaelic League, 73
    gentlemen pipers in, 61
    national identity, 191–2
    poetry in, 40
    uilleann pipes, 45–6, 49, 73,
        149, 150, 162, 176

US, influence on, 186
    War of Independence (1919–
        21), 126
Irish Pipe Band Association, 191
Islamic culture, 12
Israel, 172
Italy, 28, 115, 131
ivory, 61

Jacobite movement (1688–
    c. 1760s), 1, 4, 44, 45–56, 64,
    65–6
    Act of Proscription (1746), 65–
        6
    Grange kidnapping (1732), 51
    religion and, 47–8, 50, 54–5
    uprising (1689–92), 97
    uprising (1745–46), 1, 47–50,
        52–5
    Woodhouselee manuscript
        (1745), 55
James I, King of Scotland, 27
James VI and I, King of Scotland
    and England, 27–8, 43, 47
James VII and II, King of Scotland
    and England, 47
Jay, Archy, 186–7
Jean de Berry, 14
'Jeanie's March', 110
Jedburgh, Roxburghshire, 33–4,
    35
Jennett, Jimmy, 125, 126
Jennings, Ross O'Connell, 183–5
'Jessie's Dream', 91
Jesus, 14–15
jigs, 39, 85, 87
jirba, 185
John of Fordun, 21

John of Salisbury, 14
Johnson, Samuel, 22
Johnston, Anne, 140
Jones, Malcolm, 132
'Journey to Skye' (Thompson), 158
Julia, Shyopat, 94, 95
Just for Seumas (Duncan), 159, 164

Kailyard school, 128
Kala, Chukwu Oba, 184
Kames, Henry Home, Lord, 65
Keenan, Paddy, 162
kelping, 72
Kennedy, John Randolph Wilson, 126
Kennedy, MacGregor, 126
Kentigern, 143
Kerr, Gilbert, 102
Kidd, John, 96
kilts, 68, 71, 75, 98, 112, 134, 174
King's Foundation, 177
King's Own Scottish Borderers, 67, 99, 100, 105, 112
Kington, Miles, 75–6
'Kinmont Willie', 33
Kirkhill, Highland, 41

Labhruidh, Griogair, 188
Ladakh, India, 93
Ladies' World Championship, 113, 173
Laidlaw, Daniel, 99, 100–101, 104, 105, 120
'Laird o'Logie, The', 33
'Lament for Mary MacLeod', 164
Laocoön and His Sons, 15

'Last of the Clan, The' (Faed), 72
Latvia, 190
Laurie, William, 110
Le Pardons festival, 14
League of Young Scots, 125, 126
Lennox, Louisa, 72
Leofric, Bishop of Exeter, 25
Lewis, Malin, 176
Leyden, John, 34–5
'Life and Death of the Piper of Kilbarchan' (Sempill), 32
light music, 39–40, 65, 83, 107, 110, 114
Lightfoot, Rona, 139–40
Lindsay System Chanter, 176
Lindsay, Donald, 176
Linlithgow, West Lothian, 27
    Folk Club, 147
Lisburn, Northern Ireland, 172
Lismore, New South Wales, 113
literacy, 62
'Little Cascade, The' (McLennan), 157
Liverpool, Merseyside, 32
living tradition, 107
Livingstone, William, 40, 129, 134, 140, 157–8
Local Authorities, 170
'Lochaber No More' (Watson), 72
Logan, James, 76
London, England, 26, 48, 52, 55, 58, 59, 65
    Bratach Gorm contest, 139
    Highland Society, 48, 58, 65, 67, 68, 76, 82
Lone Piper (Watson), 112
Longest Day, The (1962 film), 119

Lord of Misrule, 14
Lordship of the Isles, 37–8
Lorient Festival, 143, 161
Lorn Ossianic Society Games, 110
Lothian Lasses, 111
Loudoun, John Campbell, 4th
    Earl, 52, 53, 54
Louis XIV, King of France, 28
Lovat, Simon Fraser, 15th Lord,
    119–20, 121
Lowland and Border Pipers
    Society (LBPS), 150
Lowland pipes, 34–6, 37, 63–4,
    145–6, 176
Lowlands, Scotland, 4, 21, 31–6,
    37, 42, 44, 64
Loyal North Britons, 86
Luther, Martin, 33

Mac Dhomhnuill, Aonghas, 55
Mac Mhaighstir, Alasdair, 56
macadam roads, 88
MacArthur dynasty, 22, 40
MacColl, John, 84–5, 110
MacCrimmon, Bess, 110
MacCrimmon, Donald Bàn, 52,
    53, 54
MacCrimmon, Euan, 81
MacCrimmon, Euphemia, 110
MacCrimmon, John, 3, 41
MacCrimmon, Malcolm, 52
MacCrimmon dynasty, 3, 22, 40,
    41, 50, 52–4, 61, 76–81, 110,
    128, 189, 191
    Boreraig college, 40, 76, 78–9,
    81
MacCrimmon Legend, The
    (Campsie), 76–81

'MacCrimmon Will Never
    Return', 54
MacDiarmid, Hugh, 128
MacDonald dynasty, 37, 49, 51,
    56
MacDonald, Alexander, 51–2, 56
MacDonald, Allan, 39, 150, 165,
    181
MacDonald, Angus, 107
MacDonald, Donald, 64, 83
MacDonald, Eilidh, 173
MacDonald, Finlay, 168, 179
MacDonald, Hector, 95
MacDonald, Helen, 110
MacDonald, Iain (of Glenuig), 150
MacDonald, Iain (of Neilston),
    150–51, 168
MacDonald, John, 85, 106, 110,
    141–2, 184
MacDonald, Joseph, 39, 40, 48,
    70
MacDonald, Patrick, 48, 69–70
MacDonald, Rona, 139–40
MacDonald, Sileas, 55–6
Macdonough, Terence, 125
Macedonia, 8
MacFadyen, John, 127, 128
MacGillivray, Donald, 141
MacGillivray, Duncan, 141–3,
    150
MacGowan, Shane, 161, 165
MacGregor dynasty, 22, 40
MacGregor, Patrick, 67
Macgurmen, John, 41
MacInnes, Iain, 142
MacIntyre, Duncan, 116–17, 121
MacIntyre, Sue, 131–2
MacKay dynasty, 61

MacKay, Angus, 28, 74, 76–7, 79–81
MacKay, John, 92
MacKay, John (of Raasay), 80, 84, 92, 110
MacKay, Kenneth, 103, 167
'Mackay's Memoirs' (Bennett), 167, 168
MacKenzie, Angus, 155
MacKenzie, John Bàn, 48, 82–3
MacKenzie, Kenneth, 155
Mackintosh, Aeneas, 52
Mackintosh, Anne, 52, 53
Mackintosh, Donald, 125
MacLellan, Christine, 77–8
MacLellan, Colin, 156
MacLellan, John, 77–8, 122, 150
MacLennan, John, 83
MacLeod dynasty, 3, 50–54
MacLeod, Alan, 141, 143, 162
MacLeod, Donald, 123
MacLeod, John, 52
MacLeod, Norman, 50, 51–2, 53
MacLeod, Roderick, 51
MacNeil, Robert Lister, 136
MacNeill, Seumas, 40, 79, 122–30, 137, 139–40, 141, 142, 162, 163
MacPherson, Angus, 133, 189
MacPherson, Cluny, 85
MacPherson, Edith, 113
Macpherson, James, 42, 59, 152
MacPherson, John, 22–3
MacPherson, Malcolm Jr, 133, 136
MacPherson, Malcolm Sr (Calum Pìobaire), 63, 84–7, 110
'Mairi's Wedding', 130

Malaysia, 172
Malta, 8
Manson, Fiona, 172
'March of the Cameron Men, The', 118
marches, 62, 88–9, 97, 100, 102, 110, 113, 116–17, 139, 163
Margolyes, Miriam, 192–3
Mars with Venus (Richardson), 131
Mary, Mother of Jesus, 14–15
Mary, Queen of Scots, 4
mashki, 94, 95
McAdam, John Loudon, 88
McAvoy, Meghan, 180
McCallum Bagpipes, 93
McCartney, Andy, 178
McCartney, Paul, 145
McGregor, Ewan, 166
McIntosh, Farquhar, 131–2
McLennan, George Stewart, 106, 157
McLeod, Wilson, 4
Medieval period (c. 500–1450), 11–15, 16, 24, 25–6
medleys, 139
Meerut, India, 92–3
Melrose Abbey, Roxburghshire, 20, 35, 151
Menuhin, Yehudi, 6
#MeToo moment, 174
Metropolitan Museum, New York, 8
mezoued, 183–4, 185, 192
Mhic Raghnaill, Sìleas Nighean, 55–6
Michael Colliery Prize Pipe Band, 109
military, 2, 36, 37–8, 42–4, 65–9

First World War (1914–18),
91, 98, 99–106
  pipe bands, 86–91, 96–8
  revolution (1590–1640), 42–3
  Second World War (1939–
    45), 114, 115–21, 123
Military History of British India
  (Bhatia), 95
Military Tattoo, 2, 127
Millin, Bill, 119–20, 121
Millin, John, 120
minstrels, 14
Mòd festival, 110–11, 144
Moidart, Highland, 150
monastic texts, 12
Montgomery, Bernard, 115
Montreal, Quebec, 68
Montrose, James Graham, 1st
  Marquess, 121
'Monymusk', 116
Mooney, Gordon, 147–9
Moore, Hamish, 145, 148,
  163–4, 176
Moore, John, 68
Moravia, 18
Morrison, Fred, 165, 181
Morton, Graeme, 72–3
Moving Hearts, 163
Mowat, Christina, 113
Moy Hall, Highland, 52–4
Muirhead and Sons, 143, 145, 147
'Mull of Kintyre' (Wings), 145
Mull, Inner Hebrides, 111
Murray, David, 66, 88, 99, 121,
  135–6
Murray, Kylie, 20
Murray Cup, 112
musette, 28, 60, 91

Na Fianna Éireann, 126
Nadir Ali & Company, 92–3
Nantes, Brittany, 154
Napier, J. E., 89
Napoleon: Bisexual Emperor
  (Richardson), 131
Napoleonic Wars (1803–15), 68,
  72, 88, 97, 103
National Centre of Excellence in
  Traditional Music, 169
National Library of Scotland, 79
National Mòd, 111, 144
National Museum of Antiquities
  of Scotland, 62–3, 75, 148–9
National Piping Centre, Glasgow,
  48, 168, 169, 177, 179
National Youth Pipe Band of
  Scotland, 177
nationalism, 23, 50, 70, 73, 109,
  124–30, 169, 191
Nazi Germany (1933–45), 114,
  115–21, 153
Neilston and District Pipe Band,
  151
'Nellie Dean', 130
Nero, Roman Emperor, 9–10
Netherlands, 21, 42
New York City Fire Department,
  186
New Zealand, 19, 72, 172
Newcastle, Tyne and Wear, 32,
  63
Nicol, Robert, 123
Nigeria, 184
'91st at Modder River, The', 95
Normandy landings (1944), 119–
  21
Norse culture, 40, 70

North African Campaign (1940–43), 115–17
North Britain, 67–8
Northern Ireland, 172
Northern Meeting, 84, 117, 134, 142
Northumbrian smallpipes, 7, 60, 64, 73–4, 146–8, 150, 176
Nova Scotia, 83, 124, 128, 155, 158, 176
Núñez, Carlos, 153, 155, 190

O-Level, 127
Oban Times, The, 62, 117
Oban, Argyll and Bute, 84, 110, 139, 142, 157, 178–9
oboes, 60
Ochtertyre, Perth and Kinross, 36, 63, 69
'Of the Influence of Poetry and Music' (Ramsay), 69–70
'Old Rustic Bridge, The', 130
Oman, 93
Ontario, Canada, 156, 157, 159, 190
opera, 60
'Oran Brosnachaidh do na Gàidheil' (Mac Dhomhnuill), 55
orchestral chanters, 143–4
organs, 21
Orkney Wedding, An (Davies), 144
Osborne, George, 192
Ossian, 42, 59, 152
Ossian (band), 150
Oswald, James, 64
Ourense, Galicia, 154
Outlander series (Gabaldon), 45–7, 49

Ox and Bucks Light Infantry, 120
Oxford, Oxfordshire, 63

Pakistan, 92–3, 95, 96
Palestine, 192
Pallas Armata (Turner), 43
Pashtuns, 93
pastoral pipes, 46, 59–61, 63, 65, 149
pastorale music, 60
Patiala State (1762–1947), 92
Patterson, Mark, 17
Pearston, Tommy, 122, 124, 125, 127
Peasant Cantata (Bach), 33
Peck, Cyrus, 102
Peel, John, 147
Pegasus Bridge, Caen Canal, 119–20
Perthshire, Scotland, 67
Peter I, Emperor of Russia, 8
phagotum, 28
'Phantom Piper of Corrieyairack, The', 121, 122
Pibroch Network, 175, 177
Pied Piper, 16
Pigg, Billy, 147
pigs, 12, 14, 20, 26, 35
Pincock, Dougie, 129, 143, 147, 150
Piob Mhòr, 36
piobaireachd, 38–42, 65, 106, 108, 175
    Cameron school, 83
    canntaireachd, 38, 85, 110, 177
    competitions, 38, 48, 57, 62, 75, 80, 129, 157
    First World War and, 114

Mackay and, 76, 77, 79–80
MacNeill and, 128–9
Norse culture and, 40, 70
Piobaireachd (MacNeill), 128
Piobaireachd and Its Interpretation
(MacNeill and Richardson), 130
Piobaireachd Society, 79, 106,
108, 114
pipe bands, 86–91, 96–8, 107–
14, 128
civilian, 107–9
military, 86–91, 96–8
women and, 110–14
Pipeline, 109, 171, 190
Piper, Andro, 31
Piper's House, Jedburgh, 33–4,
35
'Piper's Maggot, The', 64
Piper's Tune, The (1983 TV
series), 137
Pipers' Persuasion, 136
Pipes of War, The (Seton), 105
Pipes|Drums, 188
piping dynasties, 3, 22
MacCrimmons, 3, 22, 40, 41,
50, 52–4, 61, 76–81, 110,
128, 189, 191
Piping Faun (Praxiteles), 15
Piping for Boys (Sturrock), 108
Piping for Health, 177
Piping Live! festival, 169, 175
Piping Sounds, 171
Piping Times, 49, 122, 123–4, 125,
126, 129
pitches, 60, 62, 143, 146
Pitlochry, Perthshire, 75, 78, 159,
161, 162
Pittock, Murray, 59

Planxty, 141, 163
Plockton High School, Wester
Ross, 169, 174
Poems, Chiefly in the Scottish Dialect
(Burns), 59
poetry, 22, 23, 32, 40, 42
Pogues, The, 161
Poland, 8, 18, 117
Pollard, Tony, 49–50
Pompey, 10
Portree Games, 85
Prachen tradition, 18
Praxiteles, 15
'Pressed for Time' (Duncan), 164
Preston Lodge High School, East
Lothian, 177–8
Prize Pipes, 65, 76, 82, 84, 93
Prussia, 42
Puhoi, New Zealand, 19
Purrok, Rob, 31

Queen Elizabeth, RMS, 113
Queen's Own Cameron
Highlanders, 100, 103
Queen's Own Lowland
Yeomanry, 135
Quigg, Gerry, 157

Raasay, Inner Hebrides, 48, 84,
92, 110
Ramsay, John, 36, 63, 69
Rankin dynasty, 22, 40
Real World Records, 167
Red Hot Chilli Pipers, 180–81,
186
reeds, 8, 10, 12, 60, 118, 144
reel dances, 64
reels, 39, 92, 110, 117, 139, 163

Reformation (1517–1648), 15, 32–3, 152

Regiment of Foot, 25th, 72

regulators, 60

Reid, John, 33

Reid, Robert (b. 1784), 73

Reid, Robert (b. 1876), 39

Renfrew, Renfrewshire, 113

Renfrewshire Rifle Volunteers, 86

Resentidos, Os, 155

Rexurdimento, 152–3

Režný, Josef, 17–18, 151, 189

Richardson, Frank, 130–31

Richardson, James Cleland, 101–2, 104, 105

Rigler, Eric, 45

Rimmer, Joan, 21

'Road to the Isles, The', 119

Robert I 'the Bruce', King of Scots, 127

Roberts, Frederick, 89

Robertson, Alexander, 55–6

Robertson, Hugh, 65, 93

Robertson, Jeannie, 111

Robertson, Katie, 177

Romania, 8

Romanticism, 58–9, 72, 152, 153

Rome, ancient, 9–11

Rosie, William Sinclair, 118

Ross, Colin, 147–8

Ross, Donald, 83

Ross, Roddy, 132–4

Ross, Uilleam, 83

Ross, Willie, 106, 108, 110, 122, 134, 136

Rosslyn Chapel, Midlothian, 20, 35, 151

Rothbury Traditional Music Festival, 151

Rothesay ferry, 162

Rothiemurchus, Highlands, 121

Rough Wooing (1543–51), 28

Rout of Moy (1746), 52–4

Rowan, Mike, 149–50

'Royal Chance, The', 62

Royal Conservatoire of Scotland, 166, 175

Royal Dick Veterinary College, 134

Royal Edinburgh Military Tattoo, 2, 127

Royal Highland Fusiliers, 163

Royal Mile, Edinburgh, 3

Royal National Mòd, 111, 144

Royal North British Dragoons, 67

Royal North British Fusiliers, 67–8

Royal Regiment of Scots Dragoons, 67

Royal Scots Dragoon Guards, 145

Royal Scots Fusiliers, 67

Royal Scots Greys, 67

Royal Scots, 67, 89, 102

Royal Scottish Academy of Music and Drama, 166

Royal Scottish Pipe Band Association (RSPBA), 109, 173

Royal Scottish Pipers' Society, 85–6, 134

rumba, 155

Runrig, 132

Russia, 8, 42

Sabhal Mòr Ostaig, 175

Salerno landings (1943), 118

Sandy Bell's, Edinburgh, 141
School of Scottish Studies, Edinburgh, 127
Scotia bar, Glasgow, 141
Scotland, 16, 18, 19–29
  Acts of Union (1707), 47, 65, 67
  devolution (1979), 148
  Europe, connections with, 20–21, 32
  Gaelic, *see* Gaelic
  Highlands, 1, 4, 21, 28–44, 46, 72–3
  Ireland, connections with, 21–4, 126, 141, 146
  Jacobite movement (1688–c. 1760s), 1, 4, 45–56, 64, 65–6
  Lowlands, 4, 21, 31–6, 37, 42, 44, 63–4, 145–6
  nationalism, 23, 50, 70, 73, 109, 124–30, 191
  Parliament, 167, 169
  piping dynasties, 3, 22
  Rough Wooing (1543–51), 28
  Singing for Health Network, 177
  Union of the Crowns (1603), 20, 42
Scots Guards, 100, 107, 131
'Scots Wha Hae', 127, 129
Scott, Kathleen, 12, 26
Scott, Walter, 3, 21, 55, 59, 68, 70, 111, 152
Scottish Assembly, 148
Scottish Enlightenment (c. 1740–1800), 57–8, 59, 65, 70
'Scottish Horse, The', 110

Scottish National Party, 191
Scottish Parliament, 167, 169
Scottish Pipe Band Association (SPBA), 109
Scottish Pipers' Association, 163
Scottish Pipers' Society, 85–6
Scottish Power Nigeria, 184
Scottish Rifles, 99
Scottish Schools Pipes and Drums Trust, 170, 177
Scottish smallpipes, 147–8, 150, 173, 176
Scottish Traditional Music Hall of Fame, 111, 146
Seaforth Highlanders, 89, 91, 99, 118
Second World War (1939–45), 114, 115–21, 123, 130–31, 153
Select Society, 58
Sempill the Younger, Robert, 32
Serbia, 91
sernai, 95
Seton, Bruce, 105
Seven Years War (1756–63), 66
Sex Discrimination Act (1975), 140
Sharples, Robert, 126
Shaw, George Bernard, 85
Sheffield, South Yorkshire, 32
shepherds, 7, 8, 14, 60
'Ship of the People' plan (1739), 51–2
Shotts and Dykehead Caledonia Pipe Band, 139
Sialkot, Punjab, 92–3
Siege of Boulogne (1544), 28
'Siege of Delhi, The', 95
Siege of Pondicherry (1793), 90

Sikhs, 93

Silly Wizard, 163

Simon Fraser University, 159

Simpson, Habbie, 32, 34

Singing for Health Network, 177

Sketches of the History of Man
  (Kames), 65

Skirling, Peeblesshire, 20, 151

Sky Arts, 171

Skye, Inner Hebrides, 3, 40, 131
  Boreraig, 40, 76, 78–9, 81
  Dunvegan, 3, 50, 51
  Portree Games, 85
  Waternish, 51

slavery, 51

Sleat, Skye, 51

Smith, Adam, 57, 58, 65, 70

Snake Charmer, 186–7

social media, 186

solo piping, 49, 57, 75, 86, 107–
  8, 113, 128

sordellina, 28

South and Port Ladies Band, 112

South Uist Games, 136, 139, 176

South West Scotland Piping and
  Drumming Academy, 170, 178

Spa Hotel, Pitlochry, 75, 78

Spain, 18, 20, 151, 152–3, 154–5

Spalding, Anne, 140

Spanish Armada (1588), 37

Special Service Brigade, 119

St Andrews, Fife, 109

St Kilda, Outer Hebrides, 51

St Patrick's Day, 186

St. Laurence O'Toole Pipe Band,
  192

Stalag 383, Bavaria, 117

Statutes of Kilkenny, 24

Stewart, George, 83

Stewart, Jackie, 166

Stewart, Pete, 35, 36

Stewart, Sheila, 167

Sting, 7

Stirling, Scotland, 41

Stone of Scone, 126

Strachan, Hew, 66, 90

Strakonice, Bohemia, 17, 151

*Strange Death of Scottish History,
  The* (Ash), 4

Strathclyde Police Pipe Band, 158

strathspeys, 92, 97, 110, 117, 137,
  139, 163

Stuart, Charles Edward, 47, 49,
  50, 52

Sturrock, J. Percy, 108

Sudan, 95

Suetonius, 9

suffragettes, 111–12

Summer of Love (1994), 166

swashers, 32

Sweden, 42

Sydney, New South Wales, 8

Tain pipes, 49

'Tam O'Shanter' (Burns), 13

tam-o-shanters, 112

tamboril, 152

Tannahill Weavers, The, 141,
  161, 163

Tartan Tavern, Oban, 179

tartan, 68, 71, 90, 112

Tartantry, 128

Taylor, Ronald Robertson Kerr,
  126

Taymouth Castle, Perthshire, 82

Telfer, Seoras MacDonald, 126

Temple Records, 150–51

Thompson, Don, 158
Thomson, John, 125
Thoreau, Henry David, 59
Threave Castle,
  Kirkcudbrightshire, 35
Thunderstruck (Duncan), 164
Tickell, Kathryn, 7
Tirah Campaign (1897–8), 96
Todoroski, Risto, 8
Torloisk, Mull, 111
Toronto Police, 159
torupill, 190
town clocks, 73
town pipers, 27, 32, 34, 73, 148
Traditional Music of Scotland, The
  (Collinson), 145
Treacherous Orchestra, 180
Trevor-Roper, Hugh, 23
Trewin, Mark, 93
trews, 62, 71, 90, 92
Triumph of the Lord, The (Hume),
  37
tropical hardwoods, 61
Tulloch, Angus, 170
Tunisia, 183–4, 185, 192
Turner, James, 43
Twelfth Night, 14
tympanum, 11–12

uilleann pipes, 45–6, 49, 73, 149,
  150, 162, 176
Uist, Outer Hebrides, 22–3
Union of the Crowns (1603), 20,
  42
union pipes, 46, 59, 61, 63, 65
United States, 172, 173, 186
University of Edinburgh, 4, 127
University of Glasgow, 21, 45,
  127

University of the Highlands and
  Islands, 175
urbanisation, 28

Vale of Atholl Pipe Band, 159,
  162, 163, 165
Vancouver, British Columbia, 190
Vereno, Michael Peter, 9, 11,
  18–19
veuze, 151, 153–4
Victoria bar, Glasgow, 141
Victoria Cross, 96, 101, 103
Victoria, Queen of the United
  Kingdom, 28, 76, 77, 82, 83,
  96
Victorian Highland Pipe Band
  Association, 109
Virgin Mary, 14–15
Voice of the Wind, The (Vereno), 9
volynka, 8
Votes for Women, 111

wacian, 32
Wales, 110
Walker, Gordon, 163
Wallace, Hamish, 48
Wallace, Robert 'Rab', 79, 142,
  144, 145–6, 147, 150
Wallace, William, 127
Walsh, John, 157
War of American Independence
  (1775–83), 66
'War or Peace', 103–4
Ward, Mike, 141
Wardlaw, Highland, 41
Warriors of Scotland, 125
Waternish, Skye, 51
Watson, Elizabeth, 112, 113
Watson, John Nicol, 72

INDEX

Waverley (Scott), 152

Wealth of Nations, The (Smith), 70

Wellington, Arthur Wellesley,
 1st Duke, 89

Welz, Norman, 48

Weoley Castle, Birmingham, 25

West, Gary, 109, 144, 190

Wester Ross, Highland, 169

Western Park, Renfrew, 113

Westminster Abbey, London, 126

Whistlebinkies, The, 145–6, 147

Wilkie, Rona, 174

Williams, Vivien, 4–5, 28, 55

Wilson, Anne Campbell, 94

Wilson, Helen, 113

Wings, 145

'Within a Mile of Edinburgh
 Toun', 64

Wolfstone, 162

women, 6, 83, 92, 109–14, 123–
 4, 139, 172–4, 186–7

wood turners, 49

Wood, Thomas, 35

Woodward, Richard, 28

woodwork, 61

World Cup, 166

World Pipe Band Championship,
 107, 113, 118, 139, 143, 171,
 172

Wormald, Jenny, 20, 21, 33, 43

written pipe music, 6, 38, 83

xenophobia, 70, 109

Xunta de Galicia, 154

Yar'Adua, Umaru, 184

York, archbishop of, 20

YouTube, 7, 100, 134, 136, 188,
 190

żaqq, 8

Zimbabwe, 172